D1549663

The Bravest Man in the British Army

To all the unknown, unrecognized and forgotten heroes of the Great War
and to the women who loved them

The Bravest Man in the British Army

The Extraordinary Life and Death of
John Sherwood Kelly

Philip Bujak

Pen & Sword
MILITARY

First published in Great Britain in 2018 by
PEN AND SWORD MILITARY
an imprint of
Pen and Sword Books Ltd
47 Church Street
Barnsley
South Yorkshire S70 2AS

Copyright © Philip Bujak 2018

ISBN 978 1 47389 576 8

The right of Philip Bujak to be identified
as the author of this work has been asserted by him
in accordance with the Copyright, Designs and Patents Act 1988.

A CIP record for this book is available from the British Library.

All rights reserved. No part of this book may be reproduced or transmitted
in any form or by any means, electronic or mechanical including
photocopying, recording or by any information storage and retrieval
system, without permission from the Publisher in writing.

Printed and bound in England by
TJ International Ltd, Padstow, Cornwall

Typeset in Times by CHIC GRAPHICS

Pen & Sword Books Ltd incorporates the imprints of
Pen & Sword Books Ltd incorporates the imprints of Pen & Sword
Archaeology, Atlas, Aviation, Battleground, Discovery,
Family History, History, Maritime, Military, Naval, Politics,
Railways, Select, Social History, Transport, True Crime,
Claymore Press, Frontline Books, Leo Cooper, Praetorian Press,
Remember When, Seaforth Publishing and Wharncliffe.

For a complete list of Pen and Sword titles please contact
Pen and Sword Books Limited
47 Church Street, Barnsley, South Yorkshire, S70 2AS, England
E-mail: enquiries@pen-and-sword.co.uk
Website: www.pen-and-sword.co.uk

Contents

Acknowledgements

The collecting of information and development of my understanding of Jack in order to write this book has spanned two decades. Along the way I have been supported and helped by so many individuals that time and again my faith in the intrinsic goodness of people, what some would call Christian spirit, has been rebuilt, when in so many other ways it has been let down. In paying tribute to some of the builders here, I recognize that some have since passed away.

To my long-suffering extended family – Anne, Alex, Eleanor – who have heard the name Jack Kelly so often he must seem like a long-lost relation; and to my mother, Phyllis, whose idea it was to record Jack's life in the first place.

Without the help of John Kelly of Walmer, South Africa, whom I had the pleasure to once meet, I would not have had access to many of the sources that have been used to place Jack in the timetable of his life. In addition, I would like to thank the following: Julia and Peter Walsh of New South Wales (who, in a chance meeting, provided much of the information on Nellie and Mount Oriel); Burgess Winter (whose sense of the Irish temperament provided a much-needed empathy with the inherent dangers of Irish passion); Mr Peter Long of Farnham (who researched the wedding of Nellie's younger sister) and the late Mr W. M. Morris (who, having seen an article in the *Eastern Daily Press*, called me to come and see him and sat in his chair, telling me what he had seen of Jack as a young solicitor's clerk, thereby providing me with a ray of insight into the voice and character of the man himself).

The following public bodies and people were immensely helpful in providing source material and photographs on which to build a chronology of events: Dr Frank Millard, Mr Richard Berrett, Mr Geoff Simmons, Mr Blyth Thompson, Mrs Barbara Wilmott, Mrs Ruth Wheeler, Mrs Fiona Fouracre, the South African National Museum of Military History, the British Library, the Victoria Cross and George Cross Association, the Kelly family, the National Army Museum, The National Archives in Kew, the National Newspaper Library, St Andrew's School SA, the Imperial War Museum and the administrators of Brookwood Cemetery in Surrey. Without the help of the various regimental museums and records, I would not have been able to chart Jack's journey through the British army – most notably: the Royal Norfolk Regiment, the Royal Hampshire Regiment (especially Lieutenant Colonel C. D. Darroch DL, who provided valuable photographs of Jack and members of the 2nd Battalion in North Russia), the Suffolk and Norfolk

Yeomanry Trust (especially Lieutenant Colonel J. H. Boag OBE, MC, TD, DL) and the regimental records of the King's Own Scottish Borderers. To Pen & Sword Books for believing this is a story worth telling, Mrs Ana Pollard, my excellent editor and proofreader, and finally to Helena, Skye and Cameron who lost me for many a day writing this story.

PEB
March 2018

Chapter 1

The Imperial Adventure, 1830–1902
Part 1: Nature or Nurture?

'A man of character in peace is a man of courage in war.'
General Sir James Glover

It can take courage to fight the myriad challenges that face us in ordinary life – but it takes a certain sort of courage to fight a battle we think impossible to win. Very often we do not know such courage lies within us. Courage displays itself in countless forms. The courage to take a stand and speak out in public against something we know is wrong is a different sort of courage to staying silent, whilst we ourselves are being attacked. Courage is invisible to the naked eye and, like a mist in the morning of the autumn sun, can appear and disappear just as quickly. Courage provides a glimpse into a person's soul and a testament to their character. For some, showing courage in the face of adversity requires great effort, for others, it comes with ease. Sometimes, therefore, courage comes naturally and sometimes it has to be nurtured and grown in the garden of our souls. In peace, courage can come in many forms, and so it is in war. But in both peace and war one thing is constant and that is that courage comes from within and is formed through nature and nurture – through inheritance from our forebears and through the experiences of our lives and the world around us.

So it was for John Sherwood Kelly. Nicknamed 'Jack', his life of 51 years ended on 18 August 1931, and was a life rich in a variety of forms of courage – some ill-advised, some heroic and some unexpected, even to him. Jack is buried in a quiet corner of the very large public cemetery of Brookwood in Surrey. There was a time when his grave, like the story of his life, lay neglected. In this vast expanse of a cemetery, Jack is joined by at least twelve other winners of the Victoria Cross (VC), but, unlike them, he does not lie under a massive tomb or statue crediting his exploits and life. Indeed, when I first came across his final resting place, I was saddened by the moss and lichen that covered his grave, to the point where the crest of his VC could not even be seen – his life story as neglected as his resting place. His body lies under a tree in a corner of the cemetery, almost as if the space had been given grudgingly, rather than gladly – it is as if he has been deliberately hidden. Given the nature of what Jack did with his 51 years, this may indeed have been the case – and yet closer examination of his life shows that he inspired hundreds of thousands with the tales of his courage, touched the souls of others in immense pain and confusion, and had such impact on the life of one global icon of the twentieth century that he nearly changed the course of history.

This account of his relatively short life covers an epic sweep of history and geography. Beginning in the heat and dust of the South African veldt and on to the deserts of Somalia, then from the blood-soaked beaches of Gallipoli to the killing fields of Northern France, on via The Ritz and first-class cabins on luxurious cruise liners to the frozen wastes of North Russia, leading on to love and wealth alongside poverty and illness in the steaming jungles of Bolivia – and then finally to Bognor Regis. To the historian, this itinerary provides the backdrop to Jack's series of interactions with the developing political career of Winston Spencer Churchill. To the psychologist, Jack's life contains clues to what drives a man with volcanic energy and equally powerful emotions towards self-destruction. To the reader, I hope it provides a sense of understanding life's contradictory journey and the nature of courage.

South Africa, 1830–1900

Jack's grandfather, James Kelly, was a native of Newbridge in County Kildare, Ireland. We know little about him except that he was at one time a regular soldier. James had served in the British army throughout the 1840s and his son, John James Kelly, was born in June 1850 (Jack's father, who from now on shall be referred to as John Kelly). James went on to serve in the Crimea – taking part and subsequently surviving the Charge of the Light Brigade at Balaclava in October 1854.

As a young man, James possibly saw a better future for himself and his family overseas, staking a claim in one of the many colonies, rather than returning to England, or an impoverished and starving Ireland, to begin his civilian life. The population exodus from England and Ireland was encouraged by successive governments. Like the Roman Empire 1,900 years before, shortages of food and employment at home were matched by manpower needs overseas, and tens of thousands of families emigrated to America, Canada, India, Australia and South Africa in this middle period of the nineteenth century. Why South Africa became the focus of James' attention is not known, but during the 1860s he emigrated with his family from Ireland and settled in Queenstown, Cape Colony at some point in the early 1870s.

On the 30 July 1877, his son, the next John Kelly, married Emily Jane Didcott, who was born in Winchester, England, in June 1858. This young couple, aged 27 and 19 years old respectively, very quickly began what was to become a family of ten children, with Emily Nuovo Abele Kelly being born on 18 May 1878 in Queenstown. Two years later, in 1880, Emily gave birth to twin boys – John (Jack) Sherwood Kelly and Herbert Henry Kelly. The family then moved to Buffle Doorns, where another brother and sister were added between 1880 and 1882. The reason for their subsequent move north-east from the growing area of the Cape into the far more rugged, yet beautiful interior of the Transkei, where John and Emily were to live for the rest of their lives, is unknown. However here, under the evening shadows of Mount Frere and the little wooden collection of huts of Lady Frere, a further five children were added to the family.

Like a number of young men keen on horse riding and carrying a rifle, John had joined the Frontier Armed and Mounted Police in 1868. Signs of his own personal courage became evident, when, at the age of 24, a strong gale hit the south-eastern Cape area on the Transkei coastline on the 6 December 1874. It is not known how Sergeant John Kelly happened to be in this area, but perhaps word reached his local police garrison headquarters that a ship was aground. An Italian wooden barque of 690 tons, the *Nuovo Abele*, commanded by Captain Cuneo Francisco, had foundered and was breaking up off shore, having hit some rocks.[1]

The *Nuovo Abele* was on a trip from Batavia to London with a cargo of sugar and a crew of ten. Arriving at the scene and in the midst of the storm, it was clear that the ship would be destroyed and the crew lost, unless some way of linking them with the shore could be found. With little or no thought for his own life, John tied a rope to his waist and swam out through the violent waves and wash to the ship, clambering over the rocks and taking the men off one at a time by rope. This was achieved and all ten crew members, including the captain, were saved. For this heroic rescue, John was awarded the Royal Society's Bronze Medal for Gallantry. Later he was to record the event personally, and four years later named their firstborn child, Emily Nuovo Abele Kelly, after the ship – possibly in gratitude for his survival.

The development of policing throughout the colonies of South Africa was a long and by no means comprehensive process. The Cape Mounted Police (CMP) replaced the Frontier Armed and Mounted Police in 1878, in the year following John's marriage to Emily. Sergeant John Kelly remained a member. There were nine mounted police garrisons throughout the Cape, with a further three in the Transkei, and it may have been for this reason that his family resettled in the Transkei sometime after 1882, possibly posted there by his employers, the CMP.[2] These mounted police garrisons doubled as mounted local police forces (composed of volunteers) and a mounted militia and their members were expected to support the enforcement of British policy at all times, and to join the regular units when and if the time arose.

It was in this unforgiving landscape of the Transkei, that John would start work as the local law agent – until his death on 18 August 1926. The interior of South Africa was populated by numerous tribes, which meant it was essential to try to assimilate the colonists and work with the indigenous people, who for the most part did not reject the new technology and progress that the colonists brought with them. Just as today in South Africa, there were exceptions and violence and rejection, but it was the responsibility of local law agents to try to keep the peace and to settle disputes when they arose. Acting as arbiter, enforcer and representative of British Law was a vital role for law agents such as John.

In the only surviving picture, John was a short, thickset and determined-looking man. His Irish temperament served him well at times, but not so well at others, and his character was to have a strong influence over his children – Jack in particular. Like any son, whose own values, emotions and experiences were so influenced by those of his father, it is fair to assume that Jack inherited (through nature and nurture) both his father's explosive temper and fearless nature.

A small and undated work entitled *The Life and People of Lady Frere* gives a valuable insight into the life of this small colonial community and the role played in it by Jack's father, John:

> His [John Kelly's] true Irish temperament revealed itself in his courage at all times, whether it be courage to speak up in the defence of his fellow man or courage to save the lives of those in distress. He also had the courage to go against those whom he thought had stepped out of line and then his attack was relentless even though they were his friends.[3]

This extract is particularly poignant in relation to Jack. His father's 'courage' in the 'relentless' pursuit of those whom he perceived to have erred from the path of Justice, was a key characteristic that Jack himself was to inherit and display – even to the point of his own destruction. He saw injustice as the greatest evil of all and, despite this being a wonderfully laudable attribute, it also made him extremely vulnerable to the realities of life in a world in which we all have to live. The brutal reality of human nature was not something that Jack was prepared for.

The area in which Jack spent his childhood comprised a combination of differing religious and ethnic groups, and was populated by a simmering mixture of white Christian settlers of various denominations, all sharing the same community church, and the local Xhosa tribes people, whose own needs and grievances had to be balanced with those of the rest of the community.

The whole area was also a boiling pot of potential hazards and tribal friction. Aggression and even localized rebellion were always brewing beneath the surface. However, John built a reputation amongst all groups for being a firm, but very fair judge of circumstance, not afraid to speak up for the most influential white man or the humblest native of the area: 'he never deviated from giving each and every individual his services and a fair hearing'.[4] Blending the local tribal laws and customs, which had sufficed for centuries, with the new 'white man's' laws must have been a tremendously difficult task when attempting to keep the peace by consensus amongst people who did not consent to their changed circumstances.

One example, which serves to illustrate John's sense of fairness and justice, concerns the passing of the Glen Grey Act of 1894. Glen Grey was the former name for the area around Lady Frere and the area east of Queenstown. Legislation was passed by the totally white government of the then prime minister, Cecil Rhodes, creating individual land ownership (by white settlers), ending the traditional community system of tribal land ownership. In addition to this radical upheaval for the tribes' people of the Xhosa, the act also created a labour tax to force Xhosa tribesmen into employment on commercial farms – farms now owned by white settlers – in other words a legitimate form of slavery.[5] John publically challenged Rhodes in parliament over what he saw as the unfair implementation of this law. He reminded the government that their high-handedness was undermining the efforts of all those in the rural areas, who were trying to work with the local people, and that the Act needed to consider tribal laws and customs and not just impose white control over the indigenous peoples. Interestingly, John made this open attack by writing to the *Cape Argus*, which published his letters across South Africa. Such an open and courageous style was both admirable, but also personally dangerous and an act that no doubt had an impact on his son Jack, who saw what bravery his father was able to show in the face of considerable odds, in the pursuit of justice. It was also a course of action that Jack would follow himself in 1919, when his life collided with that of Churchill. 'Here was truly a lone voice in the wilderness, but a man who honestly displayed courage and tenacity unequalled and he did this for the cause of seeing justice and fair play done in all walks of life in the small town of Lady Frere, a mere speck on the map.'[6] It is clear from his epitaph, that John held justice above all things, as sacred, and this strong principle must have had a profound effect on the shaping of the characters of all his children, not least his son, Jack.

John's strength of character showed itself again during the Influenza Pandemic that affected much of the world in the wake of the First World War and which took its toll on the region. Lady Frere was badly affected with over ninety people at one time disabled and dying. A public meeting was held outside the town hall, where the mayor tried to co-ordinate a plan. Only the store remained open and it was here that John heard of the rumour, circulating in the district, that the white population of Lady Frere was in fact only interested in looking after its own and nothing was being done for the black community. John was incensed and again sent a long and direct letter to the *Daily Representative and Free Press*, in which he wrote about a group of five ladies, 'God Bless them', who volunteered to make soup in spite of being ill themselves. With no help, they stood from dawn to dusk making 12–15 gallons of soup for daily distribution around the community and surrounding Xhosa villages. Many natives would have surely died, but for the delivery of this nourishment by the well-known law agent, John, who carried the soup in his wagon.

It was, therefore, into this life of working with the native populations, heat and hard work and high moral expectations and discipline that Jack was born on 13 January 1880 in Queenstown, Cape Colony. His twin brother Herbert Henry was born a few minutes later. The origins of Jack's middle name 'Sherwood' remain unknown, but he never served with the Sherwood Foresters as has often been stated.

Jack's father was a strong, but not overbearing influence: a busy man with a large family of ten children and many commitments. With his great sense of justice and moral and physical courage, he was a firm and guiding influence. He was sometimes outspoken but had considerable qualities of leadership. It is fair to say that Jack inherited all of these characteristics in good measure. Indeed, one could extend this to say that Jack was the product and epitome of his age. At a time when strength of character and vision were vital to exploiting the opportunities of the age, of equal importance were the Victorian principles of fair play and the tenacity to see things through to their conclusion. Neither Jack nor his father were interested in playing at politics, where economies with the truth and manipulation of circumstance and people for personal gain were bywords for a successful career.

From the dust of the Transkei, an heroic figure was to emerge: a man who, like his father, achieved noble deeds, who led a full life, epic in scale, who played his part in several of the great theatres of politics and war of the early twentieth century, and whose life was to encompass vast swathes of human emotion and experience. But he was also a man who, in his achievements, was to be cut down and ruined in his efforts to stand for what he viewed as justice. Jack was a man clear-sighted in what he saw as his duty to defend, but blind to his own emotions. This made him unable to separate the courage needed to defend a principle from the emotional impact of the event or action itself and as such created a very vulnerable man – especially in the world of political intrigue, where conscience and moral justice were and are often missing from the actions of men and women in power.

If it is true that 'the child is father of the man', in order to understand the man, whom Jack became, it is necessary to look at the child that Jack was, and his relationship not only with his father, but also with his mother, Emily. Often in life one meets a person who is so shaped by the impact of their own parents that they never really become themselves – who they might have become. With overbearing and dominant fathers or mothers, children can retreat into anonymity, frightened and in awe of their parents' achievements. Paralysed in their personal development for fear of doing wrong, a personality cannot mature and grow as they constantly feel in the shade of fear. Whilst Jack had inherited much from his father – his short and hot temper and his sense of justice – so, luckily, he received the opposite from his mother, who provided understanding of his mistakes and tolerance of Jack's over-sensitized sense of injustice. As such it was his mother on whom Jack depended and she was crucial in helping him navigate the tortured and treacherous emotional pathways of growing up.

The frustrations of youth ran deep with Jack, as they do for all young men of all ages and all times. It is likely that Jack fell foul of his father on many occasions. Although in biography one should always stick to the path of what is known, sometimes conjecture has to be added and it is down to the reader to sense whether such assumptions are fair and reasonable. In Jack's case, and although we have only one small piece of evidence, the immovable object of the dominant father meeting the irresistible force of the growing son must have ended in combustion on numerous occasions. It was inevitable. We can deduce this from the likely state of relationships as Jack grew older and more independent and probably became the tearaway of the family. The pivotal point, however, in Jack's young life was when tragedy struck when he was only 12 years of age. The date was 8 August 1892. On that day his mother was driving a horse and cart when the horse bolted. Unable to control it, she struggled with the reins in vain, until the whole cart was overturned and landed on top of her. She was killed.

There is no age that can withstand such a tragic event with equanimity, but for a child of 12, especially one with a frayed temper and strong sense of fair play, nothing worse could have happened. Jack was probably emotionally defenceless. On a single day, his entire world was shattered at a stroke and there was no one to protect him from the extremes of that grief. The one person who could have comforted him was the very person he had lost. For a young man, for whom justice was one of his watchwords in life, where was the justice in this? How do we consider all this? There is a memorial to Emily in the local church in Lady Frere – but, unusually, it is not from the whole family but from one particular son. It reads:

> She was a true Christian woman, noble, fond, loving affectionate mother and a staunch friend.
>
> Jack, 8th August, 1892.

How many 12-year-old children could call their mother a 'staunch friend'? Was she the one who protected him when the explosion of his temper attracted the fury of his father? Was she the one who put his side of the argument over the dispute with his brothers and sisters? Was she the one who always stood by him when he had made a total mess of a situation, simply because he could not help it? To lose the one person who was tolerant of his failings and who understood his emotional frailties, must have been devastating. He also lost the one person to whom he felt able to show his emotions. In a world and family where male heroism and dominance would have been so strong, what happens to the little boy who wants to cry but cannot? He would run to his mother who would welcome him with open arms and always forgive him. This was Emily. How did losing his mother shape Jack's emotional development and nurture his own version of courage? I would suggest that it made him a very angry young man, resentful of everything and opposed to authority. After all, what did authority do to protect his mother? So, he became particularly carefree with his own existence and aggressive with those who tried to shape him.

One of the necessary prerequisites for the sort of courage that one is aware of (that sits at the front of one's consciousness, ready to be used – as opposed to the unknown courage that appears from within unexpectedly) is a conscious disregard for danger. Now, whether Jack was born with this characteristic, inherited perhaps from his father, or whether it was something that appeared as the result of the death of his mother, we can only guess. For the author, it is likely that it was the latter. Death had met Jack at such an early age and introduced itself so completely that he felt he had nothing to fear by meeting it again. Maybe it even set him apart from others and on a path to a lonely existence where he was only prepared to depend on himself, and where giving his love to another person was too risky in case it was again ripped away. We find few examples of friendship in his story and virtually no warm reminiscences of him from people we could assume were friends. We might even begin to understand that what we see as courage and heroism was in fact something else. That the medals we give for bravery are in fact not for that at all – we simply don't see what drives the hero to act in the way he does. We can examine later the undoubtedly heroic and courageous nature of Jack's actions on the Western Front, in Gallipoli or North Russia – but, after the pain of losing his mother, he became, quite possibly, immune to the pain of the battlefield. What we award medals for is, after all, purely subjective, depending on society's view at that time. The criteria for commemoration is not a science.

This then was the environment and the history that shaped Jack's early years. It was a version uncommon to most and specific to him. It was his persistent struggle to understand and accept that would live with him for the rest of his life and an anger that would drive him to meet injustice head on. The injustice of the death of his mother was ever-present in his psyche. Circumstances had conspired to place Jack in a setting where courage was needed – and he responded with an emotional intensity and resilience that can only come from experiencing deep loss.

Australia, 1842–1900

Another family deciding that the opportunity imperial expansion offered was too good to ignore was the Greene family of County Louth, also in Ireland. Here we trace the history of another family and another individual who would become central to Jack's life, but whose emotional development and experience was so very different.

In the closing years of the eighteenth century, William Greene of County Louth married Mary Yorke on an unknown date. William had achieved distinction in the diplomatic corps, having also served in the Indian army. In 1797, his son William Pomeroy Greene was born. Late Georgian England gave opportunity for great and fast advancement for those already from a privileged background, and William Pomeroy joined the Royal Navy as a midshipman. By 1816 he was so well thought of that he was part of the British guard for Napoleon during his exile on St Helena. Later William was part of Lord Exmouth's expedition to Algiers and by 1824 Lieutenant Pomeroy Greene was in Burma taking part in the capture of Rangoon – all by the age of 27. Having been invalided out of the service due to malaria, in 1826 William married Miss Anne Griffith and they moved to Collon House in Louth. Collon was owned by his cousin, Lord Oriel, who decided to sell it to him at a reduced rate. Over time William's health stabilized, and so it was that he and Anne had seven children – one girl and six boys – one being George, who was born on 20 July 1838. Two years later William was advised that the damp climate of County Louth was not good for his condition and a decision was made that the whole family would seize the opportunity for adventure and emigrate to Australia.

> Lt Greene, as he was still known, chose Australia and arranged to charter a ship in which to make the journey. Besides his family and two friends, Sir William Stawell and Mr Walker, Lt Greene brought out his butler, grooms, cowherd, gardener and his family, man cook and his family, laundress, housemaids, nurse and governess. He also brought out two racehorses, his hunters, two bulls and a cow. Besides this, he brought his library and an entire house packed in sections which he had had built in London.[7]

Clearly the Greene family came from a significantly different background and heritage to John, but both families were making their way building new lives in the 1850s. The Greene family locked the stable doors to Collon House and set off on their epic journey in 1842. One can only imagine the mixture of excitement and trepidation as this family and followers watched the shores of Ireland disappear behind them.

For something like six months George and his family looked ahead at the horizon and journeyed across the oceans of the world. They probably faced bad weather and danger along the way, and many members of the party no doubt longed for home, thinking what a mistake they had made. There being no Suez Canal at that time, their route would have taken them around the Cape in South

Africa, where they would almost certainly have stopped for a while. We do not know if everyone in the party survived the trip, but we do know that they erected the little house they had brought with them near Melbourne, where they settled for many years: 'It became famous for the old world hospitality and sportsmanship of its owners who also went on to found the once famous Woodland Steeplechase'.[8]

Taking full advantage of the opportunities that the expanding and cosmopolitan Melbourne had to offer, George attended the best school and graduated from the University of Melbourne in 1860 at the age of 22. Australia, like South Africa, was a land of hardship and adventure, and, for some, discovery and success. So it was that George spent the next ten years farming in Victoria with a loan from his father. As a young man he decided to make his fortune in New South Wales, where he moved in 1870, together with his new wife, Ellen Elizabeth Crawford – thereafter changing the family name to Crawford Greene. Ellen was the daughter of Colonel Crawford. Together they took on the vast tracts of dust and desert of the outback and put signposts where none existed. Nestling to the west of the Blue Mountains, George and Ellen built their first modest home and established ownership over some land. They approached a Mr J. A. MacKinnon who happened to own 34,000 acres. Offering him 6*s*. 6*d*. for each acre, George bought the lot and set out to map this vast new estate and decide what to do with it. Part of the land now in his ownership was a small area called Iandra Station. Iandra looked out over a wide plain in all directions and the Blue Mountains could be seen through the sunny morning mists. Settling on a small rise, Ellen and George named their new home Mount Oriel – in memory perhaps of George's uncle, who had made the trip to Australia possible in the first place. It was here that George and Ellen would make their lives and build a considerable fortune, raising one son and three daughters in the process.

George spent his life transforming the landscape of his new landholding. After much hard work and tough times financially, thousands of acres were ready for planting with wheat. By 1880 – the year Jack was born in South Africa – production was in full swing and money began to flow in in large amounts. Travel across the estate from one side to the other took six days by wagon, so George was often away from home. Despite this a normal family life was established and his reputation as a pioneer followed. It was George who, in the 1890s, experimented with the use of fertilizers and added 50lb of superphosphate to each acre, which doubled the wheat harvest. Despite periods of serious drought and millions of rabbits, George made it a great success. He was also the first to encourage the use of mechanization, and when capital investment allowed, he brought in threshing and harvesting machinery. But size was still a problem. The estate was just too big – thus it was that the concept of share farming was developed by George. The *Sydney Morning Herald* described the scheme as simplicity itself. George provided the land ready to be ploughed from the estate, to willing tenants who signed a share agreement. George also provided the seed and fertilizer. The farmer had to provide the labour and machinery and the land was then cropped and profits shared between the two men. There being no rent to pay, the tenant was motivated to work hard to increase the profits. So, George saw more of his landholding intensively farmed. By 1909 there were 61 tenant farmers on the Iandra estate and 600 workers. By 1900, 100,000 bags of wheat were being shipped off the station at Greenethorpe – an entire town and railway built by George to enable the flow in and out of supplies (including that for the 19,000 sheep that George also introduced to Iandra in the parts unsuitable for wheat farming).

All of this, of course, made George a very wealthy and influential man. He was propelled into politics at local and then state level, become a Member of the Legislative Assembly, and in 1908 entertained the Governor General of Australia, Lord Northcote, at his new and impressive house. The first building work had begun on Mount Oriel in 1880, and Iandra House grew from those early buildings into one of the most impressive houses anywhere in Australia at that time. Built in Victorian Gothic majesty, Iandra House was part home, office, library, castle, viewpoint and tourist attraction. The design incorporated 17 miles of steel reinforced concrete and every state of the art convenience was installed. Electricity was created by generators with extensive copper piping, and sewage systems were installed. There were fifty-seven rooms all with wood panelled interiors and stained-glass windows. The total cost of the building was £63,000 – millions in today's equivalent.

So, what of the four children? We know much about their early life from a book published in 1911 by George's sister Mary (who married William Stawell, one of the passengers who travelled with her father).[9] Mary tells a tale of a gentle and talented family, supporting their father, and brought up in all the social graces. This was a family environment without the explosive outburst of temper and family tragedy of the Kelly family, thousands of miles away in South Africa. There was peace, tranquillity, calm, a belief in God and a certainty of stability. William was born on 28 June 1884. Unlike his father, William was sent to England for school and university – Haileybury and Trinity Cambridge – and was expected to inherit the estate. William joined the army and travelled in the Near East and India. Of the daughters our story moves to the fourth and youngest, who was named after her mother – Nellie Elizabeth. Nature and nurture inspired a steely resilience, as they faced a sometimes harsh and uncertain future in the Australian outback, underpinned by devotion to family and a structure that financial security brings. Nellie was taught not to be weak in the face of adversity. Challenges for Nellie were to be met with a calm and quiet resilience, relying on the certainty that God was with her, and borne of a true pioneering family. So, like her mother in manner as well as name. What photographs exist of Nellie show a tall, slim and elegant woman. She was graceful and cultured, sensitive, keen on needlework and reading, a devoted Christian for whom life was good. She had been protected from adversity and heartbreak. She was a daughter to be proud of and hopefully to be married to a suitable gentleman for whom she would make a very suitable wife and mother. Thus it was that all seemed set fair for George Henry Crawford Greene and his family, as the nineteenth century came to an end. How then did the life of Nellie become irrevocably entwined with that of Jack's? How did they meet? And what would the consequences of having experienced such differing early lives be?

The Boy Becomes a Man

Hardly a year had passed after the tragedy of the death of Emily, before another tragedy struck the Kelly family. Jack's twin brother Herbert, to whom Jack must have been very close, was killed in a riding accident on 21 July 1893. To lose his twin brother so soon after losing his mother would have been overwhelming. At just 13 years of age Jack's character and attitude to life were being dramatically changed as he coped with the tragic loss of yet another person he loved, just at the age when it was hard enough to cope with growing up.

It seems that Jack's brother Edward (known as Ted or 'The Skipper') became Jack's best friend in the family, replacing Herbert. With ten children to bring up, Jack's father had employed the services of a Miss Selina Collins as governess-cum-housekeeper to the children. Soon after, maybe predictably, he announced that he intended to marry her. They married on 11 April 1894. One might assume that there were many arguments between Jack and his father regarding his re-marriage so soon after the loss of his brother, and only two years after the death of his beloved mother. Jack had to see another woman take her place in the household. He had hardly got used to not seeing his brother wake in the mornings, before seeing his belongings removed to trunks and a cuckoo arrive in the nest. This is not to say that possibly they had a positive relationship but, given what was to happen next in his life, his sense of vulnerability, resentment and depression clearly remained. According to family recollections it was from this time onwards that Jack 'became unhinged during his teens'. Such a rollercoaster of emotions in the space of four years, and at a crucial time of development, significantly affected the emotional temperament of an insecure and volatile young man.

His first schools were Queenstown Grammar School and then Dale College – but before the age of 16 he had been expelled from both, his strong temperament already well-developed and fiery. Victorian public schools were not renowned for their ability to understand emotional problems or even young volatile men. It would have been a certainty that, whilst being aware of the tragedies that had befallen him, the schools would have expected the 15-year-old Jack to get on with his lot in life and conform. Although he enjoyed and excelled at the sports offered in school, especially opportunities to ride (he was an exceptionally gifted horseman), he found himself at odds with the often rigid discipline required.

Avoiding a return home, Jack volunteered for the defence forces being raised to deal with the Matabeleland Rebellion, which broke out on the borders of the Transkei in 1896. Inflamed by a local oracle, Matabele warriors set out to raid and murder local white settlers. This was Jack's first taste of real action. We have no details of his involvement, save that he was there and no doubt preferred action and riding to school. He was awarded the British South Africa Medal (Matabeleland), which was to be the first of his ten medal decorations with nine bars.

Maybe keen to have Jack out of the house or possibly trying to do his best for Jack, his father enrolled him as a boarding pupil at the famous St Andrew's College. In the meantime, his father and stepmother provided Jack with three step siblings: Dorothy, Henry and Patrick, in 1895, 1898 and 1901 respectively. Again, we can only surmise how Jack reacted, but it would not be unexpected for him to have found it very difficult to relate to a new family so quickly after the death of his mother. St Andrew's College had been founded in 1855 and was, in the words of one 'Old Andrean': 'a typical Victorian public school, populated by the rough, tough sons of Eastern Cape farmer's and equally wealthy sons of Johannesburg businessmen'.[10] At the end of 1896, Jack joined the school and it was not to be a complete waste of time. Yet again, Jack excelled at sports, as his father had done before him, most notably boxing and riding. There was more here to suit Jack's talents and enthusiasm than he could have expected: a Cadet Force, which in 1890 numbered 126 cadets. With their field-grey uniforms with black piping and officers drawn from the master's common room, this was an attractive diversion from academic studies for Jack. Most schools could boast such units and they further embodied the notion of self-defence, in a land where native insurrection was as likely as foreign invasion. With relations with the nearby Boer states always strained, it is no surprise that a Captain Cherry, when inspecting the unit in 1880 commented, 'Volunteer forces form a very important part of the colonial army now that we are to expect little aid from Imperial troops in future disturbances'.

Unfortunately, Jack's career at St Andrew's was also cut short by expulsion from the college. According to Jean Coulter writing in 1989: 'he was not amenable to discipline'.[11] Another 'troubled youth' of this time, who found school not to his liking and preferred the open field to the classroom, was Churchill. The lives of these two young men were to become intertwined and it is important to note that they were of a similar disposition, if not background. Churchill longed to indulge in activities outside the classroom, as opposed to those which 'seemed of the slightest use or interest'.[12] Like Jack, Churchill found the harsh discipline of the masters and the use of the birch alienated him from the community, and he longed to leave school at the earliest opportunity – failing most examinations along the way. However, unlike Churchill, who found a way into the army after a very undistinguished career at Harrow, Jack had to fend for himself. The year 1896 thus saw Jack leave school with no qualifications, save that of experiencing the style of Victorian discipline that framed the character and attitude of generations of British officers.

Having found excitement and freedom in conflict, and again, rather than return home to more friction and strife, Jack decided to follow his father's lead and enlisted, in 1896, at the age of 16, in the CMP. This was a crucial time to make such a decision. Soon after the Matabeleland Rebellion was put down, relations began to deteriorate quickly between Britain and the Boers. The imperial ambitions of Rhodes and Sir Alfred Milner were well known and hardly disguised, while the increasingly hostile resistance of the Boers, led by Transvaal President Paul Kruger, made a clash inevitable. The abortive Jameson Raid of 1896 had indeed been a signal flare that conflict was imminent.

Between 1896 and 1899 Jack, as a member of the CMP, filled his time with patrols, arrests and travelling the region on horseback. Later, one of his first major roles was to escort Alfred Milner when he visited the Transkei in early 1899. In an article found in an obscure journal called the *Nongqai*, dated February 1918, there is also a reference to Jack being a 'rough rider' for the CMP. Although there is no evidence to substantiate this, it would come as no surprise. Rough riders were used to transmit letters and orders into areas with no communications at all and where danger was ever present. Described as 'a man of exceptional nerve', such a job would have suited the outstanding horseman that he was and given Jack a lone but exciting role.[13]

Unfortunately, a career in the CMP was not to be and, as if to keep up his record of dismissals, Jack was ordered out of the CMP in February 1899. This must have exasperated his father and although we do not know what caused it, it was almost certainly another rebellion against authority. Between 25 February and 17 March, his father is known to have written a series of letters, trying to find him employment either back in the CMP or with the Native Department. Admitting to Jack's 'nasty temper' and his 'insubordination', but also emphasizing his many good points, John used whatever contacts he could, and in July 1899, at the age of 19, Jack joined the Native Department in the Cape. Given that the Boer War broke out in September, not even Jack had time to be dismissed before the Cape was thrown into turmoil.

The background to the outbreak of the Boer War was simple enough. President Kruger of the Transvaal wanted to extend his borders, but was continually frustrated by the British, most notably Rhodes. Rhodes had arrived in South Africa in 1870 aged only 17 and went to Natal for a health cure for tuberculosis. He became involved in diamond mining and, by 1881, he had secured control of virtually all of the important diamond mines in and around Kimberly for his company – the DeBeers Corporation. Having become extremely rich, he set out on a political path and became Prime Minister of Cape Colony in 1890. Amongst his many grand designs he established a British territorial corridor between the Cape and Cairo in Egypt, by means of a new railway line. However, the Transvaal stood in the way. The discovery of gold in the Transvaal in 1886 had hugely complicated an already tense situation. If Rhodes was to have his way, then the Transvaal would have to become part of the British Empire.

By 1894, it had seemed to Rhodes that the Transvaal was becoming richer than the Cape. It was also becoming less dependent on the Cape, as the Boers were able to export and import increasing amounts of goods along their own new railway to secure their complete independence. Kruger was strongly supported by Germany. The kaiser himself, involved in an arms race and imperial struggle with Britain during the 1890s, was sending him arms and military advisors. The trigger for a sharp deterioration in relations was Kruger's attack on the 'uitlanders', or outsiders. There were tens of thousands of workers mining gold in the Transvaal, many of whom were British, and Kruger was concerned that they would soon outnumber the Boers themselves. Kruger therefore introduced a two-tier system, where all uitlanders were denied political rights and were taxed more heavily than Boers. Rhodes therefore seized this opportunity to 'protect' British citizens and the British military/political machine engaged itself in overthrowing Kruger.

Unfortunately for Rhodes, he made a serious error by plotting with a friend, one Dr Leander Starr Jameson, to lead a raid into the Transvaal via nearby Bechuanaland, which was set to coincide with a rising of uitlanders in Johannesburg. The raid took place in December 1895, but was a complete failure. The British Colonial Secretary, Joseph Chamberlain, disowned all knowledge of the raid and Rhodes was forced to resign. Subsequent research, most notably by Elizabeth Longford, suggests that Chamberlain in fact knew all about the raid. This event saw the end of Rhodes' career, by the galvanizing of the two Boer states into harmony – the Transvaal and Orange Free State – who were both now receiving aid from Germany. Kruger even received an open telegram from the kaiser, congratulating him on the crushing of the Jameson Raid. For a short while, the British abandoned their designs on the Transvaal. However, the appointment of Sir Alfred Milner as High Commissioner for South Africa was to change all that. In 1898, the uitlanders were 'encouraged' to write to Queen Victoria, protesting at their treatment by the Boers. A conference was arranged at Bloemfontain in Orange Free State in June 1899. The belligerent Kruger was in fact prepared to make concessions, but these were stretched by Milner into an impossible situation and the conference broke up with no agreement. Milner was not the right man for this job, if genuine reconciliation was what was wanted. He was himself an ardent imperialist, impatient and every bit as obstinate as Kruger himself.

Kruger could see what was coming and suggested independent arbitration and also the withdrawal of British troops, not just from the borders with the Transvaal, but also the Cape. When his ultimatum failed, the Boers had to make a choice, one so often made in history, to await events, or to take the initiative away from a much stronger enemy by making the first move. This they did, and Transvaal and Orange Free State Boers immediately attacked Natal and the Cape. Kruger had played into Milner's hands and as British Prime Minister, Lord Salisbury, put it long after, 'liberated us from the necessity of explaining to the people of England why we are at war'.

British regiments had been arriving in the Cape for many months as part of a build-up of military strength prior to action against the Boers. But the British were very badly prepared, with only 14,000 regular troops in South Africa in July 1899. By October, 47,000 troops would arrive under the command of General Redvers Buller. However, this would be too late to stop the Boers seizing the initiative and throwing sieges around Ladysmith and Mafeking and taking Kimberley altogether.

In Lady Frere, as in hundreds of similar communities, local levies and militias were raised and led by either serving or past-serving members of the military. In Lady Frere, it was John who took on this role, building up and leading 'The Lady Frere Company' of the Glen Grey Forces. This ragtag, but well-intentioned group was formed primarily for the defence of their own area from the Boers. Records pay testimony to John's efforts to impose some minimal discipline on his unit with great difficulty – his main task being to issue defaulter sheets to nearly every man for breaches of discipline.

Meanwhile the real war had begun, and an increasingly vicious war it was going to be. The British army was to lose not only significant numbers of men to disease, but also to the new tactics of mounted guerrilla warfare to which they were unaccustomed. It was not unreasonably assumed at the outset of hostilities, that the British professional soldier would be more than a match for the irregular Boer farmer. Nevertheless, serious defeats at Magersfontein, Stormburg and Colenso were humiliating and it became clear that the army reserve should be called up. The hope of a quick victory was rapidly turning into the very real prospect of defeat.

The inability of the British troops to pin down and erase their enemy swiftly was soon exposed. The tactical awareness and rigid inflexibility of the British army should have sent alarm bells ringing throughout the War Department in London. But it was an alarm bell that did not ring loudly enough or did not get heard until July 1916, when on the Somme the lesson was finally driven home. Rather than make wholesale changes to the way the British army was officered and fought, a localized change in tactics was developed just for South Africa. It was clear that a new wing of the army was needed – that of the long-range, mounted soldier. The Boers were not interested in lining up like gentlemen to have their bottoms smacked or men shot honourably. The majority of the 48,000 or so Boer troops were mounted, enabling them to carry out lightning attacks and then disappear in the worst traditions of the British army – they fired and left the scene to fight another day. They knew the land while the British did not, and it was a tactic designed to kill not chalk up runs. Lord Roberts was ordered to South Africa as Commander-in-Chief with Kitchener as his chief-of-staff, and between them the tactics changed and became far harder. Requests went out throughout the Empire for experienced horsemen to join this imperial struggle.[14] Volunteers began arriving from Canada and Australia, while the CMP also provided 2,000 men. Altogether, 28,000 men were home-grown from the Cape, with colourful names such as Montmorency's Scouts, the Transkei Mounted Rifles and the Pioneer Railway Corps.[15] However, it was the home-grown Imperial Light Horse (ILH) that stole the show, the headlines and Churchill's admiration. It was almost inevitable that it was to this unit that Jack volunteered and enlisted, having spent barely two months with the Native Department.

Men of the ILH took part in most of the famous and infamous events of the Boer War. In his role as War Correspondent for the *Morning Post*, the young Churchill built up a great admiration for the men of the ILH, serving with them in his capacity on a number of occasions and describing them as, 'the bravest men I have ever seen'.[16] Whether Churchill actually met Jack is a fascinating question, although there is no evidence that he did. However, it is not inconceivable that Jack would, at least, have been aware of Churchill's writings and his presence as a journalist with the ILH. By a strange twist of fate, they had already led parallel lives in a number of respects. Both had rebelled against school and preferred the outdoor life and adventure, both were strong and stubborn personalities and both were impetuous. Both were also now sitting on horses in a war maybe only a few yards from each other. However, much later, their paths were to cross in a head-on clash and a national scandal that was to end Jack's career, but also threaten to end Churchill's future political ambitions, thus potentially altering the course of history.

The ILH had been formed in September 1899 with the approval of Queen Victoria and was co-ordinated by Colonel Aubrey Woolls-Sampson, Sir Percy Fitzpatrick and Major Walter Karri-Davies – all local colonial figures with strong British pedigrees. A call went out for volunteers to join this new regiment and 5,000 men put themselves forward with only an elite 440 being selected – Jack was one. Following the regular troops around in their engagements was dangerous in itself, but Churchill also had ample opportunity to watch and work with the men of the ILH. The ILH were fast, lightly equipped, well-led and brave – this was their kind of warfare and they were a good match for the Boers on most fronts across the huge areas upon which the wars were fought. Two VCs were awarded for actions at Elandsgate in October 1899. Over the next two years, Jack was everywhere he could be as a member of the ILH. It is likely that at a young age, Jack may have made a pact with himself that if he ever got the chance, he would risk all he had to win his own VC (which indeed he did in 1917).[17] In uniform, armed and able to lead from the front, he must have realized that here was a vocation in which he could finally express himself. His medals began to accumulate and his first decorations read in order: 'Orange Free State', 'Transvaal', 'Rhodesia' and 'Relief of Mafeking'.

Many miles of hard living and fighting would have gone into this collection of honours and this for a man of only 19 years of age. The war was hard and saw many atrocities to soldiers and civilians alike. The life of the mounted soldier was harsh, with endless nights out in the field, torrents of rain, shortages of food, loss of horses, fever, bogs, insects and of course deadly bullets from the Boer sharpshooters. Something of the nature of the fighting can be sensed in these excerpts from the recently unearthed diary of Private Horace Bell of the 14th Regiment of Hussars, who served in the Transvaal:

> Went up to a farmhouse where they were hiding. They opened fire on us at 1,000 yards and a bullet struck my horse Hoff. Fighting all day: got pom pommed while we were feeding. Routed the enemy and captured it when it was dark. Next day to Bloemfontain: got up and cut the railway. Buried our old and respected colonel, Col. Hon Hugh Gough CB who lost his reason through overwork and shot himself.
>
> 22 April on a flying column with General French and the Lancer's Brigade to Thabanchu, where we lost Captain Denny, shot dead through the heart, Sergeant Cunningham, hit by a pom pom and killed, Privates Pragnell and Amoore only lived a few hours and died of their wounds. I was lying beside a chap named Smith when he was hit in the neck and a lot of our squadron wounded including Corporal Spring shot through both legs and calf, Private Sheppard shot through both feet, Sergeant McQueen shot through the thigh, Sergeant Piper shot through the seat. We buried Captain Denny at the foot of the kopje with a sergeant Soterton of the 17th Lancers. Return to Donkers Hoek where we heard of the death of a lot of my comrades from fever including 2922 Woods, Underhill, Hawkes, Akin, Hyde and Kenworthy. Private Watson was drowned at Mooi River.[18]

Despite dangers everywhere, so successful was Jack in his service with the ILH, that on 8 January 1901 he was commissioned in the field. Already his leadership qualities had been recognized, even though his superior officers had had to combat his often uncontrollable temper at the same time. Such decisions were not taken lightly, being a signal honour given the elite nature of the 440-man regiment. There was no doubt that it was his strong personal qualities of leadership and his style that attracted the attention of his superiors. A cavalier approach was just what was needed here and Jack certainly offered that. With John's young son stationed so close to his home town, John could only have wondered at the achievements of his son, who so recently had been expelled from school. Perhaps there was a new closeness of mutual respect, we will never know.

In the early phases of the war the Boers had surrounded a number of towns with British populations, such as Mafeking, which lay deep in the Transvaal itself, and Ladysmith to the east in Natal. Lord Baden-Powell's reports from the besieged Mafeking, reaching British Headquarters, were desperate, and from the perspective of public morale back in Britain, something urgent had to be done. A flying column was, therefore, dispatched from Lady Frere, under the command of Lieutenant Colonel Plumer, with the objective of breaking through Boer lines and relieving the town. Jack was a member of this column. On 17 May 1900, a column of troopers from the ILH rode proudly into Mafeking, led by Major Karri-Davies, with Jack close by. Jack had been specially chosen for this mission, along with an elite group of men from the ILH.

At 930am the next day, a Reuters message arrived in London, announcing that the siege of Mafeking was over and jubilant celebrations broke out all over London and the United Kingdom. At last there was something to celebrate. The war was, however, destined to last for another two long years, during which time many more lives would be lost on all sides. On 8 January 1901 Jack was commissioned as a lieutenant in the ILH – an honour for Jack and, of course, for his family and father. The feeling of pride and relief was to be short-lived. Only five months later, on 5 June 1901, Jack resigned his commission in a fit of temper and pique, having had a heated exchange with one of his superior officers. Frustration was probably one of the causes – not helped by his explosive temper. However, a lack of understanding on the part of his higher commanders was no doubt also a factor. In future years it was to be the case that Jack needed a certain approach and handling to get the best from him, but such understanding or visionary leadership was to be rare. Indeed, it was not to be until 1917 that we first discover someone in the higher command that appreciated the necessity for flexibility in what came with the sort of courage that Jack brought to the table. In any event, Jack was now interested in the next war which was brewing in the Sudan.

The war could not go on forever, and in the end the Boers were worn out and the peace negotiations that followed, led in part by Kitchener, resulted in the Treaty of Vereeniging, which was signed in May 1902. For tens of thousands of men in uniform, the war was thankfully over. For Jack, this was a mixed blessing, as the units of the ILH were one by one disbanded. Jack had started the war a boy and now ended it only two years later a young man, rich in experience and aware of what lit his fire. How was he going to lead his life now?

Chapter 2

The Imperial Adventure, 1902–13
Part 1: Finding his Way

'There were some who thought he was too eager for fame, and indeed the
desire of glory is the last infirmity cast off even by the wise.'

Cornelius Tacitus, AD 98

After the general demobilization was ordered in 1902, thousands of men in South
Africa were now left with a long walk or ride home. For a young man such as Jack
the war had taught him many lessons, not least that there was an alternative to
seemingly pointless study and the unreasonable discipline of the schoolroom. More
importantly, there was a world to be seen and met. His schooldays and father's
discipline were now far behind him, and on his journey home he had a few days
to contemplate his future and what he had learned. Experience with the CMP had
shown him that relative discipline combined with fear was a drug that appealed to
him – but how could this be replicated in civilian life and times of peace? Young
men need challenges and goals, something to aspire to as well as something to
burn their energies.

A future with the British army – if he could keep his temper – would no doubt
have appealed to Jack, but this army was contracting not expanding. Even after
their strong performance in the field, colonial troops were regarded as second- or
even third-class troops. There would be little chance of either action or
advancement. A commission was out of the question, as Sandhurst was a world
away from accepting colonials into its ranks. Thus, Jack's discarded field
commission was in any event worthless in peacetime and effective only for the
duration of hostilities. The old corruption of the purchasing of commissions may
have ended in the British army with Cardwell's Army Reforms of the 1870s, but
the patronage associated with it remained as strong as ever in colonial forces. Entry
into this precious club was not on merit but background and breeding – and as far
as entry to the British officer class was concerned, Jack had neither to qualify.
Thus, although by the age of 20 he could boast the British South Africa Companies

Medal for Service 1890–7, the Queen's South Africa Medal and the King's South Africa Medal, as well as Mentions in Dispatches and a field commission, Jack was considered fit only for the rank of sergeant when he decided to seize the opportunity to serve in an expedition to Somaliland, rather than continue on his journey home to Lady Frere.

Bounded as it is by the Gulf of Aden, Somaliland was a long way from the Transkei. The territory of Somaliland is a barren environment, but its strategic position with the Indian Ocean to the south had often made it a site of interest to Imperial powers keen to secure their route to India. This was especially so once the French opened the Suez Canal in 1878, linking the Mediterranean to the Red Sea. By the mid-nineteenth century, Somaliland, with its 700-year-old Muslim culture, was divided up between three of the great European Imperial powers: France, Italy and Great Britain. The often moral and legal questions notwithstanding regarding control by foreign powers, there could also be significant advantages in terms of social and economic development and stability. However, foreign dominance could also act as a catalyst for awakening dormant nationalist sympathies amongst the people. Thus, the Italians had purged their country of Austrian intrusion (and then set out to replicate that dominance on others), the Mexicans had removed the French . . . and now Muhammed Abdille Hassan began his ride to death and glory in a campaign to rid Somaliland of the British. In a similar vein to his predecessor in the Sudan (the 'Mad Mahdi'), Hassan set about torturing, burning and terrorizing his way around the country. Very soon he also was awarded the title of 'Mad' by the British press and became the 'Mad Mullah' – clearly any nationalist leader had to be mad in the eyes of the British press. The Mad Mullah of course represented a serious threat to British interests, and finding him at the end of a British bayonet was the government objective. An expedition was ordered against him and a call went out in Africa for men to volunteer to support the regular force sent to Somaliland. Perhaps out of some patriotic desire to protect the Empire, Jack was a product of the Empire after all. More likely it was a desire not to return home. And so, Sergeant Jack Kelly, aged 22, made his way northwards out of the Cape, across central Africa, to take part in another conflict. In the words of Tacitus, he was now heading firmly towards one objective: his 'desire for glory'.[1]

In the Burger Corps Jack was again employed as a mounted infantryman and scout. Long distances had to be travelled to locate their quarry, and the mullah was adept at quick raids followed by equally rapid disappearing tricks (which he himself put down to his supernatural powers) – as was reported at the time:

The notorious Mad Mullah who has been seeking to stir up rebellion in British Somaliland has fled across the border into Italian territory and a British flying column has taken up the hunt accompanied by an Italian observer Count Lovatelli. The Mullah appeals to the credulity of the pastoral Somalis by telling them that he has supernatural powers. If they resist his demands then he returns with a raiding party to rob and kill. He then vanishes into the bush to lie low for months.

From his arrival in November 1902 to the end of the campaign in July 1903, Jack was involved in the tracking down of the mullah. In an article dated February 1918, in the *Nongqai*, we have a reference to his being wounded whilst in Somaliland. The article was probably written from a selection of quotations about Jack and we have no way of substantiating whether he was in fact wounded or not.[2] What Jack lacked in schooling and examination certificates, he more than made up for in medals. As the rising was put down Jack was awarded another decoration: the Africa General Service Medal 1902–4 with Somaliland clasp. However, as Jean Coulter also pointed out, inevitably again matters did not go smoothly – he may have begun as a sergeant, but he returned to the Transkei as a private soldier. This was the result of another breakdown in personal discipline, although it may not have been without good reason. As Coulter and his great-nephew pointed out, his demotion was the result of 'speaking out at his commanding officer'. As a man in his early twenties one could argue that Jack should have begun to learn to control his emotions. We do not know, however, whether this latest brush with authority was born of bad temper, or whether again it was the result of what Jack perceived as injustice. The British army was and is full of injustice, learning to cope with it is all part of the process. Jack had much to learn if he was to ever fit comfortably into such a place again. Loyalty to the Crown, however, was felt very intensely by British imperial subjects around the world. The culture of the motherland, its values, attitudes, moral ambitions and history were fostered and developed by those transforming the Empire into its own image. The books and poems of Rudyard Kipling, the music of Edward Elgar, the art of Landseer, all were moving and emotional evocations of their vision of Empire. Loyalty was perhaps strongest where it was most threatened, and for people like Jack and his father, devotion to the British Empire and its way of life was a central feature of their lives. Now with the Somaliland expedition over, it was time for Jack to return home to Lady Frere and attempt to start a civilian life. This was to be one of the few periods in his life that he was out of uniform.

It is reasonable to assume that Jack did not want to return home. The new family his father had created was not close to him, and there may have been a very strong resentment towards his father, dating back to 1894 when he had re-married so quickly. So, between 1904 and 1906, Jack was to be found working as a trader and recruiter of native labour, serving the extensive mine works of the Cape and beyond. This was not to prevent him from involvement in the crushing of the Zula Bambatta uprising in 1905–6. This inclination or need to rush to any scene of conflict had become an established part of Jack's personality and character. It was something that would stay with him to the end of his life. There was something of the buccaneering spirit so deeply ingrained in him that Jack was always ready to drop what he was doing at any time, and look for the next adventure on the horizon. Life, it seems, was not big enough to hold him and a quest for challenge was ever present. It must have been hard, therefore, between 1906 and 1912, to have experienced a period of relative normality and stability, as he continued to work in Butterworth alongside his younger brother Edward, in the family labour trade. Even these six years could not remain uneventful. His life was rapidly becoming as turbulent as the times in which he lived.

Fortunately, we are able to peer into Jack's world between 1902 and 1912 through a number of events that give us some flavour of life for Jack in South Africa at this time. Prior to a court hearing in 1909, when Jack was due to give evidence in a local magistrates' court, he was found to be missing. The court was all assembled and the magistrate, dressed in his suit and winged collared shirt, not at all happy that a key witness was not there. Giving him the benefit of the doubt, a constable was sent to look for him, only to discover that he was, in fact, playing a tennis match (which he had hoped to complete before running down the road to make his other 'court' appearance) – after all, they were in the final set of a close match. Having been summoned to report to the court, Jack jogged into town and arrived complete with tennis whites, white shoes and racquet under his arm. The magistrate was by all accounts furious and taken aback with this apparent disrespect for his court. He shouted at 'Mr Kelly' to retire immediately from his court and to return more appropriately dressed and showing due respect to the court. Most people would have taken the hint and direction as it was meant, but not Jack. As a local newspaper report described: 'The magistrate was this time too shocked to even respond when the debonair young man returned to the court arriving in a full length morning coat, with top hat and lavender coloured trousers. The final artistic touches were given by the addition of his white gloves and walking cane.' The assembled audience broke out into a fit of loud laughter and applause for the audacity of this young man, who stood silently smiling in the dock with top hat in hand, chin in the air and a smiling glint in his eye as he taunted authority. After significant amounts of banging of the hammer on the bench and trying to quieten down the crowd, he was of course fined for contempt of court. But his reputation locally – which was already pretty well established as a comedian, puller of the nose of authority and someone not to pick an argument with – spread even further. Jack was a local hero and, at such a young age, already a decorated leader of men, liberated and charismatic, a drinker, a sportsman and a character – intoxicated by his own success and local popularity.

At around the same time as he was trying to earn a living trading in slave labour, Jack threw himself into any sports that he could find. In later life in the 1920s, even after being gassed and severely wounded on the Western Front, he was able to reduce his golf score to zero after only six months. As we know he was already playing tennis (when he should have been somewhere else) and, as well as riding, he had another passion as a young man and that was cricket. Lady Frere may have lacked all the conveniences of a 1900 city like Port Elizabeth or Cape Town, but the English influence pervaded, and apart from sandy, dusty tennis courts there were also hard, brown, cricket pitches where that typically English game could be played out as if they were in any rural village in any county in England. It is from one of these matches that we are able to gain another glimpse into the character of the charismatic leader, Jack, aged 22, in 1902.

Writing at the age of 92 in 2015, Blythe Thompson recounted a story to the author which had been told him by his father, F. R. B. Thompson:[3]

> My father F.R.B. Thompson, popularly known as Fred, captained the Transkei at cricket for thirteen seasons. Cricket in the Transkei in those days was pretty active with a thriving, robust and competitive internal league consisting of the various village teams from which a combined side was selected to compete in the Border League. As far as I know, the Kelly brothers Jack and Ted were passionate cricketers, unusually so for a couple of Irishmen. I conclude that this story told to me by my dad related to earlier times when my dad was one of the youngsters in the Butterworth team captained by Jack.

This was no mean feat for the young man. Butterworth, in the Eastern Cape, was a thriving and expanding area by 1900. According to the Cape Census of 1891, Butterworth, far from being a small village, was in fact a large town with just over 15,000 inhabitants (the white population of which was estimated at around 1,500).[4]

> The Butterworth team had somehow reached the finals of the Transkei league and they were due to meet Idutywa in the finals to be played on the Idutywa ground two or three miles outside the village.
>
>   Jack Kelly, as captain of Butterworth, was proud and very keen that his team should do well. Consequently he arranged that the whole team should spend the night before the match at the Idutywa Hotel which was at that stage owned by a man named Alf Baker. Jack wanted all his players to be fresh for the game so they travelled the afternoon before and Jack got them all to bed early. Well nearly all. Furthermore Jack had a particular 'Nerve Pain Specific', so called strong drink, that he wanted all the players to sample before they went to bed to settle their nerves for the next day's play. Jack as captain of the cricket team and in life generally, demanded obedience and had the tough physique and disposition to back up his

demands even though only in his early twenties. There were very few who would not do what Jack instructed but one of those was his brother Ted.

Ted, who was one of the opening bats for the Butterworth team, got involved in a late night poker game in the Lounge next to the bar where there was a liberal flow of whiskey and soda. When Jack discovered his brother well sauced and red faced he was highly annoyed and rebuked his brother who, for the sake of peace, gave up the game and went to bed. However, as soon as he was satisfied Jack had himself gone to bed, Ted returned to the game and continued on the whisky well into the early hours.

The next morning, the morning of the game, Jack woke to discover that Ted had only recently gone to bed and what was worse he was 'pretty full of ink' . . . It would have been normal for there to be a massive fight between the brothers but Jack did not make a fuss in front of everybody and instead held his temper and thought of a better plan. They walked off to the game and Jack duly won the toss at which point Ted went to put on his pads as he was the opening bat. At this point Jack said 'What are you putting the pads on for?' Ted replied 'I usually open don't I?' 'Not today you don't' came the reply from Jack, 'Have a look in the scorebook' . . . Ted grabbed the book and saw that his brother had put him down to bat number 11! The rest of the team watched and took cover and knew that the explosion of two Kelly tempers going off at the same time could happen at any moment. Ted said nothing, ignored Jack and continued to put on his pads and walked out to the middle and stood and waited. By now spectators were filling the stand and carts and some early vintage cars were arriving on the boundary roped with their picnics.

The sun beat down as mid morning start approached. Ted stood on the dry grass matting which was laid over the dusty ground to replicate the grass wicket and turned towards the main stand and started to shout 'If my brother Jack does not let me open the batting I will tear the whole mat and wicket up!' It may have been his temper but it was probably the drink still pulsing through his veins – plus his temper – but he clearly was now causing an embarrassment to Jack and the whole team. Jack's natural instinct was to march out there and knock Ted out and drag him back but he decided to let him have his way and the opposing team took his nod and came out for the match to begin.

Then began the pantomime. Ted was too drunk to even hit a ball. He swung wildly at every ball and missed toppling over many times to the amusement of the crowd and to Jack's simmering temper as he watched from the boundary rope. But no matter how often he missed, the bowlers just could not hit his wicket no matter how ridiculous his shots were. Ted miraculously began to sober up as the sweat poured from his head and much to Jack's annoyance, even began to notch up runs as his colleagues started losing their wickets. Ted, far from being a drunk embarrassment, was becoming the hero of the match. Eventually Jack came in to join his brother but disaster struck and he was bowled first ball by a stinker of an in swinging Yorker. Can you imagine the scene, his disgust and his temper about to explode – god knows if Ted smiled at him from the other end . . . anyway on his way back to the pavilion a chap in the crowd shouted 'What price Kelly's Nerve Pain Specific versus Alf Bakers's Dope & Soda!' There was a huge laugh amongst the crowd at which point Jack, pads on still, started to run at the stand with his bat swirling around his head and chased the man right up through the wooden seating to the top and was seen jumping off the end in hot pursuit across the fields back towards the town. We don't know who won that game but we can guess what happened to that chap when Jack caught up with him . . . which he would have done!

This story tells us much. Jack was marked out as a leader of men in peacetime as well as in war. He did have some control over his emotional pressure cooker, but only as long as people did as they were told – if not, he was prone to lose that control. It also tells us that his temper was well-known and his fearless character was backed up by a pretty imposing physique. Today, the thought of a cricketer running off the pitch to give a member of the crowd a good hiding would be unheard of, and such actions would result in law suits, fines, charges of GBH and compensation. Neither could you get away with it in 1902, but it was an age where the individual quality of a man was judged by his actions. Where justice and honour were at stake, men such as Jack (and he was not alone) were simply not concerned about the consequences. The action was necessary so the cost had to be paid.

What all this did for the relationship between Ted and Jack we can only guess. Perhaps it smouldered on for some time . . . There is another story: when given out lbw by a ball that Jack felt was nowhere near hitting his stumps, he argued with the umpire, using language not usually heard on the cricket field, even questioning the parentage of said umpire who happened to be . . . Ted Kelly. On his way past the umpire, walking into the pavilion, it seems somehow Jack managed to direct a left hook at Ted, which laid him out unconscious, and another umpire had to be found so that the match could continue. One can only imagine how that would increase the audience at test matches today.

As mentioned in Chapter 1, Edward was born on 28 November 1882 and became Jack's closest friend after the tragic death of Jack's twin brother Herbert in 1893, at the tender age of 13. Edward took his name from his grandfather, who, we may recall, had fought in the Crimea. At his funeral in 1948, one Archdeacon

Powell gave an oration which provides a fleeting but meaningful insight into the character and personality of Edward:

> Edward Charles, or as we liked to call him 'Skipper Kelly' met his death as he and perhaps we ourselves, would like to meet it, without ceremony, without fuss, without pain. Death comes in many forms, but the form in which the door opens and shuts quickly is the best . . . so long as we are ready for the hereafter.
>
> Skipper Kelly inherited a fighting legacy and he never dishonoured it. An ancestor of his took part in The Charge of Light Brigade; he himself joined Montmorency's Scouts when he was a mere schoolboy. He later joined Hartigan's Horse in World War Number One and was bitterly disappointed that an operation for appendicitis prevented him from seeing much of the fighting in German South West. But he was not to be denied and paying his own passage to England he joined the 10th Norfolk Regiment where he later commanded a company. And what a commander he was! He was severely wounded some six weeks after he was married in London and after the war he returned again to the Transkei transferring to Port Elizabeth in 1935. War disabilities hardened the hearts of the authorities and he settled down without uniform to do his civilian work; he had been rejected but had the physical energy of half a dozen soldiers.
>
> What underlay this somewhat blustering and impetuous exterior? A tremendous amount of chivalry and gentleness and real goodness. He was tough and yet gentle with a most charming chivalry to old people, especially poor people, perhaps his outstanding characteristic was his generosity: he never did anything by halves: he was a great giver.

Archdeacon Powell concluded, 'The Skipper loved his home, his life and children and his like we shall not easily meet again.'[5]

Through these words it is possible to discern an essence that was also found in Jack. Impetuosity certainly has a resonance, but chivalry and toughness are also marks of the Kelly brothers. Ted was to be alongside Jack throughout his life. Perhaps unable to control him much, but there to reason with and to understand what made someone like Jack the man he was. They were to share tragedy and pain as young brothers without a mother, and hilarious experiences as brothers on the cricket pitch, as well as brothers fighting on the Western Front. They would go on to lead men in the British army in their own way, the way they had learnt and practised on the frontiers of the Empire, rather than the parade grounds of the colleges of Sandhurst. They were to become heroes to the men they led, irritations to the men that tried to lead them and markers to a world we have lost.

But to return once more to the young Jack. Young men need challenge and direction, or so it is said. One can see that the young Jack, between the ages of 20 and 30 (1900–10), was someone who had developed a devil-may-care attitude. He had survived under fire to the point where he was a local hero and had built his reputation for courage. But his underlying anger at the world set him on various paths of confrontation. Together a heady mix. A sense of invincibility – but if not invincible, who cared anyway. Alongside the reality came humour and legend. This can be sensed from the stories that are still remembered and passed down from father to son, even now in families who have roots in the Lady Frere and Transkei region. Like Viking legends, Jack still has a place in the folklore of the area.

Jack's humour had a wild, some would say extreme, side. Pushing boundaries with little care for the consequences, as another story illustrates. Jack and Ted, despite their own rough quarrels and drinking, worked closely together and had probably relocated. Jack himself was based in Butterworth, Transkei, the homeland of the Xhosa people (and of Nelson Mandela). After the Boer War, rather than return home, Jack and Ted entered the service of the NRC – National Recruiting Corporation – the purpose of which was to recruit African labourers to work the mines in the Witwatersrand. Jack had a network of agents, mostly Transkei traders, who covered the most remote areas. One of those agents was Neil Mills, a much respected and successful trader in the Kentani District, on the road to the popular seaside resorts at the mouth of the Qolora River.

Mills would regularly make his way to Butterworth to purchase supplies for his trading station or wait for goods to arrive by train from East London, the nearest port. He would always call at Jack's office to sort papers, get money for new labourers and then off to the Bungalow Hotel for a drink or two – or being a hard drinker, many more.

On one occasion, they were sharing the bar with 'Spongy Piet' (Pete). Piet de Jagger was so called because he was always sponging drinks and never paying for his own. After a while, Jack and Mills moved on to the Masonic Hotel, and sure enough Spongy Piet arrived soon after. Jack gave a wink to Mills and offered Spongy one of his 'specials' – a combination of whiskey and brandy that was strong enough to anaesthetize the most hardened of drinkers. Spongy Piet, already rolling from the drinks at the Bungalow, accepted a series of these from Jack, then slowly closed his eyes and keeled over backwards onto the floor unconscious. Jack and Mills carried poor Spongy to his home, a small hut on the edge of town, where they left him on the porch and went. Mills mentioned to Jack as they left that he was worried about him, but Jack just waived it off in his dismissive manner and said he would be fine. Now, not to allow the fun of the evening to end, Jack got it into his head to put the wind up Mills. So, first thing in the morning – Jack was an early riser no matter how much drink he had had the night before – Jack saw the local constable doing his rounds on his horse, a young chap also in his twenties and not the most gifted. Given Jack's background (sergeant in the Cape Police and local war hero) and strong character, the constable was rather in awe of him. Calling him over, Jack said he should go over to Mills' house and tell him that Spongy Piet had been found dead on his porch from alcoholic poisoning the night before. This was Jack's sense of devilish humour – borne of hard drinking and a devil-may-care willingness to play jokes on friends. The constable knew it was a put-up, but as it was Jack, and he thought it was quite funny too, he went along with it and did exactly as he was told. He told Mills that he would be back in an hour or so to arrest him.

What Jack had thought was a splendid practical joke, planning to go and tell Mills later in the day, had the reverse effect. The constable had done such a convincing job that poor Mills was beside himself and frightened out of his wits. South Africa at that time had the death sentence for murder. Mills panicked, grabbed some belongings, ran from the house and rode out of town. Mills disappeared totally and Jack saw his joke rebound. Mills was gone for nearly two weeks and the local newspapers carried reports of 'The Disappearance of a Transkei Trader' as their headlines. Mills only returned after Jack had put adverts in all the same newspapers that Spongy Piet was in fact fine and that Mills should come home to his family. We can only imagine what Mills had to say to him when he arrived back – and what his wife had to say to Jack. I suspect that after a pretty strong row, they were back drinking in the local hotel bars just as before – whether Spongy Piet kept turning up as well we will never know.

So, by 1910, Jack had been a fairly wild young man. Now aged 30, he was fearless and to an extent careless in so far as he cared little for what people thought of him. But he was also highly admired and regarded as a man of courage and hard drinking, with a local reputation that spread far and wide. So it was natural that his thoughts now turned to creating his own family and he began to give some serious thought to a local widow. The fortune and assets of one Emily Sarah Snodgrass (née Lawlor) seemed particularly appealing. Recalling this period in Jack's life, his stepbrother Henry James Collins (who died in 1983) remembered that, although able to show a romantic side, Jack was attracted to Emily for other reasons. Emily was a young widow with considerable financial assets, who was no doubt swept away by the attentions of the dashing 32-year-old hero. Marriage between a widow and a young man of 32 was not necessarily a problem, but Edwardian social conventions frowned upon such matches/alliances, as did Jack's father who wrote that 'he should be ashamed of himself'. This did, of course, not stop Jack marrying Emily. However, she was clearly astute enough to realize that she needed to protect her assets from the unpredictable but attractive Jack. According to records in the Royal Norfolk Regimental Museum, 'An ante-nuptial contract was signed between Emily Sarah Lawlor and Jack Sherwood Kelly on 15th May 1912'. This proved to be far-sighted as, after a whirlwind relationship and marriage, they were divorced soon after. What possessed Emily to create such a contract we will never know. It may have been that she had children, but it may also have been that Jack came with such a reputation that she sensibly judged he might be hard to hold on to for any length of time.

After the excitement of the Boer War, Jack's life was characterized by flirting with danger, challenging authority, playing to the crowd (regardless of the consequences) and indulging his wicked sense of humour. Many would applaud the sentiment, but lack the courage to commit such acts. While the sentiment may be applauded, we can also see that the limits which he chose to surpass often catapulted him into grave problems, even destruction. Jack was 32 years of age by 1912, and between then and 1919 he was to experience a tidal wave of challenges, opportunities, dangers and happiness – enough for several lifetimes and not just seven years. It is a dramatic period in his life, full of incident, trials and a disregard for peril that some saw as heroism. But for those who knew his past, Jack was simply living life to the full, regardless of consequence. He had given up worrying about repercussions when he buried his mother and brother.

Events now unfolding in faraway Europe would create a rollercoaster ride that would take him from the dust, heat and predictability of life in the Eastern Cape of South Africa, on to the family homeland of Ireland, to Turkey, Flanders and then North Russia. By 1919, just seven years after his failed marriage and attempts to drink Spongy Piet to death, he would be attending his own court hearing: a court martial in central London, as a colonel, with the VC, the DSO and the CMG – and one where he was antagonistic not only towards the entire British military establishment, but also his nemesis, Churchill. Jack's brushes with authority and the establishment, which he paradoxically fought to defend, had only just begun. His real journey was about to begin and it would end in the destruction of his career – but even that was only a precursor to even more adventure. He was at 32, ready and explosive, the sort of man you wanted beside you if life had put you on the ropes and an ideal person to throw into the mix of another war – something he had been missing in his life since 1902.

Chapter 3

Ireland, 1912–14
The Ulster Crisis and the Road to War

'While war is terribly destructive, monstrously cruel, and horrible beyond expression, it nevertheless causes the divine spark in men to glow, to kindle, and to burst into a living flame, and enables them to attain heights of devotion to duty, sheer heroism, and sublime unselfishness that in all probability they would never have reached in the prosecution of peaceful pursuits.'

Major General John A. Lejeune, 1929

To fully understand the elements of chance and circumstance, which directed Jack and Edward to Europe in time to be caught up in the maelstrom of global conflict, it is necessary to be aware of a more parochial, yet viciously intractable, problem which had (and would continue to) beset successive British governments – the so-called 'Irish question'.

Ireland and Irish nationalism had broken the careers of numerous politicians and even ended the lives of others, yet all attempts at finding a lasting solution to the problem had, by 1910, failed. Like a rumbling volcano, Irish affairs were always liable to explode in the faces of the most stable of British governments, but for unstable governments the consequences could be catastrophic.

After his first appointment as prime minister in 1868, W. E. Gladstone worked tirelessly to find an answer to the Irish question. At this time, the Kelly family were settling into life in South Africa and the Crawford Greene family were doing the same in Australia. Gladstone's initial aims of pacifying the Irish failed as miserably as his later attempts to give the Irish nationalists what they wanted – Home Rule. It was over this issue that Gladstone not only gave up finally, but split the Liberal Party irrevocably in the process. Gladstone's failure had in some ways highlighted the impasse that existed between the demands of nationalist passions in both the north and the south – the south wanting a united and independent Ireland and the north loyally determined to remain British. By 1910 the Irish question was reaching another explosive phase. Similar to the period between 1960 and 2000, sporadic and shocking violence produced a cycle that by 1910 had the British government in turmoil. The appointment of Sir Edward

Carson as leader of the Ulster Unionists further increased tension, and led to public pledges to protect the north and to retain strong links with Great Britain. Tension between Republican and Unionist factions grew and this time civil war loomed.

In Edwardian England, there was a new atmosphere of liberation and hope, contrasting sharply with the social control that had been exerted by Queen Victoria and her key prime minister, Lord Salisbury – the effect of which had reached its apogee in the 1890s. In his book on European history after 1880, J. M. Roberts characterizes this period as one 'swept by gusts of sentiment and anger, unstable and insecure'.[1] It certainly was a period of uncertainty and a crisis of identity for Great Britain. Increased communication, education, ambition and social change at home became mixed with a greater awareness of the vulnerability of Britain's place in the world, the pressures of maintaining the Empire and, closer to home, a real concern about the growing threat posed by Germany as she sought her 'rightful place in the sun'. This heady mix demanded flexibility and vision from government. It was a time when new problems needed new responses and approaches, for to attempt to deal with these new tensions in the old ways was to court disaster.

It was against this backdrop that the lives of millions depended and British relations with Europe mirrored the growing temperature created by the Irish problem. The once enforceable and impregnable positions of 'Splendid Isolation', where Britain with its naval and military reputation built on the myths of Waterloo (but exposed by Crimea and South Africa) were waning fast. The efforts of Edward VII to play a more leading role in European politics led him to closer ties with France (the *Entente Cordiale* in 1906) and with Russia through naval agreements. Inevitably the combination of the two drove Germany further away. The performance of the British military in South Africa, despite the colonial support of people such as Jack, had at least resulted in the arrival of Lord Haldane to he War Office. With 10,000 British troops killed and a further 16,000 dead from disease whilst fighting an army of Dutch farmers in South Africa, Haldane's series of major military reforms were urgently required. These went a long way towards creating the effective, well-trained and motivated army that was at the disposal of ministers in the summer of 1914. The British Expeditionary Force (BEF) may have been small and was largely slaughtered within months, but it bought the time needed to create a new, nationally recruited army to be led by Field Marshal Lord Kitchener.

The new Irish problem developing in 1912–13 should be seen against a background of problems piling up for H. H. Asquith (who had succeeded to the leadership of the Liberal Party in 1908) and his new Edwardian government. His predecessor's election victory in 1905 may have been a landslide victory against Conservatism, giving the Liberals 377 seats, but it was also marked by the establishment of Radicalism in British politics. The new 'Labour Party' (formerly the Labour Representation Committee, or LRC) had won twenty-nine seats and could no longer be ignored. Their voice was to be a loud one in the years ahead. However, the concern in some quarters over the growth of socialism was overshadowed by various crises between 1909 and 1911. A series of related issues came together to create the crisis that was to bring Jack and Edward to London to fight for an 'Ulster that will fight and an Ulster that will be right'.

First came David Lloyd George's budget. The financial requirements of funding both the massive legislation introduced by the Liberals and the cost of building more and more battleships in the arms race with the kaiser, meant the need for a radical budget – which the Conservative-dominated House of Lords chose to reject. This in turn led the Liberals to lean on the support of the Irish Nationalist MPs, and they in turn saw the price for this as new demands for independence from Britain at a point where John Edward Redmond (the leader of the Irish nationalist MPs in Parliament) was no longer interested in partial independence, but wanted nothing less than a self-governing and united Ireland.

In Ulster reaction was swift and calls went out for the creation of a volunteer force for the defence of the province should the British government surrender, as they saw it, in the face of Irish nationalist blackmail. A request went around the world for loyal patriotic unionists to return home to join a new paramilitary organization. Civil war was now creeping closer and individuals such as Andrew Bonar Law, leader of the Unionist Party, fanned the flames, declaring that 'the unionists were the "national party", the party of The South African War, the party of Empire, the party of the assertion of British interests'.[2] The call reached as far as Lady Frere and Butterworth in South Africa, and sure enough both Jack and Edward answered. According to the memoirs of Henry Kelly, 'He [Jack] couldn't get there quickly enough – nor could Uncle Ted'.[3]

Their enthusiasm was not, of course, out of character. Jack was 33 years old in 1913 and had already fought in four conflicts in various parts of Africa. Both Jack and Ted were at that age when now was the time, if they were going to do it. It was probably a fairly easy decision to leave a business that neither of them liked and to take a trip to Europe, maybe get in a fight or two in Ireland, and then return home. Of course, with the world of synchronicity surrounding them, it was not going to work out like that.

It is probable that Jack and Ted set sail for Ireland sometime early in 1913. Saying goodbye to friends and family in Butterworth and Lady Frere, they set off on their adventure. Who knows what dreams they had – perhaps of adventure and glory and to make something more of their lives. They were expecting to enter into a possible civil war in Ireland. But within a year, the most disastrous war in history was about to break out across Europe – placing them both in exactly the right place at the right time.

Synchronicity is another aspect of heroism most often overlooked by its neighbours: courage, devotion and impulse. Without timing, none of these other factors that go to make up the hero would be of any use. Ten minutes before or after, a left turn rather than a right, an order misheard through the gunfire . . . the variety of inter-related factors that create the exact circumstance at exactly the right time is vital. This thing called synchronicity, where everything conspires at the same time to create a circumstance where the hero inside of us rises up, is in fact one of the universal laws of history. Virtually all major events in a person's life or events in history are the result of good or bad timing. The right place at the wrong time is no good, the wrong place at the right time is equally of little use, but the right place at the right time and the potential impact is incalculable. So, Jack and Ted stepped off their boat in Belfast docks into a world that was changing all around them, a world where politically great events were potentially about to happen in Ireland, but also a world where, in the corridors of power across Europe, war was being planned.

Both Jack and Edward would have been witnesses to the increasing tension and atmosphere of friction throughout Ireland. For two years, since its introduction into the House of Commons in April 1912, the Third Home Rule Bill attempted to make its difficult way through parliamentary procedure. To both sides, Asquith's position seemed to be one of vulnerability and both sides mistrusted him. To compound the problem, Asquith had his own problems with trust. He had been warned more than once that the loyalty of the British army, if called upon to act against the Ulster volunteers, should not be taken for granted. Indeed, a number of British officers were in complete sympathy with the Unionist cause – they too believed in the defence of the Empire and its inhabitants. In March 1914, a cavalry brigadier general told the government that he and his officers would rather leave the army altogether than carry out orders to coerce the north. The Curragh Mutiny – as it became known – was one of the last pieces in the drama that was unfolding in Northern Ireland, leading, inexorably it seemed, towards civil war and bloodshed. The Ulster Volunteer Force was then forming up in Belfast, and it was there that Jack and Ted joined up and once more were in uniform. As fate would have it, and just as they thought they knew where the fight was coming from, another nationalist cause created major instability in Europe, which was to overshadow all events in Ireland.

Ireland Eclipsed by Sarajevo

The assassination of the Austrian Archduke Franz Ferdinand and his wife in Sarajevo on 28 June 1914 sent a shock wave throughout Continental Europe. This action ignited the frustrations, anger and fears of the Austro-Hungarian Empire. It also provided a timely excuse for other nations to act, so closely in competition with each other and so closely connected by the treaties and pacts signed in previous years.

What should have been a long, hot, summer break in England and Ireland, offering people respite from mounting domestic issues, instead turned into a frantic international political disaster. Events in Ireland took second place as the August Bank Holiday approached, with the foreign ministries of the major powers working at fever pitch to contain what was now an international crisis. Instead of reading the news on events in Ireland or listening to speeches in the pubs of Belfast, Jack and Ted were increasingly aware that a major international dispute was unfolding. It soon became clear to Asquith and his Foreign Secretary, Sir Edward Grey, that German support for Austria in her demands on Serbia had elevated this issue to a far higher and more dangerous level. By the last week of July 1914, Austrian troops were fighting in Serbia and Russian and French orders for full mobilization had been issued. The kaiser had pledged his support for Austria and a conflict with France seemed inevitable. If German troops passed through Belgium then this automatically brought Britain into the conflict, as Belgian neutrality was guaranteed by international treaty (1836).

In the main, the loyal and trusting public knew little of these events. Throughout Britain the main thought was still: 'What to do with the sunshine?' Farmers planned their harvest, fathers planned their family holiday and mothers planned their summer recipes. From Yarmouth in the east to Blackpool in the north and Folkestone in the south, thousands of people had arrived to enjoy what was one of the hottest summers on record. The newspapers, however, carried increasingly disturbing reports of troop movements and the aggressive posture of the kaiser.

The potential for war had a long pedigree and was not just the product of the assassination. It does not fall within the scope of this work to even try to explain the mass of conflicting aims, jealousies and intrigues in order to determine who or what was ultimately responsible for the slaughter that was to come. It is, however, necessary to examine a little more closely the political world, which would determine the fate of millions.

In the final days and hours before the British declaration of war, it was clear that Asquith and many of his closest advisors, both inside and out of the Cabinet, had grave reservations about what needed to be done. Naturally the burden of taking the nation into war was far from straightforward, but equally clear was the role that decisive and clear action could play in averting a crisis. In his book, *Dreadnought*, Robert Massie offers a most readable account of those final hours and concludes that, 'Asquith allowed events on the continent to outpace and influence decisions of the British government.' This suggests a controlled and calculated indecision, in terms of British involvement, regardless of the military consequences in the short term.[4] But this was not a methodology confined to Asquith, as his successor as prime minister, Lloyd George, was to employ a similar approach with events in North Russia later in 1919 – although that indecision was to be ruthlessly exposed to the British public by one, Jack Kelly.

Most people were well aware of the problems in Ireland and expected that if there was going to be a conflict, that this was where it would surface. News that war was imminent in Europe came as a real shock – as though the world was sleepwalking into war. On 1 August, Germany declared war on Russia and the die was cast when German troops moved into Luxembourg two days later. That same day Germany also declared war on France. The long overdue re-match, threatened since the defeat of France by Prussia and the German states in 1871, was about to begin.

In Belfast, Jack and Edward, like thousands of others, knew that greater events were unfolding. Very soon men ready to fight in Ireland were packing their belongings and saying their goodbyes as they headed for London to enlist. The situation changed daily and the momentum of events built up quicker than governments were now able to control. Jack and Ted travelled by ferry to Liverpool and then onto a buzzing and confused London by train, arriving in late July. Unaware of the scale of what was about to happen to Europe and the world, they arrived excited and eager to join in somehow. While ministers rushed around the corridors of Whitehall, they were soon aware that events were passing them by. Even before the government had made up its mind to declare war on Germany, eight German army corps were moving across the Belgian borders as the Schlieffen Plan unfolded. In Britain, tens of thousands of volunteers were queuing up to enlist in regiments in centres hastily being set up in church halls and schools. As German troops poured into Luxembourg and Belgium, thousands of people dressed in straw boaters and cloth caps waving Union Jacks gathered in Whitehall, waiting for news and direction from the government. The excitement of war was everywhere, the mood was positive, the sun shone and confidence in the army and the navy was supreme.

Although Churchill, as First Sea Lord, had already issued a stream of orders to the fleet, and Haldane at the War Office had been sending out mobilization papers, recalling soldiers from leave and calling up reservists, Foreign Secretary Sir Edward Grey had as yet not made a statement to the House. He did so, however, just after 3pm on 3 August. He had walked to the House through the patriotic crowds milling and singing in Westminster and began his speech to a packed House. He began at 3.10 and one hour fifteen minutes later he concluded a rational and calculated speech, detailing where Britain stood on an issue that was already out of control. Far too late, as many historians agree, Britain made its position clear. Britain had to act both in defence of its own interests, as a moral obligation to France and as a treaty obligation to Belgium – which by now had received an ultimatum from Germany to stand aside and allow its troops across its borders to invade France (movements that had in fact already been initiated). To paraphrase that excellent writer on this period, Barbara Tuchman, Grey spoke to posterity, whom he knew well would analyse his every move. Grey's words ensured that an ultimatum would now be sent to Berlin via the British Embassy. However, this was far too late. It was delivered by the British Ambassador to Berlin, Sir Edward Goschen. But by 7pm on 3 August 1914, Britain was at war with Germany. The roots of the conflict had been forgotten, the tensions between nations had not, and the fuses had been lit all over Europe.

As a postscript to this briefest of summaries, it is worth noting that one of the replies given to Sir Edward Grey in the House that day came from Redmond, who said: 'I say to the government that they may withdraw every one of their soldiers from Ireland. The coasts of Ireland will be defended by her armed sons . . . the armed nationalist Catholics in the south will be only too glad to join the armed Protestant Ulstermen in the north.' At two minutes past eight in the morning on 4 August 1914, the first waves of German troops in their field grey and (at that time) pickelhaube helmets crossed the Belgian border and the British army initiated their strategy, designed to meet such a threat.

The meticulous plans, drawn up by General Sir Henry Wilson, had been in existence for some time, but ministers now realized that it was time to read and understand them. Based on his observations, the availability of manpower and the known elements of the Schlieffen Plan, Sir Henry had devised a scheme that was based on putting a small army of six divisions into the field (much like a rapid mobile brigade of today), as soon as possible, to form a block. The BEF (British Expeditionary Force) was now hastily assembled and famous regiments began forming in camps all over southern England. Before it could move, however:

> On August 5th, the first day of The Great War, the General Staff's plans, already worked out to the last detail by Henry Wilson, instead of going into action immediately like the Continental war plans, had to be approved first by The Committee of Imperial Defence. When the committee convened as a War Council at 4 o'clock that afternoon, it included the usual civilian as well as military leaders and one splendid colossus (Kitchener) taking his seat amongst them for the first time.[5]

From his position as the new Secretary of State for War, Lord Kitchener saw it as his duty to propound his deep apprehensions about placing the small but very well trained BEF in the hands of the French, holding the left of their line. How would they fare against almost seventy German divisions heading for them? He feared that if this force was severely weakened, or lost, then there would be no time left to train the hundreds of thousands of volunteers that were now heading for the enlistment centres – they would be arriving too late. His premonitions were echoed by Field Marshal Sir John French, whose 'mercurial temperament commonly associated with Irishmen and Cavalry soldiers' led him to believe that a sudden change of plan was essential to preserve the British force, and give it an opportunity to make a real impact, as opposed to being swept away in the tide of German field grey. On the opposite side was Sir Henry, whose plan was on the table. However, time was vital and was not on their side. To Sir Henry the council members were 'mostly ignorant of their subjects' and 'fell to discussing their subjects like idiots'. His plan for the BEF had been worked out over many years, down to a level of detail that any German staff officer would be proud, but the Germans were not controlled by committee. An alternative plan to land part or all of the BEF at Antwerp, to save the port and push to cut the German advance in two, was put forward. It was at this point that Churchill stepped forward with a clear and unequivocal objection that the navy could not guarantee a secure crossing for such a large force over that distance – Calais was far safer. And so it was that orders were issued for Wilson's plan to be put into operation immediately and the BEF began moving.

It is of interest and relevance to our story that only two months later Churchill, having initially dismissed the idea of using Antwerp, went on to implement the plan when it was far too late, despite many protests from senior officers. Churchill was, arguably, always prepared to take risks with the lives of others to secure victory. This is no doubt a mark of leadership, making important decisions is never easy and Churchill can never be accused of shirking the big decisions, despite the cost. However, his decision-making process was often reckless and cost many thousands of lives over the years in which he held positions of authority.

The grand Schlieffen Plan failed to encircle Paris and cut the Allies off. The resulting stalemate culminated in the dismissal of Helmuth von Moltke and the arrival of Erich von Falkenhayn, who identified the siege now going on around the key post of Antwerp as a potential disaster to the advance. So did Churchill. Not having access to the army, Churchill did however have access to the Royal Marines, and a force of 3,000 was sent to Antwerp to support the Belgians, on his orders. So enthusiastic was Churchill that, according to A. J. P. Taylor, he even wanted to command the force himself.[6] As Robert Rhodes James pointed out, Churchill offered to resign from his post at the Admiralty (which many would no doubt have readily accepted) and take field command. He was met with 'roars of incredulous laughter'.[7] How strange that two men could wish to sacrifice everything in order to rush to war: this determination of Churchill to lead his troops into battle was no different from Jack's to trek to the other end of Africa to fight in Somaliland. This was the cavalier spirit in Churchill trying to escape from the politician's body. In any event, and in typical Churchillian style, the attack was rushed and poorly planned. The brave marines ended up either dead or in German prison camps and the German attack swept on.

Given that Jack and Churchill had already served together in South Africa, it was another twist of fate that their lives were now to become inextricably linked again for the next five years. The Antwerp fiasco has been all-but-forgotten, along with many of Churchill's blunders, in the tidal wave of the British need for heroes and victories, despite failures. This gives us a valuable insight into the character of Churchill, as do the unmitigated disasters at Antwerp in 1914, Gallipoli in 1915 and the rushed and ill-thought-out Narvik campaign in 1940. All were failures and were launched without proper planning and against the advice of many around him. Hidden from history amongst these disasters was the Archangel Campaign of 1919, an attack in which Churchill was to discover that not all his campaigns could so easily be washed away by the tide of history – especially when Jack was playing his part.

In London, the heady excitement and anticipation of war had now translated itself into a city at fever pitch. Excitement gripped the nation and across the cities of the United Kingdom recruits began swarming to local centres to sign up. Regimental recruiting teams began their exhausting work of coping with the onslaught of eager applicants. It was in these early days that young men, many under age, saw their great chance of excitement, glory and an opportunity to bloody the nose of the kaiser. Their enlistment became possible because of hugely over-worked recruiting officers and sergeants. One such unit which began forming was King Edward's Horse in central London. The new energy and furore of the time was exemplified by recruiting dinners and parties. Old officers came out of retirement, patriotic songs were written, newspapers inflamed passions, mothers said tearful goodbyes to sons, fathers shook hands with their heirs, and pals walked arm-in-arm and signed on together. Into this frenetic melting pot Jack and Edward arrived at Charing Cross station in the heat of a July summer's day.

When Jack stepped off on to the platform, London and the world expanded before his eyes and ears. He had never seen a city of this size – this was the centre of the Empire. Buildings seemed to stand taller than the mountains of the Transkei. As he breathed the London air for the first time, his lungs took in the air of a brave new world of opportunity. He arrived full of youthful energy, expectation and dreams, but also something familiar to him – a determination to make his mark and name and grab the opportunity that was now on offer. He expected much from London and was prepared to make whatever sacrifice was necessary. His ambitions were framed even before he left South Africa, but now they were given a real hope of becoming a reality. He had left South Africa for one cause and now he had another. Perhaps here in England and specifically in London, Jack's restless spirit would find a home. All around him he saw colour, people, energy and an opportunity to make his name and fortune.

One of Jack's main characteristics was his overpowering energy. As a youth he had been irrepressible. Now he was simply stronger, larger than life and louder. He never just walked into a room, he strode in with a charismatic sense of certainty and confidence that enabled him to win over those around him, impressing them with his strong personality and humour. Contemporary accounts also paint a picture of him, similar to that of his brother, 'The Skipper'. In virtually every photograph we have of Jack, we see a man in a state of calmness and certainty – a clinical look in his eyes. He knew himself and this was enough to lean on. Such traits were magnificent for leading men – but potentially combustible when being led. Jack was spontaneous, dynamic, clear-thinking and direct, and he made decisions with ease and a self-assurance that often unsettled or disabled his superiors. This speed of decision-making also extended to his personality. He was quick-witted and amusing in company, his sense of fun and the absurd made him attractive in groups but, as we know, he was also quick to anger. He was described as courteous to his inferiors – his soldiers adored him for his care and affection for them. To his equals he was magnanimous and respectful, but to his superiors he could appear rude and undiplomatic. Not for him the niceties of double standards, multiple faces, arrogance and nasty back-stabbing, back-handed compliments, and all the other personality traits sadly so common amongst English society. He was the product of a different world and had no intention of becoming part of this new one. This new world would have to accommodate him.

He was a man of magnetic charm, a refreshing and open contrast to the strict Edwardian codes of behaviour into which he had stepped. He was the life and soul of a social gathering – hugely attractive to men and women alike. He was not eccentric, but he was extraordinary in his devotion to duty. We know that in early life there was nothing more intolerable for him than injustice. This was something he was now going to meet with first hand, and so often that his ability to contain himself would be tested over and over again. Finally he was a cavalier of old, confident in the certainty that this was going to be his war – or mean his death.

Not just in South Africa, but also in the colonies of Canada, Australia and India, the mounted equivalent of the English Yeomanry detachments were known as the Light Horse units. They were local formations formed for the defence of their homelands in support of often sparse police detachments. They were usually mounted and of course armed. In the majority of cases both the English Yeomanry and the colonial Light Horse units were led by leading members of the local aristocracy, gentlemen farmers and squirearchy. Gentlemen farmers, landlords and their estate workers swelled the ranks of these part-time units that existed in addition to the territorial formations of the cities.

In 1901, Kind Edward VII had supported the raising of the Kings Overseas Dominions Regiment. By 1905 the regimental headquarters was based in London and consisted of four squadrons:

'A' Squadron – British Asian with an Elephant cap badge
'B' Squadron – Canadian with a beaver and scroll cap badge
'C' Squadron – Australian with a kangaroo and fern cap badge
'D' Squadron – South African with an ostrich cap badge.[8]

The size and distribution of these squadrons varied enormously from country to country. However, by 1909 'colony' squadrons were becoming associated with a past age, and relations between Britain and the colonies were becoming more sensitive. So, individual squadrons were abolished and replaced by King Edward's Horse (KEH), with a unified cap badge composed of a shield with all the former squadron names embossed on a series of scrolls.

With the influx of volunteers arriving in London with colonial experience, a second echelon of the regiment – 2/KEH – was raised in London. Having made their enquiries as to where they could best serve in the new conflict, Jack and Edward were directed to the recruiting office enlisted in 2/KEH in the second week of August 1914. Thus, the journey was now complete: Jack, who had left the British army twelve years previously, was aged 32 and once more subject to the authority of the king.

Synchronicity Plays its Hand Again
It was into this cauldron of events that the kind, charming and scholarly Nellie Elizabeth Crawford Greene stepped in, in July 1914. Her father George suffered a gradual decline in his health and died aged 73, on 22 December 1911. It was no doubt his intention that his family would continue to run and develop his wonderful legacy. He left two sons, George Cyril (born in 1878) and William (born in 1884), and three daughters, Nellie Elizabeth (born in 1871), Georgina Maria (born in 1874) and Gladys (born in 1888). We do not know what happened to his son George, so it was William who took the lead and indeed was appointed by his father as an executor of his estate. In his will, he directed that his wife and family could continue to reside at Mount Oriel, with expenses for the massive property defrayed from his personal estate. Further, he bequeathed a lump sum to each of his children and a substantial annuity to each of his three daughters. The net value of his personal estate was sworn at £83,937 5s. 5d. The value of Iandra lands and equipment, however, was far more and estimated in 1910 at a further £228,740. The will, therefore, made each of his children financally independent for the rest of their lives – indeed each would be very wealthy in their own right. What to do with their wealth? William was cut from a different cloth – shaped by his Cambridge degree, education at Haileybury School and his experience as a yeomanry officer in the King Edward's Light Horse in Australia. He was determined that the family's future did not lie in the dust of New South Wales but back in England, and, the estate having been sold for a massive sum, it was there that the entire family relocated in 1912. Just as Jack was trying to build his life in South Africa, so the Crawford Greene family were unpacking at Warren Corner House in Farnham, Surrey.[9]

By 1914 the family had been permanently resident in England for two years. William and Nellie, with their considerable fortunes behind them, spent the majority of their time in fashionable parts of London. Nellie acquired a beautiful flat in Cranley Gardens in South Kensington and had a wide circle of friends. No doubt they socialized on the London scene and built up an extensive sphere of very well-positioned and influential families. At the outbreak of war, William quite naturally immediately volunteered for service and, given his previous rank, experience and social standing in London, was offered command of the 2/KEH with the rank of lieutenant colonel – the same unit that Jack and his brother Edward were now joining. Perhaps at a party, a recruiting event or on a parade, but, within days, the two families' paths crossed, as Jack was introduced to William's family, including, of course, his sister Nellie. From two totally different backgrounds and countries, in all certainty Nellie and Jack should never have met.

In spite of its horrors, war creates as well as destroys. Within days Jack and Edward were offered the rank of lieutenant in the 2/KEH and were fitted out with their new officer's uniforms – who knows, perhaps with a loan from William. At the same time both Jack and Edward were integrated into the Crawford Greene's London social circle and from here there was no going back. Jack's new odyssey in the cradle of a landed and wealthy family had begun, and his world, and theirs, would never be the same.

Chapter 4

Gallipoli and the Odyssey Begins, 1914–16

'Good relations between commanders and the rank and file are like all other forms of friendship – if they are to be maintained and bear fruit they must be nourished. Our men are exceedingly accurate judges of an officer's worth and character, and whilst they intensely dislike the officer who does not enter into their feelings and treats them as if they had none, they have unbounded admiration for the one who treats them kindly as well as justly.'
Field Marshall Sir William Robertson, 1921

For those first few weeks of war Jack and Ted read, as did everyone else, of the bravery of the BEF on the Marne and the ever increasing casualty lists. No doubt all Jack could think about was boarding a boat and getting to the front lines, but the British army had no plans for colonial units to fight – they were going to be used to either fetch and carry or fill in the ranks of the lower battalions of the great regiments. So, the autumn of 1914 was spent training, marching, shooting, practising sword drill and running a unit that all knew was unlikely to be committed to combat. On the flip side, there was learning the social graces of parties, chit-chat, new friends and acquaintances in London. All fine and dandy, but frustrating. No doubt it was in this period that Nellie formed a liking – soon to be love – for Jack. His dashing confidence was everything she was not. His handsome features and cavalier style were a heady mix, and it is easy to see why she might have fallen under his spell. Jack, on the other hand, we might imagine, was happy to allow this friendship to prosper as it gave him a new lifestyle far beyond his dreams only a few months earlier in Butterworth. But whilst Jack was basking in the full gaze of Nellie's admiration and sharing her family's social entrée, the first phase of the Great War had come and gone with disastrous and bloody rapidity.

Initially, the regular battalions of the British army that went to France were decimated in the early battles of the war, as part of the BEF. The retreat from Mons, the Aisne and the Marne saw the flower of the army killed or wounded, and it was only the stabilizing onset of trench warfare that enabled Kitchener to build his New Army. Back in the counties new 'service' battalions were formed. These were regular units in training. Some were broken up, while others, when ready, were sent to France. Jack and Edward trained with King Edward's Horse between

August and November 1914, before the unit was broken up and officers and men sent out to staff other regular battalions forming up in the Shires. In Jack's case, he was promoted to full lieutenant and commissioned into the Norfolk Regiment. It was of course pure chance and he could have been sent anywhere, but it was to rural and very conservative Norfolk that Jack arrived just before Christmas 1914, and set about changing the collar dogs and hat badge of his uniforms – something he would do a number of times between now and 1919.

More than likely, Jack trained and drilled at the drill hall near the cattle market under the shadow of Norwich Castle. The Norfolk boys would no doubt have taken a liking to their new officer as he was, like them, plain speaking and one of them. He probably managed a pint or two in the many pubs in Norwich and settled for a while either in a guest house or perhaps billeted with one of the other officers, as they waited for their new recruits to join them and for their orders as to which battalion they would be joining. They had to wait, of course, until the harvest was in.

As with most English counties at the outbreak of war, Norfolk had been broken up into districts for recruiting purposes. Peculiar to the agricultural way of life and of course temperament, the major job to be done was not fighting the Germans, but bringing in the harvest. Once this had been done, the *Norfolk News* proclaimed on 5 September 1914: 'with the finish of the harvest, the Norfolk labourers were now rapidly making their way to the recruiting stations'.[1] We can only imagine the humour with which these lads, like so many other young and older men across the nation, went home, packed their bags, bid farewell to their wives, children and mothers and said, 'Well now, let's see about this 'ere war.' The harvest they had just collected was to be, for many, the last that they were ever to reap. They were soon to be claimed by another type of harvest, one in which they themselves would be gathered in.

It was not the weather for war. For the regular and the reservist, the first troop trains were pulling away from loved ones in stations as early as 6 August. In places such as the market town of Attleborough, by the second week of August, most of the able and fit men of the area were asked to assemble and take the train to Norwich to join the newly forming battalions – many of them never having travelled the 15 miles to the county town.[2]

Everyone now knew what had happened to the regular battalions of the regiment. The 1st Battalion of their own county regiment had formed up, had travelled to the south coast, crossed the Channel and by the 17 August was leaving for the Front from Le Havre. By the 24 August the men were already fighting for their lives, with the regiment falling back from Mons, where it had engaged with the tide of German divisions that were flooding across the flat, but scorched, green fields of Flanders. By the beginning of September, news of the first fatalities was reaching home and the first of many small brown telegrams stamped 'War Office' were being received by anxious families all over the country.

In his *Story of An Old Contemptible*, Rob Kirk writes about the head-on clash between the best in the British army and the best of the Imperial German army.

The foot soldiers (of the Norfolks) were deployed around noon, over half a mile of countryside between the mining village of Elouges and neighbouring Audregnies, among the slag heaps, rail lines, sunken roads and narrow cobbled streets of tiny terraced pit cottages. Tom Lawrence described it: 'we were on a little ridge, Cheshires on our left, 119th on our right, and a clear field of fire across cornfields to the north west. Might have been back home in Norfolk!'

   They were faced with the entire German VI Corps, outnumbered six to one in what has been called 'an extraordinary battle'. The horsemen of the Lancers and Dragoons charged, but were beaten back, horses caught up in the wires and fences of allotments and tracks which crisscrossed the countryside . . . Six thousand shells fell in two hours . . . the waves of field grey pressed forward . . . one German later recalled 'they fired like devils, simply to move was to invite destruction . . . in our first attack we lost nearly a whole battalion'.[3]

Heatstroke mixed with shellfire and blood. The British units were losing men all around and in danger of being enveloped and so the great retreat began . . . Artillery batteries called for their horses and pulled back. Infantry, under heavy fire, withdrew into streets and roads in good order, but many runners taking orders to withdraw were killed before their messages could be delivered.

   Back in Norfolk, 6,000 untrained but determined men had walked, cycled or taken the train to Norwich from all over the large wide flat county and volunteered for service in the Norfolk Regiment – a colossal number for the time. The existing two regular and one special reserve battalions were now supplemented by the formation of the 4th, 5th and 6th Territorial Battalions (the Territorial Army having been one of the reforms created by Secretary of State for War, Sir Richard Haldane).

   These part-time troops now became full-time and started making their way to the new training camps of Kitchener's 'New Army' – designed with the intention of winning the war in 1915. With the arrival of this mass of new recruits a further four battalions of 1,200 men each were drawn up to form the 7th, 8th, 9th and 10th Service Battalions.

   To train and drill these new units was a real challenge. Most officers were either straight from Sandhurst, or retired officers who had last seen service in the Boer War. Their gallantry was not in doubt, but the same could not be said for their ability to understand the new warfare that was emerging. The tactics drilled into the recruits in the barracks on Mousehold Hill, like those for countless other battalions up and down the country, were to be stretched to the limit by the mud, machine guns and gas of northern France. For now, there was still time for the drill sergeants to turn boys into men and individuals into units.

One final unit to be formed at this time was the Suffolk and Norfolk Yeomanry. This was a militia unit, based on similar lines to those of the colonial detachments of the Edwardian period. The Norfolk Yeomanry was led by a range of Norfolk landowners. Being virtually self-supporting, they provided their own uniforms and tended to recruit their own estate workers as in days of old, when retainers were the mainstay of the army. By 1914 the Norfolk Yeomanry boasted some 400 men spread across 4 squadrons. Having said their goodbyes, the Norfolk Yeomanry was sent to form up in Woodbridge in Suffolk, and it is here that Edward and Jack arrived to join their new unit which, on 7 February 1917, was re-designated as the 12th (Norfolk Yeomanry) Battalion of the Norfolk's.[4]

Churchill and Gallipoli

The winter of 1914–15 was spent in Suffolk practising sword drill, parade ground drill and fitness. However, even as the trench lines and mass graves were spreading across Flanders, there was still no call for the 12th Service Battalion. These must have been frustrating days of waiting for Jack, but they gave him a chance to take the train into London to meet with Nellie and enjoy dinners with his newfound contacts and friends.

Jack's new rank of temporary major in the Norfolk Regiment suited him well and was the result of his obvious leadership qualities and experience – he was in fact probably the most experienced combat soldier in the battalion. Sporting his new uniform, with a major's crown on his sleeve and flourishing his gloves and cane, London must have seemed like a dream to Jack. Only a year before, he was working and sweating in the heat and dust of the Eastern Cape, drinking hard, playing cricket and trying to keep himself occupied. Now here he was surrounded by huge historic buildings he had only dreamed of, green parks, thousands of motor cars, trams and buses, the hustle and bustle of people everywhere, the bridges over the Thames and of course the many hotels.

By hanging onto the coattails of the Crawford Greenes, Jack attended many drinks parties, dinners and even balls raising funds for the troops and meeting all their influential friends. The Crawford Greenes' circle would have included many very wealthy individuals and families. A good number would have been from the colonies and lived in their London town houses for part of the year – just as foreign millionaires do today. It was a world apart from where he had come from only months before, but a world he loved and breathed in as if it were a whole new life. In this new range of company, Jack had a fresh audience in which to expose his charm, huge-spirited nature and confidence – in contrast to the tight-lipped conservatism of his fellow officers. We know he had a special affection for the Ruben's Hotel in Victoria. It is still there, just as he would have known it – where evening events and dinners abounded and where Jack could network with London society. It may also have been where he met up with his aunt – a Mrs Hamilton – married to the very wealthy Sir Frederick H. Hamilton of Margery Hall.[5]

Sir Frederick was a South African himself and a millionaire in his own right. Over the next few years Jack wass often to be found residing at Margery Hall, which sits just to the north-east of Reigate in Surrey. We know that Mrs Hamilton was his aunt from various references in newspapers to his living at Margery Hall. In a report dated 12 November 1919, Nellie (by then Jack's wife) mentioned that there had been an incident at his aunt's house near Reigate.[6] Becoming a friend of the Hamilton's gave Jack and Ted even more exposure to the world of London society, with its glamour, music and vibrancy. It also drew him into a political circle as there were men with political ambitions alongside their business interests. The two young officers were seen as the young heroes, keen to get to the Front and do their bit for England. Dashing, handsome, charismatic, they were no doubt welcome additions to every party – but Jack wanted to get into the fight. He would not have long to wait.

Writing in the late twentieth century, the historian A. J. P. Taylor described Gallipoli thus: 'The Gallipoli expedition was a terrible example of an ingenious strategic idea carried through after inadequate preparation with inadequate drive.'[7] At the time, of course, it was not possible to foresee this would be the result. It was an idea driven, perhaps, by the desire to do something to break the deadlock on the Western Front. Inevitably in war, against a backdrop of complex political and personal ambitions, it is the soldiers who must fight and risk their lives, often for what they do not personally understand or believe in. The Western Front had, by the winter of 1914–15, already taken shape as a killing ground on an industrial scale where reconnaissance showed no way through, but offensives were launched anyway and ended where they had begun. Tens of thousands died proving what reconnaissance had already told them.

The cost of speaking out against such futile loss of life was severe. For any Edwardian staff or general officer to question tactics or refuse an order not only meant immediate dismissal followed by a court martial and very likely the death penalty (the first British soldier to be shot for cowardice was in August 1914), but also disgrace for his family and children. Jack, although not an Edwardian British officer, but an Irish South African with the temperament to match, had as yet not arrived on the Western Front. If he had he would either have been killed quickly in some heroic, but forgotten, attack, or rebelled and recoiled at the senseless tactics employed by the General Staff. In this deadlock situation it was not the General Staff that came up with an alternative way to win the war in 1915, but the politicians – most notably Churchill.

Many saw the Gallipoli campaign as having the potential to win the war if Asquith's government and the General Staff had the determination to see it through. However, as history judged, it became a disastrous sideshow to the catastrophic main event and saw the flower of the Australian and New Zealand armies ripped to pieces by bullet and shell, alongside their British Allies, just as the Royal Marines had been at Antwerp in 1914 in Churchill's first experiment in tactical control. Indeed, Antwerp was the first real indication of how Churchill operated as a strategic and tactical leader. Although he has been rated as the greatest Briton of all time for his role in the Second World War, for many Churchill was both the best and worst kind of leader. Synchronicity was going to raise its head once more as the lives of Jack and Churchill became entwined in the spring of 1919. It is as well at this juncture to familiarize ourselves with one of the many sides of Churchill not so well publicized.

When war broke out in August 1914, Churchill could see, like Jack, a new horizon of opportunity and excitement. Appointed as First Lord of the Admiralty in 1911 (until his resignation in 1915), he had enormous reach of authority and pushed through some valuable reforms of the Royal Navy. But his real goal was to be at the Front. Like Jack, Churchill had seen fighting on his own in the Boer War, Sudan and the North-West Frontier. Like buccaneers of old, both Jack and Churchill shared a passion for danger, which day-to-day life could not provide. They also shared a defiant belief in being right. Once either had an idea in their head their entire force and focus was directed at that aim. Thus it was that when Churchill saw the Belgian army still bravely holding on to Antwerp by October 1914, when the rest of their country had fallen, Churchill was energized into helping with a rushed intervention of British troops. He even visited Antwerp by special mission and returned to plead his case to Prime Minister Herbert Asquith. He was rebuffed. Resources, ships and men were scarce and it was inevitable that Antwerp would fall. But Churchill found a way around the problem and provided his own troops, garnered from the Royal Navy and a royal naval division. In haste, 2,000 men were hastily ordered to sail for Antwerp to support the few British troops already there. Within 5 days Antwerp had fallen, many of the troops had been killed or wounded, and 1,400 spent the rest of the war as prisoners.

In an article written in 1993, Baron Annan commented:

My own experience in the war cabinet office during World War Two confirms what I had read. Churchill was by nature bellicose. What more astonishing proposal can ever have been made by a British cabinet minister than that of Churchill on October 5th 1914 when he told Asquith he would resign from the Admiralty if he could be given senior military rank and the full powers of a commander of a detached force in the field in order to reinforce Antwerp . . . His restless mind, which fired off instructions for 'action this day', bred one scheme after another. As a member of the joint intelligence staff in the war cabinet I would arrive each morning wondering what new rabbit had jumped out of the hat during the night . . . often I would shout 'Oh God no!'[8]

We will never know what impact this event had on Churchill. What we do know is that his willingness to bypass authority or contrary advice in a cavalier and dismissive style in pursuit of his belief that something had to be done, and in his way, was a hallmark of his temperament. This was to happen now in Gallipoli just as it had already happened at Antwerp the previous year, and affect the lives of hundreds of thousands, including Jack's. It was to happen again in 1919 – though on that occasion he was to be blocked by Jack himself.

Although Turkey was never part of the British Empire, consecutive British governments during the nineteenth century treated it as if it should have been. 'The Sick Man of Europe', Turkey was always at the centre of some territorial or strategic design. Situated as it was between Russia and the Mediterranean, it represented a bastion against Russia or the entrance to the Mediterranean, depending on which side of the fence you were standing. To protect India and Africa, the British navy did not want to face a Russian fleet sailing south out of the enormous pond of the Black Sea into the Mediterranean. When this looked probable, wars broke out, such as the Crimean War (1852–5), where again thousands of lives were lost to prevent the spread of Russian expansionism. When Disraeli purchased the Suez Canal shares in 1875, Britain not only had a strategic interest in propping up 'The Sick Man', but also a financial one. By 1914 Russian ambitions in Turkey had been replaced by German ones, as Wilhelm II's imperial policy of Weltpolitik focussed on influencing and advising Turkey, thereby further increasing tension across Europe.

The outbreak of war was not a surprise – even if the pace of events was. Prior to 1914, Churchill was to be found in the vanguard of attempting to form a strong front against German imperial ambitions – he had, after all, been instrumental in supporting the naval arms race. Churchill's interventionist attitude was always very pronounced, given that he favoured failure from action to the ignominy of inaction, and this was demonstrated at great cost in human lives on numerous occasions: Antwerp, Gallipoli, Archangel and Narvik. It was of course a characteristic shared by one of his soldiers – Jack was the archetypal officer bent on doing something rather than doing nothing. The Irish statesman Edmund Burke comments that, 'No man regretted more than he who did nothing because he could only do a little'. Churchill felt he could always do something. As A. G. Gardiner wrote of Churchill:

You may cast the horoscope of anyone else: his you cannot cast. You cannot cast it because his orbit is not governed by any known laws, but by attractions that deflect his path hither and thither. It may be the attraction of war and peace, of social reform or of a social order – whatever it is he will plunge into it with all the schoolboy intensity of his nature. His loves may be many, but they will always be the passion of a first love. Whatever shrine he worships at, he will be the most fervid of his prayers. . . 'Keep your eye on Churchill' should be the watchword of these days. Remember he is a soldier first, last and always. He will write his name big on our future, let us take care he does not write it in blood.[9]

Jack was one of tens of thousands of men, who became the instruments of not just Churchill's plans, but also those of the generals on both sides. In the case of Gallipoli, the view of Churchill by Lucy Masterman captures the foundation of the campaign well:

'In nearly every case an idea enters his head from outside. It then rolls around the hollow of his brain, collecting strength like a snowball. Then after whirling winds of rhetoric, he becomes convinced that it is right; and denounces everyone who criticises it.'[10]

Prior to 1914, significant efforts by the German foreign ministry had been aimed at drawing Enver Pasha – leader of 'The Young Turks' – into a reliance on German support against the British and Russians. Although Pasha had at one time been convinced that the future of Turkey depended on a strong relationship with Britain, in 1913 he cemented a relationship with Germany.

These political events did not fundamentally alter the European strategic situation as it existed either in 1914 or as it developed later. Turkey was not a first-rate power. Indeed, Turkey might have remained on the periphery had Britain not decided to prevent two warships being built in British shipyards for Turkey from being delivered. This simply pushed Turkey into the arms of Germany. On 26 September 1914, the Dardenelles were closed by the Turks, the entire length of the Bosphorus was mined and the Turks hurried along with extensive fortifications to prevent any seaborne invasion. Despite this, a seaborne invasion was exactly what the Allies, driven by Churchill, attempted.

It was typically bold, but also typically rash and if successful, would probably have turned the entire war in France. Failure would lead to the death of many thousands. Churchill, however, was not alone in believing that British troops could and should be used to better effect than 'chewing barbed wire in Flanders'.

Churchill saw an attack on the Dardenelles as an appropriate strategy for a number of reasons. The devastating firepower of the Royal Navy could not be used in Flanders, whereas it could be used to fire at Turkish positions. Secondly, Russia was calling for supplies, which could either be delivered via a tortuous route through the ice in the Baltic, or far more easily through the Black Sea. Thirdly, an attack on the Dardenelles would draw off German troops from the Western Front. Lastly, if successful, the British and Commonwealth armies could drive into Germany from the south. Despite the problems and risks, Churchill pressed on and as Lloyd George recalled: 'When Churchill has a scheme agitating in his powerful mind . . . he is indefatigable in pressing it upon the acceptance of everyone who matters in the decision'.[11]

Whilst Churchill worked through some of the details of a plan, which he was convinced would end the war, the fate of thousands of men hung in the balance. In England, divisions formed up and started to prepare for invasion from the sea, whilst in Egypt the ANZACs (the Australian and New Zealand Army Corps) were training in the dust and heat. Along the route to opening the assault, Churchill was faced by a number of officers, who voiced considerable doubt over the entire plan. But Churchill overpowered each one, converting their doubts into possibilities. His powerful confidence and energy manoeuvred everything out of his way:

> He always retained unswerving independence of thought. He approached a problem as he himself saw it and of all the men I have ever known he was the least liable to be swayed by the views of even his most intimate counsellors . . . unless the Prime Minister (as he was then) was himself impressed by the argument, pressure by others seldom had any effect.[12]

More telling:

> He was not easy to work for, particularly during the anxious days of the war. Patience was a virtue with which he was totally unfamiliar . . . his own rapidity of thought and expression was partly responsible for this, together with the fact that having been in a position to give orders all his life, and seldom obliged to execute them, he had no conception of the practical difficulties of communication and of the administrative arrangements.[13]

By the time the troopships set sail in March 1915, the Turks knew they were coming and all surprise had been lost. Naval bombardments continued into February and March, but the serious damage to two British and one French battleship in uncharted minefields, meant that the bombardments stopped and the Turks were alerted. Whereas this might have caused many commanders to reconsider, it did not have such an effect on Churchill:

> I think I was pretty well trained to sit and manage a horse. This is one of the most important things in the world. Young men have often been ruined through owning horses or through backing horses but never through riding

them – unless of course they break their necks, which, taken at a gallop, is a very good death to die.[14]

The men who landed into the horrors of Suvla Bay and elsewhere on that horrifying coastline, were making that gallop on Churchill's behalf.

The story of the Gallipoli landings of 1915 and the massacres that developed afterwards are well documented. Often Gallipoli is the poor relation of the Somme, Verdun and the Western Front generally – although not of course to the people of Australia and New Zealand. The months between April 1915 and January 1916 saw every kind of horror, miscalculation and disaster so typical of the battles in Flanders. The huge losses on the steep cliffs and small beaches selected by General Hamilton, crippled the attacks from the start and invasion rapidly became a fight for survival. By the end of June 1916, the key British formation, the 29th Division, had been severely mauled and thousands of its experienced troops had either been killed or were in hospitals throughout the Middle East. Instead of withdrawing, it was decided to press on by reinforcing the landings.

The Suvla Bay landings in August 1916 were as much of a disaster as their predecessors. It was as if no intelligence material had reached Whitehall at all. Consequently, 1,000 men were killed on the first day and a further 2,000 over the next 2 days as they tried to get off the beach. The strategic result was far from diverting German manpower away from the Western Front. Gallipoli was instead becoming a huge drain on Allied forces. Quickly the service battalions that were being earmarked for the Western Front, suddenly started planning for their war in Turkey. Likewise, individual officers were able to request a transfer and so it was that Acting Major Jack Kelly was transferred to Gallipoli.

The First Command
The spring of 1916 saw Jack and Edward continuing to train with the 12th Service Battalion on the commons and fields of rural Suffolk, whilst at the same time taking the train to London to meet with Nellie and her family. However, in June, Jack approached his commanding officer and requested a transfer to help fill the many vacant roles in units in the 29th Division. Thus it was that Jack began his association with the 1st Battalion The Kings Own Scottish Borderers (1/KOSB), who were part of 87 Brigade, 29th Division. So, his third change of collar dogs and cap badge now took place on board a troopship bound for Turkey. Arriving ten days later, the regimental diary of the KOSB, recorded by Captain Shaw, carries the following entry: '23rd July, 1915: A new Major has joined us . . . The new major was a Herculean giant of Irish-South African origin, with a quite remarkable disregard for danger.'[15] Even from such a small piece of evidence, it is possible to see that Jack cut an impressive figure: large man with a large presence and a large temper, who within days of his arrival had already shown a reckless attitude to his

own safety. Standing tall in a remarkable and rare photograph taken in the trenches at Gallipoli, Jack was indeed huge, like an oak. With an officer's walking stick, he dwarfs those around him. The wound stripes on his sleeve at the end of the Gallipoli campaign indicate that he was wounded twice and gassed twice. Jack perhaps saw life as the battle and the Turks as an opportunity – they were just another challenge to meet head on and another opportunity to fight.

Replacing his Norfolk regiment collar dogs and flashes with that of the cross of St Andrew emblazoned with the three-turreted castle of Edinburgh (the regimental badge of the KOSB), he went about his work as a new major. During August and September Jack survived the merciless and dreadful fighting, and as an acting major would have commanded a company of over 100 men of the 1/KOSB – a crack battalion from a crack regiment.

It did not take long for Jack to make his mark in the battalion. Apart from his 'unique if not wide vocabulary' used to shout across the trenches to the Turks, he was almost an irresistible force of aggression. His first injuries came on 21 August 1915 in Suvla Bay, where he received serious bullet wounds to his right leg. Taken to the rear in frustration, the regimental diary states that he was back in the front lines by 15 September. He had received the first of his four wounds in Gallipoli.

Jack was further wounded in early September by a shell fragment in his back – as was reported in the *Scotsman* on 16 September 1915 – although this did not see him leave the line but carry on leading his company. Then tragedy struck the battalion, as was recorded in the regimental diary: 'The old routine had hardly commenced when a dreadful calamity befell the KOSBs. Their CO and the orderly officer of the day, 2nd Lt J.D. Mill were killed on 15th October by the direct explosion of a shell from Asia.'

Captain Shaw, a company commander with the KOSB, who had been half buried himself in the explosion, describes the gruesome sight which met his eyes: parts of limbs, of burned, bloodstained and shredded uniform and of the open eyes of men killed in an instant with no time to say their goodbyes. The commanding officer was badly missed. Shaw says of him:

He lived for the regiment, which was his sole thought: a strict martinet and very severe at times. Yet all respected him and most feared him too. Stoney was so tremendously energetic and strong, though a small, delicate featured, bronzed man, that we miss him exceedingly.

It may be added that he was a professional soldier and master of his profession. It was not only the hero of the landing and the disciplinarian, the calm, dignified, spick and span British officer, it was the man who knew the army machine in and out, who would see justice done to his officers, and who had a gift of clear exposition that was most missed.[16]

For October, Captain Cookson took command of the battalion and then word came through that Temporary Major J. S. Kelly was to take command of the whole battalion – this was gazetted later in 1916 as being from 28 October 1915. For Jack this was the military highlight of his life so far. His rank of major was only an acting one and only in recognition that he had previous service and that the Norfolk Yeomanry back in Suffolk needed officers of a senior rank. Although he had been commissioned in the Boer War, Jack had never had formal training or, more crucially, been to Sandhurst to be trained as a British officer. He knew little of the expectations of the mess, old school ties and stiff upper lips, but he did know what would make the men follow him and he did know how to fight. To be catapulted into command of an elite Scottish battalion means that we have to try to understand why his brigade commander suggested, ordered and approved of this significant promotion.

Major General C. H. T. Lucas
Making sense of the jigsaw of information and even evidence to produce a sound and fair biography of someone's life is no easy task. Conjecture and educated guessing (including downright guessing) all have to come into play – unless one stumbles across a small gold mine of documents hitherto never seen or read before. This is exactly what a letter from the granddaughter of Major General Cuthbert Henry Tindall Lucas provided, when she heard of the attempt being made to write about Jack. From any angle, her grandfather was the archetypal British service officer in mid-career on the outbreak of war in 1914. He was educated at Marlborough, Gentleman Cadet, Corporal and Senior Corporal at the Royal Military College, Sandhurst, and, like Jack, he saw service in the Boer War in Orange Free State and Transvaal. Whilst Jack went back home to trading labour, the then Captain Lucas went on to Egypt and the Sudan between 1902 and 1905, where again his path might have crossed with both Churchill and Jack. A plethora of jobs in various units followed before being accepted at Staff College in 1912, which is where he was based in August 1914. As a captain and then major in the BEF, Lucas commanded a company of 1st Battalion Royal Berkshire Regiment and fought at the battles of the Aisne and Ypres, before becoming brigadier major for 87 Brigade in 29th Division – this made Lucas a senior officer in the very same brigade that Jack served in as commanding officer of both 1/KOSB and 1st Battalion The Inniskilling Fusiliers (1/RIF).

As we know, Jack, however, did not land with either unit in Gallipolli in April 1915. Lucas, on the other hand, did. The first knowledge Lucas would have had of Jack would have been in July 1915 when Jack arrived in Gallipoli, posted from England to the KOSB and his brigade. On arrival, Jack would have met Lucas who was the brigade major and second in command of 87 Brigade. Lucas would have seen and heard at first hand the fighting qualities of Jack. When Lucas was promoted to command the brigade from 15 August 1915, it would therefore have been him who made the decision to promote Jack to temporary command of the battalion as 'temporary lieutenant colonel' from 28 October, when so many officers in the battalion were either killed or wounded. We can assume from this that Lucas had already formed a favorable impression of Jack – in contrast to some of the officers in the battalion. It would have been either because Lucas could not see a suitable and strong enough leader within the battalion for this role at that point in time, or because he really was impressed by 'Bomb Kelly' and his fighting spirit. It would also have been Lucas who prevented Jack from leading sixty men with bombs out to sort the Turks on an evening patrol he planned. Either way, Jack and Lucas were now to share the responsibilities of command and the horrors of war for the next eighteen months or so, as Lucas was commander of 87 Brigade from August 1915 through to January 1918 (through the battles of the Somme, Arras, Ypres and Cambrai). As we shall see, Jack and Lucas become good friends. This might be seen as something of a surprise. Lucas, with his rigidly programmed mind and experience of command structure and attitudes of the British army, and Jack, with his unorthodox and unpredictable style, meant that Lucas would have been sensitive to the fact that Jack would not be an easy fit with the officers of the KOSB. Nevertheless, he must already have formed admiration for his bravery and seen that this was what was needed, regardless of style. Lucas himself was a brave man: his own life story showed he was a courageous individual. Maybe he saw something of himself in Jack. His letters to his wife reveal a friendship with Jack and also give a valuable and rare insight into life behind the front lines, as well as events in Jack's own life.

Imagine the scene: a cold frosty morning in November 1915; men standing to order at 5.15am; biting winds with men's breath leaving their bodies – perhaps for the last time. In front across the hard, frost-covered ground, churned up by months of fighting, stood the Turks, only 100yd away, so close you could smell them. You knew that they had bayonets fixed, machine guns and hand bombs primed, ready for a rush assault to try to overwhelm the KOSBs' positions – and there would be no room for prisoners, such was the battleground in Gallipoli. A sergeant with mud-splattered helmet, worn-through brown uniform, rough, unshaven and dirty, woollen gloves with holes and carrying his Lee–Enfield rifle with a shiny 18in cold steel bayonet fixed, walks along the wooden boards whispering in his broad Glaswegian accent under his breath, 'Stand still. Mark your target well. If they reach the trench, give them the bayonet. We're going nowhere. Get it?'

At the end of one trench, on a corner, stands a young lieutenant, face blue with cold and white with fear, green scarf from his mother around his neck, brown uniform with a single brass pip on the sleeve and a revolver whose metal is so cold, he has to breathe on it and hope it will fire when needed. His calves wrapped in webbing up to his knee and his cloth, peaked hat sitting squarely on his head, he looks to his left at Lieutenant Colonel Kelly, looking twice his size, a huge man with a black moustache, square granite jaw and slightly double chin. No helmet for him, just his red, black and white tartan forage cap to give a feeling of calm control; no fear in his eyes, just an unblinking stare at the ground ahead of them. A glint in his eye tells you he has no fear of death from the Turks. This is his theatre, his battleground, his home.

'B company present and stood to Sir' salutes the sergeant.

'Thank you. Carry on,' whispers the colonel, resting his cane on the sandbagged wall and taking his revolver from his large brown leather holster on his left hip. Looking at the young lieutenant he mutters, 'Well, if they come now, we had better be ready to give them hell!' He walks along the lines himself, having to stoop as his head and shoulders would show above the parapets, tapping and slapping men on the backs as he goes, a team man, quite different from any of the other officers. Closer to the men than their previous CO, whom they feared, their awe at this CO is in wondering what he might do next. It is not unheard of for him to stand tall and shout, 'Come on you bastards, have a go at us. We're ready for you!' Unconventional and not so much a stiff upper lip than a salty tongue; not suitable for the barracks, but in Gallipoli at 'Stand To' he is ideal.

Bomb Kelly

Jack was very creative too when it came to killing the enemy. In the close hand-to-hand world of the Gallipoli trenches, it was a regular tennis match for both sides to lob explosives into the opposing trench. It was desperate stuff. Despite having the very best of the new modern weapons that were then available, the fight came down to a slog, and this was when Jack was at his best, as the regimental diary continued: 'His interest in ballistics extended to catapults, to obtain greater range. Such things would have been out of date on the Western Front, but on the Peninsula the catapult came into its own. The bold Major won the soubriquet of "Bomb Kelly" and excelled in stunts on occasions alarming even his own side.'[17] This newfound fame for the new CO of the KOSB spread throughout the 29th Division, as this extract from an article from the *Gallipoli Society* magazine explains:

Major 'Bomb' Kelly would reach for a pile of former tins of beef which were now packed with explosive and shell casings and a rough fuse through the base, light the fuse, the troops around him stood back, he stood up and holding a long stick in his left hand with a leather strap in his right would launch the home made bomb across the dead ground towards the Turks. Occasionally if he got his timing wrong, the tin would shoot off behind him or to the side and men scrambled for their lives as it went off – but it didn't half keep you on your toes. Often, when the tin hit the mark, out would jump Turkish soldiers to be shot by the KOSBs and up would go a cheer as the tin exploded. Much like a deadly game of cricket . . . The Major knew no fear and laughed and cheered if we got one right into their holes.

Jack therefore soon made a name for himself, not just in the battalion, but throughout the regiment and right up to divisional level. At one point, Jack was pulled out of the line by General de Lisle, CO of the 29th Division, to command the bombing school that had been set up, as this was becoming the only way to kill the enemy at close range.

Adapting quickly to his newfound rank and authority, Jack revelled in the role of lieutenant colonel and battalion commander. This was where he had always wanted to be. Never having had any training to command even a platoon of 30 men, let alone a company of 120 or a battalion of over 500, he reacted as if he had been born to command, but in his own way. Thus, the Herculean colonel, whilst popular with the men of the KOSB, who saw him as a team man and who felt closer to him than they had ever felt to any officer, found relations with his fellow officers more difficult. It is worth noting that his promotion was noted in the regimental diary as a 'change in mood and method'. Nevertheless, his bravery was undoubted and in October, despite having been sent to the rear after suffering in a gas attack (something which was to affect his lungs for the rest of his life) Lieutenant Colonel Kelly was Mentioned in Dispatches by General Sir Charles Munro.[18]

The contrast in styles between a traditional CO of a British front-line battalion and that of Jack could not be more stark. In an edition of the *Dundee Evening Telegraph*, published in September 1919, the journalist recalled:

An Early Bomb Enthusiast

Colonel Kelly VC . . . will be remembered by Gallipoli soldiers of the 29th Division in which he commanded 1st KOSB's during the later stages of the expedition.

He was the greatest exponent of the hand grenade when the missile was only coming into wide use. Numerous acts of personal daring were credited to him. Perhaps the most picturesque being his famous strafe when, in reply to a Turkish bomb which was lobbed into his trenches, he climbed up onto the parapet and hurled bombs and adjectives at the Turks as long as his men could find the goods to hand him.

On another occasion on two successive nights, his patrols failed to return. Colonel Kelly, in reporting this to Brigade Headquarters, announced that the next night he was personally going out with 60 men armed with bombs 'to see about it'. The Brigadier forbade the expedition as being outside a C's duties. [This was of course Lucas trying to exercise some control over Jack.]

Despite the careful phraseology of the regimental history, it is possible to see and understand that Jack was not part of the normal officer machine. This disjunction would ultimately lead to a clash of monumental proportions in 1919, and the seeds were being sown now on the muddy, blood-stained slopes of Gallipoli. Jack had been trained in the field of life in South Africa, not the playing fields either of Eton or Camberley. He fought as he thought – not how he was taught. At times, this may have saved the lives of many of his men, but possibly cost lives at other times. Breaking with the expected or traditional was not a deliberate act, it was natural for Jack, almost like a law of nature. He thought through and planned his exposure to danger – not to survive it as the normal person would do, but to exploit the opportunity. The fact that death waited with every bullet aimed at him crossed his mind without making any difference, and his fellow officers must have found the contrast in styles a challenge. He was, of course, also very fortunate that in Lucas he had a brigade commander who supported him. The frequent unorthodox actions that Jack indulged in could easily have resulted in removal from the lines by a less understanding brigade major.

Another aspect of his particular heroic style was that there were many repeat performances. His reputation grew based not on the back of one dramatic episode of bravery and courage that resulted in news headlines and a medal for gallantry, but on continuous and multiple examples of heroism. His was an ongoing drama that could have been ended at any time by that bullet meant for him. He came close of course. In February 1916, the *London Gazette* announced that 'for his fine leadership and remarkable gallantry' he was to be awarded the Distinguished Service Order (DSO). In a raid on a Turkish trench Jack had been wounded twice, but still took the trench and got his men (the remaining six) back to their own lines. Thus, in Gallipoli he was to be gassed once and wounded three times, on the Somme he was to be shot through the lung, lose a shoulder blade to shrapnel and other injuries . . . but he did not die. Maybe he was the last cavalier – a throwback to a heroic age long past, seemingly invincible to pain and mortality.

Withdrawal

The KOSB was a Scottish regiment of great repute and heritage. Like most Scottish regiments, it was led exclusively by English officers, as such regiments had always been. Clearly Jack was respected for his bravery, courage and impressive physical stature, but he was held on sufferance by his fellow officers. He had risen to his rank through chance and good fortune, and no doubt judged by Brigadier General Lucas as just what the battalion needed to see them through difficult times and the approaching winter. The command of a battalion like this one could have taken twenty years of hard work as a career officer and a good deal of other necessary attributes, such as a public school and university education. But Jack had achieved all this after expulsion from school and with no experience of Oxbridge, and his colonial background was frowned upon and almost hidden. In the regimental history, we find the delicately worded phrase: 'It may be added that he was what is called in Scotland a "character" and possessed a strikingly vigorous if not specially wealthy vocabulary.' For such a wonderful and typically British understatement read that he was a handful, swore a great deal and used only a series of key words to get his message across. This was followed by: 'It [the withdrawal from Gallipoli] was soon accomplished and the KOSB maintained their reputation throughout the Kelly interregnum.'

So, the diary expresses the view that the battalion managed to maintain its identity, discipline and character despite the leadership of its temporary CO. We can see that Jack continued to be at odds with a system of authority that had already shown him what it expected. He had crashed into it before in the Boer War and again in Somaliland. He knew full well what was expected and what to expect, but it did not really matter to him. Recklessness was a key attribute. The army needed him, but not what came with him. Similarly, at times in his career Churchill was needed, but not what he brought with him.

As November 1915 drifted into December, the weather worsened and the cold hit well below freezing. In his *Gallipoli Diary*, Major John Gillam DSO described just one night in the trenches of Gallipoli:

Last night the frost was severe and the men lying out in the mud behind the soaking trenches suffered the greatest hardship that a soldier could endure – namely to lie in soaking clothes, which freeze stiff in a biting wind, while the temperature falls to below zero.

In front of the 86th Brigade the Turks hold higher ground than we do and I think that they must have opened one or two of their sapheads when their trenches were flooded, thus allowing their water to rush over to our side engulfing all our first line dugouts and communication trenches. Officers in the line, if they were not on watch, were huddled together all night endeavouring to get warmth from each other's bodies. Telephone communication broke down and many men, cut off from the rest and having to watch the enemy, froze and died at their posts overnight.[19]

Back in London discussions had been going on for weeks about whether and how to withdraw from this disaster. In Gallipoli, however, the KOSB might have had a quiet time in the trenches, but Jack was in his element nursing the fighting spirit. Entries in the War Diary show that on the 9 and 10 November continuous catapult bombing day and night seriously damaged the parapet of a Turkish trench, and saw Turks run to the rear in fear of what might be thrown at them next.

Whereas many would hope to lay low and survive, not angering the enemy, Jack aggressively took the war single-handedly to the whole Turkish army. This did not come without cost and on 21 August 1915, Jack's lungs were badly burnt by a waft of gas sent over from the Turkish lines. He was moved to hospital on the beach the next day, but was so badly burnt that he remained there until 28 October, when he then volunteered to return to the front lines, even though he could have taken a troopship home. From then on, breathing was difficult for him for the rest of his life. His shoulders were often hunched over trying to compensate for the harshness of breath that he felt, especially in cold weather. He carried the pain of his leg wound too, and his three-wound stripes showed a man who had been in the front of the action with the scars to prove it.

In his book, Ian Uys has numerous inaccuracies on the actual movements of Jack at this time, but he was right that Jack always led from the front, pressing home attacks, including one from which only six men from a platoon returned. The rare but magnificent photograph of Jack standing full height in the trenches at Gallipoli also shows he has three wound stripes – not bad for a CO and for only six months' tour of duty.[20]

At Brigade Headquarters there was always a need for good news and Lucas was pleased that the latest escapades of Major Kelly, the mad South African, had been recognized. Jack was recommended for the award of the DSO, not the Military Cross, and the necessary papers were dispatched to go through the formal channels. Meanwhile the decision had been taken to withdraw, rather than retreat, from Gallipoli.

Even before the decision had been taken, the barrel of men was running dry. All over the slopes, cliffs and beaches of Gallipoli, men lived in the earth, baked in the sun by day and froze in the cold of each night. Poorly provisioned and constantly bombed, disease ran unchecked amongst their numbers, killing as many Allied troops as the Turks. The ANZACs suffered terribly. Into this hell and quite bizarrely, given the conditions on this front, the Norfolk and Suffolk Yeomanry were ordered in September 1915. They made for Southampton to board the SS *Olympic*, which was the sister ship of the *Titanic*. What a cruise that must have been – ten days on board the world's most luxurious liner. Passing through the Strait of Gibraltar and on into the Mediterranean, it must have felt like a journey to the other side of the world for these lads and their officers, for whom a walk to Norwich was the highlight of the year. They were typical of their type – largely estate workers such as the Sandringham Company, where all the boys worked on the estate and their officers were the senior clerks, managers, surveyors and gardeners of the royal estate in North Norfolk. The Suffolk Yeomanry was more like a company of retainers from the Middle Ages following their knights into battle. They boasted in their battalion alone, twelve existing and former members of Parliament and, in case there was time to chase the Turks on horseback, twenty-two former masters of foxhounds! What was certain, although they did not know it, as they watched the waves crash around the enormous sides of this huge ship, was that whatever they had learnt waiting for their chance to fight, it was going to be of no use at all as they stepped into the cold, wet, mud and carnage of the peninsula.

The eight-day journey ended with the sound of gunfire and smoke ahead of the ship. Setting anchor in Mudros Bay on the island of Lemnos, they disembarked with shiny boots, polished leather and oiled rifles into small ferries and landed in Suvla Bay on 10 October. They never got off the bridgehead. Pounded by artillery as they landed, there was nowhere for them to go save replacing men on the bridgehead, who were being taken back on the same boats that they had just left. Under the command of 54th East Anglian Division, they would have heard broad Norfolk accents all around them. Men from the same villages no doubt recognized each other, exchanged news from home and swore about the Turks, wondering what the hell they were doing here when it was the Germans that they had gone to war with.

Men who had worked together, laughed together, shared a pint or three in the local pub, watched each other become husbands and fathers, arrived in a landscape utterly alien to them and completely removed from their own experience of life on the estates, where they accepted that their lot was to obey orders. Here they did the same, implicitly trusting in their officers. Although assumption is the mother of mistakes, we can safely assume that Lieutenant Colonel Kelly of 1/KOSB, came over to visit his own unit – he was, after all, still listed as an officer on the roll of the Yeomanry. What a reunion it must have been on the beaches of the Gallipoli peninsula, and what a reputation he had forged in such a short time. A credit to the regiment no doubt, but it was clear to all that this could not go on.

Within a few days, 17 other ranks of the Yeomanry had already been disembarked with dysentery and within a month this number had grown to 139. Only one man had been killed by enemy fire. The sewage and stench of death, with so many men using the same facilities and such extremes of cold, were killing them without a fight. By 27 November, where further inland Lieutenant Colonel Kelly of their number was bombing the Turks by hand, they had lost 189 of their troops to disease. Had Churchill been there to see for himself what horror and cost his schemes could create, he may have moderated his impetuosity.

As for Jack, his temporary command as lieutenant colonel continued through to the spring of 1916 and then came to an end. In early December, the Norfolk Yeomanry was evacuated from Gallipoli and according to their regimental history, a Major Kelly arrived back to the Norfolks to aid them with their withdrawal from Gallipoli. This could not have been easy. He would have received the news badly but probably knew it was coming. He was relieved of command of his front-line battalion and sent to re-join the Yeomanry who had as yet not even fired a shot. No doubt parting from his fellow officers was not difficult as they were relieved to see him go, but I suspect he found it harder to shake hands with his NCOs, and possibly even some of his soldiers whom he had shared so much with in such a short time. He was a man more at ease with the other ranks and this would have been the hardest of goodbyes. He returned to a unit that had not once engaged the enemy; the only enemy they had encountered was disease, which had claimed many of their number in senseless waste. The fortunate ones who survived this ordeal, could only have looked back on those retreating shores, as they left the horrors of Gallipoli behind, with shock and grief at the pointlessness of their fruitless mission. One New Zealander commented, 'it was not our wasted energy and sweat that grieved us. In our hearts it was to know we were leaving our dead comrades behind.'

The number of killed and wounded was estimated at 117,000, along with a further 100,000 evacuated with dysentery and other diseases, of which 50,000 died. The horrific statistics of the Somme should not be allowed to overshadow the suffering that took place at Gallipoli. In our day of minimum casualties and impact on lives through the use of technology, the suffering of 1915 seems unimaginable. And yet the men went and gave their lives – many willingly, some no doubt very unwillingly.

One thing that kept them together was discipline, but another was leadership. Jack had now gone from being a tearaway of a young man in 1912, to his brand of hero, with huge responsibility, by 1915. Whatever we may think of Jack as a person, we cannot ignore that he did have tremendous powers of resourcefulness, self-belief, stamina, drive and determination – already to be thought of as one of the bravest men in the 29th Division (a division already full of brave men). He had come a long way very quickly in his personal development. As he removed the rank insignia of a lieutenant colonel and reverted back to his rank of major, he was still reckless, difficult to manage, short-tempered, a barrel of laughs when the time was right and a nightmare when it was wrong. But he was also now a recognized hero and left the Mediterranean lucky to be alive, andenergized about arriving in London where his now wife to be was waiting with open arms.

Chapter 5

The Somme, 1916 and Marriage

'Questioned as to how he had gained his great reputation, he said, "By having despised death."'
Plutarch, quoting Agesilaus II, Eurypontid king of Sparta (400–360 BC)

By January 1916, both the 12th Service Battalion and 1/KOSB were recovering in Egypt. The whole of 29th Division had been withdrawn to Egypt, leaving thousands of their friends and comrades in the sands of Gallipoli. The men were dazed, tired and shocked. Whilst the Norfolk's were on their way home, the KOSB were kept near the Suez Canal 'where it remained for two months, training and guarding the Suez Canal'.

Jack needed a rest and no doubt enjoyed some calm times with the men around him. But by the end of January Jack returned to England with the Norfolk's. Landing at Portsmouth at 5.00am on a cold and freezing English morning, he took an early train for London for an emotional reunion with Nellie. Before he left he sent a telegram to Nellie letting her know that he was alive and well and his train arrival time. His gas wounds were playing up and his bones were bruised from the two wounds he had received, so the cold January air made for a hard few months ahead.

Arriving back at Waterloo station must have been a surreal experience. Virtually every day there were military bands sitting in corners which struck up whenever a train arrived, or fresh units left for the front. When you pass through Waterloo even today, you can imagine the steam and smoke billowing up high into the cold black steel roof, together with the noise of train whistles and people everywhere – some with the look of innocence as if there was no war at all, others visibly carrying the reflections of death that they had witnessed. On this day, Nellie was there to welcome him. Standing at the end of the marble-floored platform, she looked a wonderful sight of delicate and dedicated feminine charm and understated high fashion. Her neck surrounded by her favourite light brown fox-fur collar and her head covered in a warm fur hat. The war had given him purpose, ambition, personal acclaim and success, but it also gave opportunities that in peacetime would not have been there. A homecoming to the family and the welcome that Nellie provided was all an added bonus.

The insatiable demand for officers to lead the volunteer army was in full swing by the middle of 1915. The raising of new battalions for the New Army required as many serving or experienced officers as possible, and the reserve lists were combed for aging officers still able to carry a sword or use a walking stick in no man's land. For some this was a duty that had to be met reluctantly, whilst for others it re-opened a door that had once been closed. Not only did openings occur for officers in the New Army battalions yet to fight, but also in the constant requirement for replacement officers for those killed or wounded, as shown on the daily casualty lists, as well as to allow for rotation of officers who needed leave or hospital rest. War also created social opportunity – as long as you survived.

Marriage
Whilst Jack had been waging a war in Gallipoli, he had also been conducting his own personal campaign to gain the hand of Nellie in marriage. Wrapped in her humility and innocence, but with a strong sense of character and wisdom beyond her years, Jack was a particular challenge. Almost certainly Nellie recognized the energy and carefree abandon of Jack's character and found it very attractive, but perhaps also a certainty that danger was never far away. Nevertheless, she had fallen in love with the proud, dashing, confident Jack when they had first met in the July of 1914. Their relationship was not to be a whirlwind of heady romance but rather a gradual bond, where Jack perhaps felt something of a mother figure in Nellie, her careful and studious nature a perfect counterpoint to his explosive exuberance. There were other advantages too. Nellie was a very wealthy woman in her own right, and she moved in circles someone like Jack would never, in the normal course of events, be able to penetrate. But the Great War was not a normal course of events and all bets were off. A photograph of Nellie taken in 1916 and published to announce the news of their marriage, shows Nellie to be the refined, thoughtful and gentle figure we imagine. Although not possessing classical features or a distinctive beauty, Nellie was nevertheless a strong and influential society woman and part of her mission in the early days of their romance would have been to guide Jack into her social world.

Jack was on leave now for the next two months to recover from his wounds. He arrived in London with a uniform already displaying an impressive array of decorations, and still on attachment to the KOSB as the commanding officer of the 1/KOSB. Such was the meteoric change in his fortunes that two years of war had brought to Jack's life – from obscurity to war hero and commanding officer of an elite army unit – quite a change in his fortunes from Butterworth and dusty cricket matches. Conflict brought the best out of him and he performed like a star in a new play on the West End. He walked and swaggered as a natural hero should, he had already won his spurs and now announced to his growing circle of friends that he and Nellie were to be married. However, Nellie was not to become the gentle sunshine after Jack's rainy thunderstorms. She herself proved to be a woman of determination and conviction and her strong character, as well as wealth, probably held fascinations for Jack in this new world into which he had arrived.

Between January and March 1916, Jack would have visited Nellie's home at 21 Cranley Gardens many times. London has changed dramatically in recent years, but this little corner of Knightsbridge is not easily changed. In 1916, it would have felt very similar to today, with a cultured suburban atmosphere, an island of graceful well-to-do red-brick Victorian flats, buildings and small churches. Over these weeks, it became a second home to Jack, where he met Nellie and together they received guests at dinner parties, discussed the war, Gallipoli and what was coming next. It is easy to assume that Jack would have dominated any social gathering. From Cranley Gardens there would be taxis to the West End theatres, to fashionable houses in Belgravia and restaurants along The Strand. To everyone who knew them it seemed the ideal match. As if to bless the couple, on 2 February 1916 the War Office sections of the *London Gazette* announced the award of the DSO to Lieutenant Colonel Kelly for his actions in the Gallipoli peninsula. For many years, the standard work on the DSO was that by Sir O'Moore Creagh, which carried a simple notation of the award, stating that at the time Jack was still listed as being on the strength of the Norfolk Regiment, though plainly he had never even fired a shot with them. It was the South African newspaper the *East London Daily Despatch* that carried the first recognition of Jack serving with the British army – it was to become a regular relationship with the press over the next few years.

Jack Kelly DSO

'It was the Major's fine leadership, coupled with remarkable personal bravery – to which there is ample personal testimony – that won him the DSO . . . such has been his efficient work and steady perseverance . . .'.[1] The *London Gazette* of 2 February 1916 carried a little more detail: 'For his fine leadership, remarkable gallantry displayed during an attack on a Turkish trench when, despite being twice wounded, he led his men to capture the enemy position – only 6 men returned from the action.'

The previous October another article had appeared in a newspaper in South Africa. Written by Mr Bernard Oppenheimer, he announced that he would give £100 to each of the first South African recipients of the VC and £50 to the first ten winners of the DSO. Come January 1916 Mr Oppenheimer was already out of pocket. The first to receive his medal was Major/Acting Lieutenant Colonel Jack Sherwood Kelly. On hearing of his gift Jack immediately announced that he would donate his prize to the Frontier Hospital at Queenstown, where his mother had been taken in 1892. The news of this act of generosity was not lost on Mr Oppenheimer, who again wrote:

Dear Sir,

Having heard that Lt. Col Sherwood Kelly learned about my recent offer from 'The African World' whilst on active service in Gallipoli – where he won the DSO for conspicuous gallantry – and that he desires to send the amount to the hospital at Queenstown, his native town in South Africa, it gives me great pleasure to inform you that I have despatched the amount of £50 to the secretary of the Queenstown Hospital by this week's mail with the best wishes of this gallant officer.

It was not long before the British press began to take more of an interest in Jack's career and Reuter cables carried news of his donation and that he was 'greatly admired' by the Queenstown community. His local fame still carried a currency and was now being topped up by his exploits on the Western Front.

What Makes a Hero?

Perhaps it is worth pausing to reconsider (or 're-group' in army parlance) our ongoing assessment of the nature of courage. The 'hero' can be played in many ways. For some, heroism comes suddenly and unexpectedly, and brings with it a sense of shock and wonderment that something that was done so spontaneously and often effortlessly, can have had such an impact on others. For others being a hero is simply the worst thing of all. The guilt associated with knowing that others have done even braver things, but died unrecognized as the unsung heroes, goes along with their efforts to accept this new label. It was not unknown for such guilt to have overcome the recipient of the VC, for example, and suicide happened more than once as the feeling of unworthiness became overpowering. Then there were those for whom seeking out courage in themselves was the challenge, and, having achieved hero status, they really just wanted it to go away. Their challenge had been a personal one that was hijacked by the media and propaganda machines to inspire others. It took away their anonymity and, again, often ruined lives. But what about Jack? Which category did his courage and heroism fit?

Jack displayed a different sort of courage. He was already at peace with himself but at war with the world. If he died, he probably did not care. Life had been tough so far so why not accept it and fight back. He was to seek out the challenge of courage and test it. He had done this already many times as a young man in the Boer War, and in the trenches of Gallipoli, as 'Bomb Kelly', he had stood in open view of the Turks hurling homemade bombs at them. He had been gassed and shot, but as he could still stand so he could still carry on. He was already thought of as partly reckless and partly mad, alongside being a hero, held back by his senior officers from further irrational behaviour. As a commanding officer it was no longer just about him. But danger and anger create a powerful combination of emotional drugs. One thing needs noting however: whilst he was reckless with his own life, he was above all a guardian of the lives of others. Unlike Churchill, Jack did not play or experiment with the lives of men in the pursuit of glory. He was cautious and careful with his men – if he could win the war and save the lives of his troops that would have been the perfect balance of courage. Thus, rather than waiting for events to unfold where a courageous act was needed to rescue a situation, we see in Jack a man seeking the courageous act in advance, looking for the opportunity to play what he would call the hero, but what we might call the saviour. A powerful sense of self-sacrifice thus underpinned all that he did, and whilst critics might see a man bent on self-glorification it could be quite the opposite. This is not to say he did not revel in the acclaim – but the acclaim had not been the aim. Jack was also fortunate, as we have seen, that he fell by chance into the brigade commanded by a man like Lucas, a man who was able to give ground and understood man management. He saw that heroes like Jack needed careful management to get the best from them. A different and more typical officer would have seen Jack's story (and this book) cut much shorter.

Throughout January to April 1916, therefore, Jack was able to relax into London society: a world of parties for the war effort, but also growing confidence in the big push that would see Kitchener's New Army divisions bring the Germans to heel – 1916 was to be the year of victory. Such confidence may have contributed to the blossoming romance between Jack and Nellie. He was still CO of the 1st Battalion KOSB, but on extended leave. As they walked the streets of London as a happy couple, the corridors of the War Office echoed with the rush of feet as details for the coming war-winning offensive on the Somme were being fine-tuned.

They made a wonderfully romantic and charming pair: Jack with his irresistibly strong and confident air, his laughter and devil-may-care attitude to life, a row of medal ribbons that would be the envy of many officers senior to him, and four wound stripes to show he had already seen serious action and survived. Photos depict him with hand on hip, cutting the pose of a twentieth-century cavalier. Nellie, on the other hand, is best described by an article written about her in the *Ladies Field* in February 1916, where she is described as 'a pretty, graceful woman of literary and artistic tastes'.[2]

Recent studies have focussed on the widescale spate of so-called 'hasty marriages' that broke out across 1915 and 1916. The abnormal circumstances that now surrounded romantic relationships led to a sense that time was ticking away. To be married now was better than to regret it later – perhaps when the war had ripped them apart. This may have been true for Nellie and Jack, but once the proposal had been accepted and Nellie's brother William had given his blessing, Nellie was to be married at St Peter's Church in Cranley Gardens when Jack was next on leave. They had hardly had time to really get to know each other. It had been a matter of eighteen months from their first meeting, and a very large part of that Jack had been either with his regiment training or in Gallipoli fighting. The subtleties of building a life together, living together, identifying where compromise would be needed and surviving frictions had all been passed by. There were to be unfortunate repercussions soon after.

St Peter's was closed in 1972 and is today the Armenian Church and stands less than 50yd from what was then Nellie's home. St Peter's today is still very much a pretty and ornate but small church, nestling within the imposing family residences around it. According to the marriage certificate, Jack was not resident in London but resided at Margery Hall in Reigate, Surrey – with his aunt, Mrs Hamilton. So it was that the marriage took place on 22 April 1916. There is no pictorial evidence of the event but it is likely to have made quite a sight with members of Nellie's considerably wealthy family, mixing possibly with some of Jack's fellow officers from the Norfolk's. His period as CO of the KOSB probably did not endear him enough to their officers for them to be invited, or agree to attend. But he would have invited the substantially wealthy Hamiltons, and they in turn may have invited other wealthy businessmen that Jack would have been introduced to in the light of his DSO award. Edward Kelly was probably also there – maybe even as best man.

One of the witnesses to the marriage was E. E. Greene – this was Nellie's mother. However, her brother was not a witness and had he not been serving in Palestine he almost certainly would have been. The other witnesses were H. G. Evelyn Varden (the young aspiring American film actress) and Julia Wilson. Perhaps Nellie's sister, Georgina, was also there. The certificate also records that Jack described himself as 'Lieutenant Colonel 1stt Battalion KOSB', which indicates that although he had left Gallipoli with the 12th Norfolk's, he was still listed on the strength of the KOSB. Under 'condition' Jack described himself as bachelor, which indeed he was – although for the second time, as we know. However, most interesting of all is that Jack lied about his age. Having been born in 1880 he was clearly aged 36 in 1916, however he listed himself as aged 42. This can only have been to narrow the gap between Nellie and himself. Nellie, aged 44, was that much older, which would very much have attracted the frowns of the post-Victorian and Edwardian society of which she was a part, for marrying a much younger man.

We know nothing of the honeymoon or how long it lasted, but it was quickly brought to an end. The war was never far away and the four-month period between January and April 1916 was merely an interlude of calm between two storms. In France, the Germans and French were slaughtering each other at Verdun. As the Germans attempted to 'bleed the French army white', so the French under Marshal Petain were saying 'they shall not pass'. The officers and men on both sides who fought for these semantics went through a hell and horror hitherto unknown in history, as the mountains of skulls stored in vast cellars at Verdun today testify. Meanwhile, in Britain life went on as normal. The government was harangued daily about their general strategy and the socialist threat continued to grow.

Shortages were becoming severe and supplies from overseas increasingly threatened by submarine attacks. Thus, the pressure on Field Marshall Alexander Haig to strike a severe blow capable of ending the war, mounted daily. In response, he prepared his Somme offensive and in early May, Jack was ordered back to the Front having spent only a matter of days with his new wife. The regimental diary records: 'On 19th May Lt. Col A. J. Welch, just a year and seventeen days since his wound, resumed command . . . Lt. Col. Kelly was given another command in the division . . .'.[3] This new command was to be as CO of the 1/RIF. Brigadier General Lucas wanted him back and wanted him in command of another battalion, rather than see him return as a major, as the build-up for the Battle of Somme continued. This time it was to be an Irish battalion and an easier fit.

Moving from a Scottish to a largely Irish regiment also made sense – at least he could share the same jokes, language and temperament, and argue with whom he liked. Like many Ulstermen, if there was not an argument going on he would create one – not uncommon with an Irish officer perhaps. On the strength of 1/RIF, Jack was still listed as being on attachment from the 10th Norfolk's – which he was – but again he was never to see action with the Norfolk Regiment.

One can imagine the interest and excitement as the new colonel arrived to take command, and the sense of fun and determination that Jack brought with him as he returned to where he belonged and possibly felt most at home – in a war. The Inniskillings had a long and proud fighting history that covered Badajoz in the Peninsular War, Waterloo and many others. The regiment had been formed in 1881 and had grown to twelve battalions during the Great War and was to earn eight Victoria Crosses.

During May and June 1916 the build-up for the Somme offensive continued. The 29th Division, which had arrived from Egypt in Marseilles on 29 March and marched to the Western Front, formed up in three brigades. The whole was commanded by Lucas and then a brigadier for each brigade and each of four battalions commanded by a lieutenant colonel:

86 Brigade: 2/Royal Fusiliers, 1/ Lancashire Fusiliers, 16/ Middlesex and 1/Royal Dublin Fusiliers.

87 Brigade: 2/South Wales Borderers, 1/KOSB, 1/Royal Inniskilling Fusiliers, 1/Border Regiment.

88 Brigade: 4/Worcestershire, 1/Essex, 2/Hampshires, Royal Newfoundland Regiment.[4]

So it was that Jack returned not only to his old division in Gallipoli but also to his old 87 Brigade, and his new battalion command was alongside that of his previous one. The 29th Division was a strong and experienced division, with some highly trained and professional battalions, and it formed up as a key part of the line. To illustrate the point and to help understand the slaughter that was soon to follow, one can look at the 24th Division, which again was composed of three brigades:

17 Brigade: 1/Royal Fusiliers, 3/Rifle Brigade, 8/Buffs and 12/Royal
Fusiliers.
72 Brigade: 1/North Staffs, 8/Queens Royal West Surrey, 9/East Surrey
and 8/Queens Own Royal west Kent.
73 Brigade: 2/Leinsters, 9/Sussex, 7/Northamptons, 13/Middlesex and
12/Sherwood Foresters.

The key difference was that the 24th Division was a New Army division, raised from all those volunteers even as far back as the summer of 1914. Although many men had joined the colours and trained during 1915, few if any had seen action. The 29th Division had one service battalion out of its complement of twelve, whilst the 24th Division had nine service battalions out of its thirteen and it was these poor men that would be hurled into the inferno of the Somme. The offensive potential of each division, therefore, varied enormously, depending on the mix of regular New Army units. The average division comprised 18,000 men, divided, as we have seen, into 3 infantry brigades, each of 4 or 5 battalions. The divisions were themselves then formed up into corps commanded by a major general and the corps grouped into an army. For the hammer blow that Haig expected to deliver a decisive victory on 1 July 1916, he had amassed forty-five divisions in three armies for what would be only the First Battle of the Somme.

When Jack arrived in France he would have immediately met up with Lucas again and sensed the new nature of the battlefield. It was broad and vast and ran for many miles, as opposed to Gallipoli, where he had been crushed into the line. The early spring sunshine was breaking through and the green flat fields stretched out all around him. It was only as he started to approach the rear, then front lines, that the ground turned brown and white, as the chalk and mud churned into the trenches that stretched across the horizon. We can gauge something of the routine and atmosphere of being in the front lines from another diary – this time that of Captain F. C. Hitcock who was serving in the 2nd Leinsters of the 73 Brigade:

1st August: bathing parades were the orders for the day. The weather was extremely hot and we kept our platoons on the banks of The Somme after we had dressed.

9th August: The weather broke; it rained heavily and the men got pretty wet. Watched shelling on the front.

11th August: D Company had 21 casualties from shellfire digging a communication trench through Trones Wood.

18th August: Orders to report to Battalion Headquarters. Found the Bn preparing to move off for action. Each man given sand-bags and bombs in addition to his cumbersome 'battle order'. It was a sweltering day and the men were too heavily equipped. This attack was not only a divisional operation, there was to be a general advance along the whole corps front. On our left the 14th Division and on our right the 3rd Division. The Germans fully realised its [Guillemont Ridge] importance and had turned it into an almost impregnable fortress to bar the way of the allies in their advance up the slopes of the Somme plateau in Picardy.

The men were silent and up 'til now there had only been intermittent shelling – mostly counter battery work. Suddenly a crashing roar resounded over the whole area, the bombardment of the Hun lines started punctually to the second. We passed our gunners on the way up; they were all stripped to the waist, their sweat begrimed bodies showed one the almost superhuman effort of endurance they were making under the blazing heat. The barrage lifted at Zero hour. . . . Simultaneously out got a line of forms from the British lines, the first wave, and disappeared into the smoke. The rattle of machine gun fire could now be heard above the roar of the guns. Laville and Handcock were killed, our gallant CO Lt col. R. A. H. Orpen-Palmer DSO was wounded along with 100 rank and file. Over 100 casualties just going up the ridge and without ever seeing the enemy.

Streams of wounded walking and on stretchers were now beginning to drift by; men with smashed arms, limping and worst of all to see – facial wounds. Among the stretcher cases were the CO and CSM Bennett. The former was hit badly in the groin and the latter severely in the head. I talked to them as they lay on their stretchers in a small hollow. [Both men died soon after].[5]

The sector in which Jack's battalion was formed up was tough. Every day the landscape changed as the ground was churned up and the dead bodies of weeks before were revealed and reburied in even smaller pieces. Thousands of men who died never even saw a German, but jumped out from their trench when the whistles sounded and collapsed into the rusty barbed wire – their final senses smelling the stale water of the shell holes and the cordite, and hearing the death-dealing chatter of machine guns before they died. On 1 July 1916, the first day of the Somme battle, a fellow unit of the KOSB and RIF had gone over the top. The 2nd Battalion The South Wales Borderers (2/SWB) had been training for weeks and advanced at 8.45am. As a consequence, 800 officers and men, typical of many battalions doing the same thing all along the Front, were simply cut to pieces. Within ten minutes 14 officers and 219 other ranks were killed. Another 12 officers and 374 other ranks were wounded within the hour. There were 91 men missing – blown to pieces in fractions of a second with no time to say goodbye. The terror, pain and grief was the same everywhere that day, and for many days after, as Haig pressed more divisions into the line, hoping to overwhelm the German lines with the bodies of devoted but ill-fated men – men who had long ago forgotten what they were doing there.It was into just such a storm of fire that Jack led his battalion in early June 1916 – although not for long. His headlong dash into danger meant that this first command of the battalion was to be very short-lived – and almost his only command. He may have been 36 and a strong towering figure of inspiration but, as later photographs testify, his body was absorbing a lot of punishment. It is not known exactly what happened on 4 June 1916, but the 29th Division was engaged in fighting in the infamous Beaumont Hamel sector of the line at that time. The Inniskillings' diary includes the phrase, 'he [Jack] was soon severely wounded'. In fact, Jack had been seconded over to the 88 Brigade/1st Essex and was apparently leading a raising party out personally when he was critically wounded.

Colonels did not lead raising parties – unless they were Lieutenant Colonel Kelly. His style was always to lead from the front as we now know, and he rankled about ordering junior officers to go where he wanted to be himself. It was certain that his own commanding officers were furious that he continued to place himself in such danger, but their efforts were futile, as the diary of the 29th Division states for 4 June: 'Nevertheless he was out in No Man's Land assisting the raising party back to their trenches. It was then he was shot by a shrapnel bullet which pierced his shoulder and passed through his lung breaking ribs en route. It was a terrible wound and there was little hope of recovery'. The force of the impact and the gaping wounds through his body left him sprawled in no man's land, coughing and bleeding to death. He lay there for some time and could have closed his eyes and died at any moment. The severity of his wound meant he was unable to move and this could have been the end, but for the bravery of a young stretcher bearer named Jack Johnson. Crawling around in the mud and water, still often under fire, the stretcher bearers were some of the many unsung heroes. Johnson saw the colonel lying in a pool of blood holding his chest, crawled over to him still under fire and dragged him back towards their own trenches some 50m back. This was a phenomenal effort, given Jack was such a huge man, and worthy of an award for gallantry at any time – although none was forthcoming as far as we know.

Had Jack gone over on 1 July he would have died. The numbers of casualties in the fields would have overwhelmed the ability of brave men like Johnson. As it was he had a chance – a slim chance – of survival. All wounds were potentially fatal through disease and lack of sterile conditions. The medical staff did what they could against impossible odds, but the volume of casualties was to mirror the poppies that fall from the roof of the Royal Albert Hall each year on Remembrance Day. It was impossible to comprehend so many men dying whilst waiting to be tended. Men were taken down the communication trenches to the rear, often still under fire, and brought to a Casualty Clearing Station – sometimes close to the front lines, but often a bumpy ride a mile or so back. Arriving was one thing, getting treated was another. For late arrivals the odds were against you, as the lines of walking wounded sat around behind the rows of more serious stretcher cases. No medical teams had been trained for what they encountered here and at Passchendaele, Arras and many other places. The numbers were just too great to cope with. Succumbing to shock, heart attack or simply bleeding to death was common. There were no blood transfusions and only a few operating areas.

Strange things happened at casualty clearing stations. In some operating theatres at the heat of the push, two surgeons would be working at four to six operating tables, moving from one to the other, leaving often unqualified assistants to handle routine tasks of stitching up, dressing and even anaesthetising while they concentrated on the more delicate work of repairing damaged organs and searching for shrapnel, bullets and shell splinters buried deep in muddy wounds.

I tried every means possible to restore the patient (a Colonel of tremendous size), jerking his arms round, pressing his chest and finally just when I thought I would have to give up, he took one gasp and began to breathe. When Wesley had finished with the other chap he came over to my patient and started to take his arm off at the shoulder, but as soon as the operation began he started to sink and died on the table.[6]

Jack, also a colonel of tremendous size, arrived with a label with a broad red stripe indicating 'look out for danger' tied to his uniform and was taken through the crush of dead and dying men to the operating area. A few hours later, miraculously, he was still alive. With Johnson sat beside him not sleeping and tending to him for forty-eight hours, Jack was at death's door at every moment. Having lost a lot of blood from a lung already damaged by gas in Gallipoli, Jack was very weak and dangerously ill. A day passed and then another, to the point where Jack was moved to the rear and taken by train to Rouen. Remarkably, news had reached Nellie in London. She must have dropped everything, packed a case and ran to the train station (where she had waved Jack goodbye only weeks before) and got herself to Rouen.

For virtually the whole of the Great War, Rouen was the main location for general or 'Base' hospitals. This was part of the casualty evacuation chain, and ultimately, it was a train and boat home to hospital in Britain if you made it. To the south of the city of Rouen at least eight huge hospitals sprawled in tents and makeshift wooden camps, with operating theatres and many cemeteries. It was also home to part of the General Headquarters of the army, a hospital for self-inflicted wounds (SIW) for British soldiers, and one of the largest brothels on the Western Front, with over 171,000 clients recorded before it was closed due to public outcry. Despite the proximity of the General Headquarters with the brothel, there is no evidence to suggest a link.

We know that Nellie and her not uninfluential mother were already working for the Red Cross in London. She may have received a telegram informing her of Jack's wounds, because there was also a very large Red Cross Hospital in Rouen where Jack may have been sent. In any event, it seems very likely that it was her link with the Red Cross that enabled her to travel to the front lines. The last thing the army High Command could have coped with was thousands of wives making their way across the Channel to tend to their loved ones. Jack must have seemed a sorry sight for her – a husband of only two months and now severely wounded. Indeed, Jack never fully recovered from the damage done to his body in Gallipoli and the Somme.

By way of a postscript to this episode, in late November 1923, whilst Jack was attempting to enter Parliament (of which more later), he was speaking at an election rally at Shirebrook in Derbyshire. A woman approached Nellie and told her that she was Mrs Johnson, the mother of the stretcher bearer who saved Jack's life.[7]

By some miracle Jack survived, and in June 1916 he was moved to London to one of the 'brass hats' wards. These were for senior officers only and where the best medical treatment and sanitary conditions could be found. There were sound reasons for separating officers from men, and as the historian Lynn MacDonald explained, it was easier for the other ranks not to be found alongside their officers. Whilst in London Jack was visited by numerous friends and colleagues, some of whom had attended his wedding only two months earlier. Over the summer, Jack began to rebuild his strength: 'On one occasion when he was home on leave recovering from his chest wound a friend said to him "I suppose you won't be going back out again?" To which Sherwood Kelly replied "Of course I shall, I couldn't go back to South Africa without the V.C. There is still unfinished business."'[8] A brave statement, but it was predictable and indicates that his thoughts were focussed on returning home – if not permanently, at least to show what he had achieved.

The angry young man was still very much a part of the now very experienced Lieutenant Colonel DSO. Much had changed – much had not. One thing that had changed was his regard for Nellie and her love for him. It is doubtful whether he ever really loved Nellie, but came to love her in his own way. Her selfless actions to save him were typical of the person she was, a devoted friend and admirer, if not lover. For Nellie, the experience showed her at first hand the man she had married. Brave yes, but determined, single-minded and likely to always go his own way – a man impossible to predict or tie down. At a talk on this subject (given by the author) in recent years, two women in the audience started a discussion in loud voices about Jack. One felt he was an adventurer, never to be trusted, brave yes, but also stubborn and stupid. She finished by saying that Nellie must have been mad to have married him. The other lady put it far more succinctly: 'Don't be so stupid, Caroline', she spluttered at her friend, 'you don't marry a man like Jack Kelly expecting him to come home and cut the grass at the weekend!' That was a lesson perhaps Nellie had only just learned.

During the preparations for the Somme offensive the Germans were far from silent. Instead there was a gradual increase in the hostility of the sector, which was widely considered to be a quiet one. As if fate were trying to bring the two men closer together again, Churchill now also found himself in the same area as Jack and the 87 Brigade.

The events that brought Churchill to the Front are well-known. Many heads rolled in London in the wake of the Gallipoli disaster. Some were heads that deserved their fate whilst others were not. The debate about whether Churchill was a deserving case goes on to this day. In any event, after the Dardanelles Committee of Investigation had completed its judgments in February 1916, Churchill was free to return to War Council business, along with his equally distinguished colleagues. He was, however, shunned and his services spurned by Asquith. With his previous military background and character, it should not be a surprise to learn that his main aim now was to get himself out to the front lines in France. The consternation that this action caused represents a marvellous vision of conflicting emotions amongst his political colleagues – some longing for him to disappear under some German shell, whilst others were extremely wary of letting him loose in the British lines for fear of what might happen. In some ways, the fears of this latter group were well-founded, as Corporal W. Morgan of 10/11th Highland Light Infantry recalled from his time in the lines near Armentières:

We were badly cut up at the battle of Loos in September and the 9th Scottish Division had been sent down the line to be reinforced. The casualties had been so heavy that remnants of the different regiments like the Highland Infantry and the Gordons were amalgamated. Then we went to the quietest part of the line at Armentieres, between Le Bizet and Ploegsteert. There was hardly a shot being fired from either side, it was a case of live and let live and we were to remain here and build up strength because recruiting was very slow.

I was on my way back to Company Headquarters because I was a runner and I had just been delivering a message. When I went into the front line from the communication trench I had to turn right, but in the first bay on the left there was an officer pumping rifle grenades over at the Jerry front line. When I got back to my own stretch of trench everyone was up in arms about it and the Sergeant Major asked me if I saw who was doing it. I told him it was an officer in the next line so he went along to tell him off. When he came back he said, 'You'll never believe who that was. It was Churchill.' After that the Jerries really let us have it and there were a lot of unnecessary casualties.[9]

The comparisons with the front-line behaviour exhibited by Jack on the cliff tops of Gallipoli are striking. Taking initiative, a headstrong belief in the way to fight and win, a disregard for the situation surrounding them and, of course, a seemingly reckless disregard for their own safety are just some of the parallels that can be drawn. In so many ways, therefore, the instincts and experiences of both Jack and Churchill were captured by the events of wars in which they were a part. In less than three years both men would come into conflict with each other, representing a titanic conflict of will and stubbornness, in which each man was to rely on similar instincts to win the struggle. Before that, however, Jack had more experiences to come, and at last some quality time with Nellie, his new wife of only four months, in South Africa.

Chapter 6

Cambrai and the Victoria Cross, 1916–17

'One mark of a great man is the power of making lasting impressions upon the people he meets.'

Winston S. Churchill (1874–1965)

The traumatic events of 1916 must have affected Nellie very deeply, but they also showed her the true nature of the man she had married. Difficult to love, Jack was now proving equally difficult to hold down. The events on the Somme proved to Nellie that the temperament he possessed and his devil-may-care attitude (which had so attracted her to him) was also his potential nemesis.

Over the very hot summer of 1916 in London, Nellie sat beside Jack every day until he was well enough to return to Cranley Gardens. Her tall, strong and dashing husband of almost four months had been reduced to a weak and thin shadow of himself. At least she had him to herself – albeit for the longest period that they were ever to experience. The options open to Jack now were to either be invalided out of the army (he had after all survived more wounds than the average) or to get himself fit to return to the front lines. Over these weeks, it must have been the subject of many a conversation between them over what the future might hold.

From Nellie's perspective, Jack could now apply for a job in the City, perhaps build a home together or even start a family – though time was short. It is unlikely that any of these thoughts even entered his head. The settling down, raising a family and rat race of life that Jack saw around him was just not going to be for him. The wind in his hair, the excitement of challenge and the need to vent his passions could only be served by a return to active duty. Before that, however, the two of them did discuss a convalescent trip back to South Africa – which appealed to Jack. Here at last was a way of demonstrating that, at the age of 36 he had, if not made his fortune, made his mark and reputation. Perhaps it was to show his father that he was worthy and had been misunderstood, perhaps it was to show South Africa what they had in Jack. In any event, in July 1916 Nellie and Jack embarked for South Africa – partly to recover Jack's health but also to recruit for the army, whose need for men, after the bloodbath of the Somme, was as acute as ever. For Nellie, such a trip would have been an exciting reminder of her many travels in earlier years. Whilst we may see Nellie at this stage of her life as a genteel, graceful woman of literary tastes, she also inherited much of her father's lust for life and sense of adventure (not to mention a strong determination to succeed and not give up in the face of adversity), of which there was to be plenty married to Jack. Nellie would have seen this interlude as their honeymoon, a time to enjoy together on board ship, to talk, plan and get to grips with areas of unease between them. Nellie was no shrinking violet, and she had her own very clear ideas about the future, her own adventures to tell and many more to come. Indeed, it may have been the immovable object of her strong character meeting the irresistible force of Jack's, that combusted on the trip to the Cape. According to the records of the Union-Castle Line, they embarked from London on steamship *The Walmer Castle* on 22 July 1916, listed as 'Col & Mrs Sherwood-Kelly'.

The accepted price for glory is death, which has been understood by military men embarking on gladiatorial combat ever since men first bore arms. However, the rewards can be many and varied. Jack's instinctive character, as we have seen from his very early days, was to play to the gallery – in part to demand attention but also to put himself and his body on the line. If fighting in Somaliland, the Boer Wars and now the Great War was for a cause, then the trip to South Africa was to reap the rewards from a gallery eager to bestow laurels upon heroes. So it was that Jack arrived in Cape Town to a blizzard of newspaper interviews, tours, speeches and trips, lunches, dinners and salutations. Advanced warning of the hero's return had been telegraphed to Cape Town, where Jack and Nellie landed in the last week of July 1916. Jack's ego probably overtook his interest in Nellie somewhere on the two-week cruise, and was eventually let loose on arrival. Our evidence for this assessment is based on court proceedings held against Jack in April 1919. Here we are given a valuable snapshot of the type of relationship that Nellie (the kind, gentle and intelligent woman admired by all her friends) and Jack endured. Interestingly the court hearing, surely not surprisingly, stated that: 'In July (1916) they both went out to South Africa. Difficulties arose there. He said he was tired of his marriage as he was giving up his liberty. They returned to England . . .'[1]

All relationships encounter problems, highs and lows, incompatible elements and compromises, but it seems incredible that after only four months – most of which Jack had not even been with Nellie – he felt constrained. They had hardly had a marriage, but now Jack wanted it to end. This must have been devastating for Nellie, especially as they were not incompatible at all. Jack was simply emotionally selfish or self-protecting, unable to give of himself either deliberately or due to his painful past. It is almost certain that he was also in a thunderous mood. Despite his wound still needing to heal, and despite the fact that he had been very lucky to survive, he was frustrated that he was not with his battalion in the Somme offensive, which had begun whilst he was in hospital and was still raging. What was happening to his battalion whilst he was here on board ship sailing in the opposite direction?

What was Lucas thinking about him not being there? Would he ever get another command? Hardly the relaxed sort of trip that Nellie had hoped and yearned for. His temper must have been volcanic and he lashed out at Nellie. However, once he landed in South Africa, it was also clear that he enjoyed the adoration now thrown at him from a myriad of female admirers, as another section of the divorce proceedings indicated: 'Some of the women her husband had previously rather admired began to exercise the old fascination over him.'[2]

Jack had left South Africa only three years previously as a complete unknown. He returned a dashing, uniformed and medalled lieutenant colonel in the British army – a hero, a generous benefactor of hospitals and most importantly of all . . . unavailable to women, as he was also now married. This explosive combination was not lost on Jack, who perhaps saw Nellie as rather an unnecessary obstacle to his freedom to be available, circulate and no doubt exploit. Nellie must have felt very much in his considerable shadow. She had married a man whom she idolized. London was awash with handsome men in uniform, but Nellie had been swept off her feet by Jack. She had trusted him and elevated him in her family and in London society. She had nursed him when he was near death, and now she had followed him to South Africa only to be pushed away and abandoned as he basked in the superficial glory of a moth to the brightest of lights. And, like a moth, he would eventually burn. It is all too easy to imagine his reception as he returned to Butterworth as the conquering hero, a rural town where little happened, but a town where his former rabble-rousing reputation still held. Now the hero returned resplendent with uniform, medals and a society wife – all in the three years since he had left. Like many women of understanding and sensitivity, perhaps Nellie recognized the naivety and vanity of her brave but emotionally fragile man. He did not know what he was doing to a woman of such substance beyond his experience, but it would be an injustice to Nellie for us to allow her devotion to remain silent in this history. However, there may be an alternative explanation for this very rapid deterioration in the relationship between Nellie and Jack, as another character enters this story around this time.

Born into a well-to-do family in Ceylon on 19 June 1893, Dora Aitken returned to England in the years prior to 1914. Contemporary photographs suggest a young and vibrant woman with soft blue eyes (evidenced from her passport particulars) and a gentle and warm smile, full eyebrows and a stylish dress sense, with an attractive personality to match. What records exist imply that in the years prior to 1914, Dora enjoyed a good lifestyle with a great deal of travel, especially to the South of France. Numerous stamps on her passport in 1915 illustrate a regular number of trips via Folkestone to Dieppe, and then on to Nice, where she regularly stayed in expensive hotels and was there so often she was issued a residence permit. On one trip in April 1916 (the very month that Jack and Nellie were married in London) she went 'travelling to France, Belgium, Switzerland and Italy'.[3]

In September 1913 Dora's relationship with a young army officer blossomed and she married James Frederick Cambell Cameron. As a second lieutenant in the 11th Argyle and Sutherland Highlanders, James should have offered a secure and happy future to Dora. The one photograph that exists shows James resplendent in his officer's uniform and kilt, also displaying a kindly smile. However, a long and happy marriage was simply not to be. According to divorce case papers from 31 May 1919, from the earliest days of their marriage, James and Dora did not live together in their own home, but instead spent their time travelling around visiting friends in this country, on the Continent and in Africa. They returned to London in April 1914 where, in under a year, their married life became very unhappy, 'owing to disagreements'. Matters deteriorated to the point where James returned to his parents' home in Scotland. It seems hard to believe that for the next five years they lived apart, except for a very short period in November 1916 when James was on sick leave from France. According to the evidence offered in court, they lived together for twelve days in London, but again they could not get along. After this James returned to his unit in Scotland and Dora continued with her travels to France.

At the time that Jack was severely wounded, in June 1916, Dora, with one of many military visas granted to her during this period and stamped in her passport, was working for the armed forces somewhere in France. She was able to travel throughout the military zones of occupation – something only possible with a link to the military. It is possible that their paths crossed in Treport, where Jack was trying to recover from his injuries. They had to have met somewhere in the maelstrom of the Western Front, because their love affair began somewhere around the summer of 1916.

The war affected every aspect of people's lives in some way or another. Some were directly affected by news of the death or injury of a loved one, others saw their friends leave their homes, towns or cities, never to be seen again. As a young woman in her mid-twenties, Dora could have expected to be married, settled down and having children, but her life and those of hundreds of thousands like her were disrupted by stories of pain, loss and hardship. Meeting Jack perhaps saw her swept away by the formidable and overwhelming energy and personality that Jack exuded, his confidence and determination all pointed to stability, to certainty and ultimately to love. For Jack, he had, out of the blue, been 'bowled middle stump' by his meeting with Dora – whether it was from a hospital bed, a chance meeting on a train travelling through northern France or wherever. He suddenly realized that perhaps his marriage to Nellie had been a mistake. Maybe it was Dora that had turned his head whilst he was in South Africa, and not his 'old fascinations' from the past. Dora was already playing on Jack's mind then, so there is no doubt that his trip to South Africa would have been plagued by his frustrations and short temper until he could get back.

By the beginning of September 1916, it was time for Jack and Nellie to make the long and no doubt painful trip back to England. By mid-September Nellie had arrived home to Cranley Gardens and the support of her friends, family and mother. Jack, on the other hand, may have re-connected with Dora or he may not, but in any event, he immediately reported for duty and asked to be posted back to active duty commanding the 1/RIF, who were still serving in the front lines in France. Jack was showing Nellie that he was untamable and unstoppable – at least at this stage of his life. Before Jack could get back to the Front, however, on 29 November 1916 he had to attend the first of a number of visits to Buckingham Palace to meet the king, for the award of his DSO. For a time at least, the tensions in the marriage were put on hold. We can wonder what such an occasion did to further heighten Jack's sense of self-importance and success – as if such elevation was necessary. Even after the award of the DSO and a new ribbon to add to the impressive array already on this still young man's chest, there was still no call to the Front. This was no doubt partly due to a relapse in Jack's health in the December of 1916. Still in London at Christmas, Jack and Nellie had agreed to work at their relationship. The couple were to be seen on the London social circuit. Nellie was even making a name for herself as a leading figure in the Red Cross in her own right, helping with the dispatch of tens of thousands of Christmas parcels to the troops in France that year – the now very collectable small brass tins. By the end of November 1916 Jack had been posted to Duddingstone Camp, but all was not good. Firstly, he had reverted to his substantive rank of major, as his period away meant that Lucas had had to appoint another CO for the RIF. Even worse, when he arrived to report for duty this time to the 3rd Battalion KOSB, he discovered that the 1st Battalion was in the process of also arriving in the same camp. Clearly, he was not wanted back in the 1st Battalion, otherwise he would have been able to rejoin them. Equally this should have been a good opportunity to catch up with old acquaintances, but in a letter hidden amongst his many papers in The National Archives (TNA) in Kew we find the following:

To: Commanding Officer 3rd King's Own Scottish Borderers.
5.XII.16

Sir,
I have the honour to request that you will recommend this my application for a transfer to The 10th Norfolk Reserve Battalion. My chief reason for making this request is that for 7 months I commanded the 1st KOSB in Gallipoli and France with the rank of Lieut. Colonel and find that some officers and many of the men at present in camp who served with the 1st battalion during my command.
I am Sir your obedient servant,
J. Sherwood Kelly
Major [4]

On one level it is understandable that, having held the rank of colonel and now to be returned to major, could seem a small embarrassment which Jack wanted to avoid. On another level, however, it may well have been that he was so unpopular with the remaining officers of the 1st Battalion, making his presence in the camp, where he was now possibly junior to many, acutely difficult. Either way a sign of his desperation was not to simply ask for a transfer, but to ask to be sent to the 10th Battalion of the Norfolk's – almost an impossible request to deny. This short letter offers us a valuable insight into the inner fragility of the so-called 'Colossus'. He was granted his wish.

Despite the war, the tragic losses on the Somme and the food and fuel shortages that year, London was alive and making the best of Christmas 1916. For Jack, there were still parties to attend, raising money for hospitals and returning heroes. The restaurants still managed to bring game and supplies into town from the countryside. The hotels were busy and life in many respects went on as normal. The London Gentlemen's Clubs too were active and, as though to validate his newfound place in the social order, Jack applied to and became a member of the Authors' Club. An odd choice, given that this particular club liked its members to be published authors. However, it was no doubt achieved through contacts of either Nellie or her brother William. Later references to Jack's life in the 1920s state that he was a resident member of the club – making it his home for want of other accommodation. We might assume that Jack and Nellie were on good terms over those winter months, and that Jack was resident in Cranley Gardens, but in truth it could equally have been a frosty period. Nellie was not one to give up hope though, and she determined to be patient whilst the head of her husband was still being turned by his new-found fame. Whatever Christmas gifts Jack received that year, however, were topped off by the award of yet another medal.

The Most Distinguished Order of Saint Michael and Saint George came into existence in 1818 as a response to Britain acquiring the protectorate over the Ionian Islands in the Aegean Sea. Initially this award was restricted to 'subjects which His Majesty may hold high and confidential stations in the Mediterranean world'. However, as the British Empire expanded at such a rate during the nineteenth century, the Order had grown to recognize the service of those resident or even native of the lands they served. By 1900 the Order was being given to many who had given valuable service in either foreign or colonial affairs. In addition to the medal itself came the full paraphernalia of officers of the Order and even a chapel in St Paul's Cathedral – so vital was the support on the ground needed to subdue and control the creaking Empire. There were three classes of award:

First Class or Knight Grand Cross (GCMG)
Second Class or Knight Commander (KCMG)
Third Class or Companion (CMG)

For each of the levels there was a stated limitation on the number of holders. For the CMG this was set at 600. On 1 January 1917, Lieutenant Colonel Jack Sherwood Kelly, Norfolk Regiment (for he was still on attachment), was awarded the CMG for services to the Empire – most likely his recruiting drive in South Africa the previous summer.

The Weak Point of the Line

Running alongside the public acclaim and royal presentations, Jack's ego knew no bounds and his affair with Dora blossomed. They were to be found spending increasing amounts of time at the Rubens Hotel on Buckingham Palace Road in London. His relationship with Nelly had virtually collapsed. The hotel registers openly record a Lieutenant Colonel and Mrs Sherwood Kelly as being resident in the hotel by the spring of 1917 – clearly this was not his wife Nellie, but an assumed name for Dora. In fact, one of Dora's passport stamps for 1916 actually records her place of residence at the Rubens Hotel, Buckingham Palace Road, London. Reveling in the society dinners and parties to which he would have been invited, one wonders whether he openly paraded Dora as his new love to the embarrassment, pain and discomfort of Nellie. Dora would have been living the dream and fantasy that Jack created around her. The pain and devastation of war created a parallel universe of fun and enjoyment for both of them. It is reasonable to assume they were swept away in an illusion of hope for a wonderful life together. Why would she resist the romance of such a lifestyle, versus the non-existent relationship with her husband? It is a fair assumption that by now, the spring of 1917, Jack had concluded that his marriage to Nellie was at an end. Nellie, on the other hand, perhaps decided that she had a fight on her hands to keep the man she adored.

By sometime in March 1917, Dora, age 26, was pregnant. It is possible to assume this date as her daughter, Angela, would be born in December that year – nine months or so later. The news of the pregnancy changed everything for them both. Dora was no doubt overjoyed. Who knows what promises they made to each other or what dreams they shared? But Jack, the hero of steel and blood, suddenly discovered he had feet of clay. For the first time in his life, the reality of emotional responsibility began to dawn. Up to now, Jack had been charging from the front in everything he had done. Nothing in his life, past or present, had been able to tie him down or did he have ties towards. He could pack and go whenever and wherever he liked. But no longer.

A deeper analysis of the hero often reveals a strong sense of self, what we might call 'selfish' on one level or 'selfless' on another. One of the main emotional threats to all human beings is the potential pain of the sense of loss that occurs when we lose someone close to us. One way of preventing this is not to become close to anyone. Conversely, such a stance leaves the hero or heroine able to take risks with his or her own life, as they know there is no one to grieve for them – or if there is, they do not accept the attachment. Thus, Jack's type of heroism and courage came from a care-free sense of his own mortality. He was willing to die at any moment and had no one he had tied himself to emotionally – although of course others had tied themselves to him. All this was born in the childhood experiences that shaped his psyche. To a large extent, his heroism was reckless, but with no responsibilities he probably felt this affected nobody but himself. He had no mother, his father now a distant memory and his brothers and sisters, though important to him, were thousands of miles away. Now all that had changed. Nellie had tried to love him in her own way. He was rejecting this even before he met Dora – not necessarily because he did not love Nellie in his way, but possibly because he was rejecting the emotional tie. But now he also had Dora and soon he would have Angela. The love of a child is possibly not a bond he either understood or wanted to know – at least at this stage of his life.

Jack, of course, had nothing to be proud of in the way that Nellie had been treated in the last few months. He had now created a new relationship with Dora, so how was he going to treat her? The hero, able to face steel, barbed wire, bullets and pain on the battlefield, was unable to cope with the psychological battles that fatherhood presented. He had never had to face the reality of emotional responsibility for another human being. This is not to say that he did not care about the men under his command, but that was not the same emotional connection, and held different demands on him personally. He reacted in the way his past (and arguably stunted) emotions dictated, and that was to run away from where pain and disappointment most probably awaited him – where connection to another person resulted in inevitable loss, as in the case of his mother and twin brother. These were deep-rooted emotions which, of course, poor Dora had little idea existed. For her, life was wonderful. She was having his baby – but did she have Jack?

Back to the Somme

Seldom has there been a single event in British history that all at once affected nearly every village and town in the country, but the Battle of the Somme did just that. It is fair to say that almost every war memorial in every village and town across the United Kingdom would have at least one name of someone killed on the Somme in 1916–17, and some of course have many. Telegrams arrived in large numbers to whole streets in late July as news of what had happened to the 'Pals' battalions filtered through. Not just one man here and there from a town or factory but . . . every man. The Somme offensives had failed in their key objectives and the slaughter had been both inexcusable and appalling. During 1916, some 400,000 British casualties had either been buried, patched up and returned to the Front, or were recovering in hospitals all over Britain.

Shell shock was still a new phenomenon and until it was understood and accepted, court martials and executions were running at dozens a month. If the flower of the British army had been lost in the summer of 1914, then the remaining petals and stem were destroyed in 1916. What was left was an army unrecognizable from the one that had entered the conflict two years previously.

It must have been a memorable day and one full of shouting and hoots when, in February 1917, the newly decorated T (Temporary)/Lieutenant Colonel Kelly received a letter ordering him to rejoin the 87 Brigade and resume command of the RIF. The diary of the regiment records that on 29 March 1917, Major J. S. Kelly once more took over command of the 1st Battalion from Lieutenant Colonel R. R. Willis VC.[5] Lucas wanted him back again.

So, Jack informed Nellie and then went to see Dora, packed his bags and was soon back in the front lines, well-decorated, maybe a little wiser and certainly bearing the wounds of battle. He was possibly relieved that the pain of the relationship with Nellie and the responsibility for Dora was over – at least for the present. The transition once again from a life in London to the mud, blood and hardship of France would have been dramatic, but this is where his heart still was and it was where he felt released and free. It all came so naturally to him. He was a born leader. He changed his collar dogs and flashes yet again from the Norfolk Britannia back to the Inniskilling's flaming grenade of a Fusilier Regiment, emblazoned with the Castle of Gibraltar. He then met Lucas and his junior officers in a fond reunion, then onto his sergeants, before giving talks to his new battalion. London life and rest for the last eight months had not softened him in any way – he was what he was and he was at home with this unit far more than he was with the KOSB in Gallipoli. 'Fighting like Kilkenny cats' as they were, in the fields of mud, the men of the 'Skins' lived up to their regimental motto of '*Nec Aspera Terrent*' –'By Difficulties Undaunted' or 'Difficulties be Damned'!

April saw the next major British offensives of 1917, with large-scale attacks at Vimy and Arras – in the Oise and Reims sectors respectively. These in their own way were also major battles of the Great War, although overshadowed by their Somme predecessor, they were nevertheless extensions of the same strategic plan and were beaten off in the same way with huge losses. The heady days of polished brass, shiny leather, rigid discipline and a sense of self-importance as an army, had been replaced by mud, destruction, pain, losses everywhere and madness. Much as Jack revelled in rising to a fight, even he had to cope with the reality of this war.

One in five wounded men went on to develop mental problems and many became suicidal for the rest of their lives, their nerves destroyed by the endless shelling day after day. Physical exhaustion showed in grey dirty faces, emotional collapse in bulging and dead eyes, illness through yellowing skin, men close to the edge of destruction with haunted half smiles the result of no sleep, as they could not bear the dreams of friends they had seen blown to pieces next to them. Into this hell, the new colonel came. He had seen it before but perhaps not on this scale. In his book, *Breakdown: The Crisis of Shell Shock on the Somme*, historian Taylor Downing explains how the new phenomenon of shell shock was only just beginning to be recognized, but far from understood. To the generals and brigadiers it was an excuse for malingerers, men who needed to be found and shot. To the colonels and majors nearer the front lines it meant something more tangible. They had seen it in their best officers, so why should they not see it in their men. To the captains and lieutenants (those that survived long enough) it was an ever-present state of mind. Some men coped and kept going, others pressed their faces into the dirt of the ground of their trench, as the hell arrived once more above their heads.

Downing explains that the Somme created a crisis for the General Staff. Shell shock was being recognized throughout the army – not surprising when one considers that this was the first war of stalemate, where men were being shelled endlessly for days if not weeks. The comparatively new medical corps tried to defend its corner, but surprisingly by Passchendaele in 1917, there were only 5,000 recorded cases of shell shock – a tenth of those recorded in 1916 on the Somme. Had the General Staff found a way of curing this impact on their men? No, they simply refused to accept it existed in all but the most insane and mentally collapsed of men. Shooting them did not seem to stop the problem and ignoring the doctors also failed. So, the most severe cases were sent back down the lines, put on secret and sealed blacked-out ambulance trains, and incarcerated in specially built mental hospitals or asylums such as the Maudsley.[6] In this very creative and yet contrived way, the figures dropped dramatically. For Lieutenant Colonel Kelly DSO, CMG, holding together his new battalion and driving it forward to further action was all that mattered. He would do this not by contrived means or unnecessary Victorian discipline, but by what we would call 'man management' and personal leadership – the hero trying to make heroes of them all, even if they did not want to be.

November 1917 and Cambrai

Having parted company from Lucas and the 87 Brigade in January 1916 as they left Gallpoli, Jack would have been reunited with Lucas on his return to the brigade in June 1916, and just before his almost-fatal chest wound. Whilst Jack was in South Africa and convalescing during the autumn of that year, Lucas continued to command the brigade through some very tough and costly engagements and battles. Jack was then, as we know, posted back to the front lines and from the 87 Brigade to the Inniskillings in March 1917, and their comradeship was renewed. It was not long before Jack resumed his dance with death. In April 1917, he was returned to the Inniskillings as CO and based near Monchy-le-Preux. On the 15 April, he was visiting Lucas behind the lines at Brigade Headquarters when a gas attack began and the wind took the poison straight to their position. He was gassed trying to get down the steps into the HQ trench – this may have been very near part of the trench lines called Airy Corner. He was back on duty just three days later on 18 April, his indestructible nature continuing to shine through.

It is worth a pause at this stage, just to consider the life of the battalion in their front-line sector in 1917. Thousands of books and many films have tried to capture the reality of life on the front lines in this war. Yes, there was mud, blood, death, chattering machine guns, wet, cold, hunger, lice, fear and all the other associations of this particular war. But there was also the daily routine, the steady machine that was the British army, and there was paperwork to keep everything in order and on track. In such documents as the War Diary of 1/RIF, the writer historian can glance through an open window as the diary records events at exactly the time Jack was in the line in April and May 1917:

Date	Summary
1st April	Bn marched to OUTRIEBOIS
2nd April	Bn marched to LUCHREUX. Draft of 1 officer, 102 OR's joined the Bn

The heavy casualties of 1916 and 1917 meant that regular drafts of men were needed and battalions were topped up to strength in the weeks preceding an attack, so the old timers knew something was up when the drafts arrived. It would be part of Jack's role to meet and talk to the newly arrived men in his command and then pass them onto his various companies and officers for further training in battle conditions. Sadly, many would be killed or wounded even before they saw a German. Note also the daily marching to new locations as battalions were gradually moved up to the front lines on rotation.

3rd April	Training by Company advancing under barrage
6th April	Marched to ETREE WAMAN. Further Draft of 110 OR's joined the Bn
7th April	March to SOMBRIN. Bn strength Officers 34, OR's 931
8th April	March to MONCHIET.
9th April	Lecture on forthcoming operations gas etc
10th April	Draining and improving the camp
11th April	Training
12th April	March to ARRAS resting for 3 hours before proceeding to Brigade Reserve. Bn moved into Brigade support line and occupied the trenches lately captured from the Huns. In support of repairing trenches.

The trenches were home to many memories and experiences for men of both sides. A trench that had been lived in by German troops for months would still contain their effects and their bodies (or parts of bodies) as the British troops moved in once it had been captured. It had to be re-organized and re-built after the shelling that would have torn whole sections apart. The smell of death had to be erased and it had to become part home, part canteen, part hospital, part headquarters and part firing step, facing the enemy. Then, of course, it could be shelled into pieces once more and re-taken by the Germans.

15th April   B Co detached to support 2 SWB's on the left flank of the Brigade in support of 1st KOSBs.

Note that Jack worked within the 87 Brigade so he was seeing men and officers he knew all the time from the KOSB and SWB. Of course, he would also hear of lost men and deaths just as regularly. It was on this day that Jack was gassed on his visit to the rear Brigade Headquarters.

16th April   Relieved 1st KOSBs and occupied firing line south east of MONCHY. Lieut, Aylmer and 5 OR's killed.[7]
17th April   In firing line digging continuous trench and patrolling front. 35 casualties.
              [Kelly came back to his battalion today and set about his aggressive fighting spirit . . .]
18th April   Two advanced posts established by CO [Kelly] in No Man's Land [this must have been popular with the men asked to go out there] 200 yards in advance of the front line.
19th April   Relived by 9th Gordon Highlanders and returned to ARRAS.
                                          Signed G E Framingham
                                          Lieut. & Adjutant
                                          1st Royal Inniskilling Fusliers

2nd May   5.50pm march to ARRAS
3rd May   7.05 am take position in old German trenches
6th May   Interior economy & Divine Services
7th May   10.15am march to DUISANS. Draft of 2 officers and 220 OR's.

[This new draft would replace wounded and sick men as well as be preparation for the coming attack on HOOK Trench].

Cape Mounted Police detachment, 1896. Jack is on the back row, extreme left aged 16.

Iandra House, until 1911 the astounding granite family home of Nellie Sherwood Kelly in the middle of the New South Wales outback.

'A Herculean giant of a man', the CO of 1st Battalion The Royal Inniskillen Fusiliers stands tall in the Gallipoli trenches, 1915.

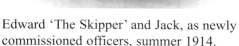

Edward 'The Skipper' and Jack, as newly commissioned officers, summer 1914.

Major General C. H. T. Lucas far right, standing with fellow officers of 87th Brigade somewhere on a Gallipoli beach in 1915. Note their worn frames and exhausted faces – but still with their ties tightly tightened.

Lieutenant Colonel
John Sherwood Kelly,
1915.

	1	2	3	4	5	6	7	8

1916. Marriage solemnized at *St Peters Church* in the *parish*
of *St Peters Cranley Gardens* in the County of *London*

Columns:—	1	2	3.	4.	5	6	7	8
No.	When Married.	Name and Surname.	Age.	Condition.	Rank or Profession	Residence at the time of Marriage.	Father's Name and Surname.	Rank or Profession of Father.
319	April 22nd 1916	John Sherwood Kelly	42	Bachelor	Lt. Col. 1st K.O.S.B.	Margery Hall Reigate	John James Sherwood Kelly	Solicitor
	1916	Nellie Elizabeth Crawford Greene	44	Spinster	~	21 Cranley Gardens	George Henry Greene	M.L.C. New South Wales

Married in the *above Church* according to the Rites and Ceremonies of the *Church of England* by *Licence or after* _____ by me,

This Marriage was solemnized between us, { *J. Sherwood Kelly* } { *Nellie Eliz: Crawford Greene* } in the Presence of us, { *E.E. Greene H.G. Evelyn Vardon* } { *Julia Wilson* }   *W.S. Swayne*

Marriage certificate for Jack and Nellie, April 1916 – note that Jack gave his age as 42
when he was in fact 36.

Dora Cameron, 1915. Taken from Dora's travel permit, which allowed her to be resident in Nice, France, but also to travel through the military lines.

Dora's young and adoring husband, James Cameron of the Argyles, *c*. 1914.

Jack on his hunter taken sometime in 1916 at a forward camp in France. This was the picture his daughter Angela kept all her life knowing he was her father but not knowing who he was.

Jack at his Victoria Cross investiture, Buckingham Palace, January 1918.

Medal group for John Sherwood Kelly in the South African Museum of Military History, Johannesburg.

With six other VC winners en route from Tilbury Docks bound for Archangel on board SS *Stephen*. Back row, left to right: Lieutenant Colonel D. G. Johnson VC, DSO, MC (South Wales Borderers), Brigadier General G. W. St George Grogan VC, CMG, DSO and Bar (Worcestershire Regiment), Lieutenant Colonel J. Sherwood Kelly VC, CMG, DSO (Norfolk Regiment), Captain A. C. T. White VC, MC (Yorkshire Regiment); front row, sitting: Lieutenant M. S. S. Moore VC (Hampshire Regiment), Captain A. M. Toye VC, MC (Middlesex Regiment).

Private Stanley Berrett, who went to North Russia with Jack and is typical of the average soldier who adored him.

Jack being escorted to his court martial, Middlesex Guildhall, October 1919.

'Kelly's Mystery Ships', North Russia, summer 1919.

Angela Cameron,
1922.

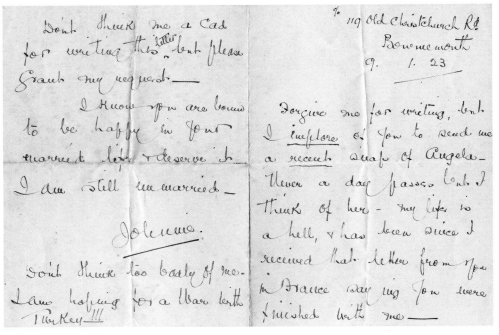

The last known letter from Jack to Dora, dated January 1923.

14th May   8.30am marched from ARRAS to front line to take over from 1st Gordons.

15th May   Officers patrols go out nightly. Enemy holds HOOK TRENCH. Snipers active and intermittent shelling. 4 killed, 8 wounded, 7 missing.

19th May   19.00hrs attack carried out in accordance with BO 17. The attack fails owing to severe casualties from M G fire. Centre party reaches their objective but are outnumbered. Lieut Aitcheson effects a lodgment in HOOK TRENCH with about 20 men but nothing more heard of them. Casualties: Capt Osman, 2Lt. Grame, Lieut Hepworth killed, 2Lt Somers died of wounds, 2Lt Clancey and 2Lt Horringe missing. Lieut Hall, Lieut Aitcheson missing. 192 OR's killed or missing.

This was a typically bloody attack to try to gain part of the German line only a few hundred yards in front of them. It was the sort of action Jack wanted to lead and did lead himself. He would have known the officers well – he would have worked with the junior subalterns, planned with the captains and wished them well. In a day, he lost 200 of his men and 8 of his officers. The unexplained loss of the 19-year-old Lieutenant Aitcheson (who made it to the German trench) and twenty men would not have sat well with him.

No doubt he mused on leading a raid to find them.

20th May   Relived by 16th Middlesex and march to ARRAS

20th–29th   Training

29th   Order received to capture HOOK TRENCH. This order is cancelled.

This order was cancelled, perhaps, through a conversation between Jack and Lucas back at Brigade Headquarters as to just how feasible gaining this objective was.

31st May   Moved to Brigade reserve in Brown Line.

Signed Sherwood Kelly
Lt Col
1/R Inniskilling Fusiliers.

The 1/RIF moved back into the line in June and July of 1917 and it is at this point that another vignette appears. The lives of men entwine from all sorts of different directions, last for a time and then diverge on their varying journeys. This must be especially acute in times of great events in history and of course in war. A rare photograph exists of Jack and his officers from November 1917. Jack is seated in the middle with walking stick and great beaming smile on his face, surrounded by senior officers of great service and young lieutenants of none so far. Forth from the right, on the back row, is a Captain Alan Cane Lendrum. In September 1920, Alan would be murdered by the IRA whilst he was serving as a magistrate in County Clare, but here he was as a young officer serving in Jack's battalion. Born in 1885 at Irvinestown, County Tyrone, Alan was only five years younger than his famed CO. He had been schooled in Enniskillen and as a young man he too, like his CO, had seen the world, serving as a Marine in India and Malaya. In 1917, he was only 32 years of age and had joined the regiment in July 1915. He knew many of the enlisted men by name as Enniskillen was a small and communal place, and he was a popular officer. Thus it was that in July, with Jack as CO, Private Robert Hope was court-martialled and ordered to be shot. Private Hope had left the battalion without leave and been on the run, in France, for eleven weeks, before being arrested and tried. We know little of Robert and cannot judge why he had run, but we do know he was also a regular and had served with the 1st Battalion in Egypt, Gallipoli and France – as such he would have been well-known to Jack, as well as to Alan Lendrum. After the sentence, Jack ordered the then Captain Alan Lendrum to take charge of the firing squad, which he refused to do on the grounds that he knew Private Hope. We do not know the details, but we do know that Private Hope of 1/RIF, was executed by firing squad on the morning of 5 July 1917. He is buried at Ferme-Olivier cemetery near Ypres. We also know that Captain Alan Lendrum must have clashed very badly with Jack as, rather than select an alternative officer and allow the matter to rest, Captain Lendrum was court-martialled on 24 July and reduced in rank to lieutenant. He was severely reprimanded on the grounds of 'conduct to the prejudice of good order and military discipline' – perversely, exactly the same sentence to be meted out to Jack at his own court martial two years later. We will meet Captain Lendrum again later in this story.

On 18 July 1917 Jack was recorded as being wounded yet again near Wancourt, but once more was back on duty within days. However, the first record of an entry in Lucas' letters recording his time with Jack in the brigade comes in August 1917. Here Lucas comments in an almost wry and humorous fashion to his future wife Poppy (née Holdsworth of Widdicombe in South Devon), that she should not be concerned when she meets Jack and sees him covered in bandages, as it is a regular thing and bullets seem to bounce off him: 'France, August 6th 1917: Don't worry when you see that he is wounded because that happens at least once a month. Last time he got a shrapnel bullet in the shoulder blade which bounced off again, and left a crater the size of a tumbler, but he took no notice of it.' The next day, and rather more personally, Lucas wrote: 'France, August 7th 1917: Col Kelly is now married, has been married just over a year, it was a rotten business, she should never have been married to anybody, and won't live with him, she has gone to America to get some weird form of divorce to set him free.'[8]

The 'hasty marriage' had come apart very quickly and Jack had clearly spoken in some detail and with some anger about Nellie. Interestingly, there is no mention of Dora and her ongoing pregnancy. Whether Lucas was aware and did not mention it, or whether Jack kept this to himself we shall never know. Typically, when relationships break down, the truth is somewhere in the middle and we do not know how difficult Nellie was to live with. We do know, however, much already about how hard it would have been to tie Jack down in any way. Nellie had already had plenty to cope with in the way Jack had treated her. In any event, taking a trip to the USA in 1917, even before submarine warfare had broken out, was either a measure of how much she cared for Jack in wanting to 'set him free' (an interesting phrase to use), or a measure of how desperate she was to get him out of her life. Time would tell which. Lucas went on: 'He is a perfect white man who has very high ideals, and is a waster. You will find it hard to make his two characters fit in.'[9]

Here at last the biographer has something concrete to work with. Someone who knew him well, almost intimately in terms of his personal life, admitting to his wife, his closest confidante, that Jack was a contradiction. On the one hand a man of high ideals – with high expectations of himself and others. Patriotic, intensely loyal to his soldiers, high personal standards and plenty of courage. Amongst these attributes (which it is safe to bestow on Jack even after 100 years of distance) was a strong if not overpowering sense of justice. This was to be so in the Boer War, as we have already seen, where he fell out with senior officers over orders he felt were wrong; in Gallipoli, reaping retribution by bombing party on the Turks when his troops had gone missing; and later, in 1919, it would ultimately bring his life and career crashing to the ground, when he took on Churchill in a national campaign all about what he saw as the injustice of poorly planned campaigns costing the lives of brave men. The early seeds of this Achilles heel were sown here and identified by Lucas.

But what about his contrasting nature: that of being a 'waster'? The word then carried the same meaning as today: a person of talent or intelligence who deliberately steers a course towards squandering friends, opportunities or money. A vandal of relationships. A wrecker of image. To his fellow officers and men, he was brave – brave beyond anyone they had ever seen. But with this bravery came a carefree disregard for expectations, for reputation or for friendships. He was what he was. The bravest man in the British army – and a waster. Yet it was hard not to admire him, as Lucas went on: 'In spite of his lax ideas on so called morality I would trust him before any man I know . . . Now you know more about Col Kelly than most people.'[10]

I wonder whether Lucas took the time to write at such length about any other man in his command? He may have done . . . or possibly this was the result of the impact that Jack's character had had upon him. This major general (to be) trusted Jack more than any other man he knew. This can only be because, above all, despite his feet of clay, Jack was courageous beyond measure – except when it came to his closest relationships. When people became too close to him he was mortal, fragile and vulnerable.

Cambrai

The French were far from inactive. Having held Verdun at terrible cost throughout 1916, they also pushed forward with their 'Nivelle Offensive' and yet another 40,000 lives were lost in the ensuing slaughter. It was beginning to seem that the generals had no idea how to break the deadlock, except to wear out each side until there were no men left. The French 16th Army Corps experienced a series of mutinies, which were ruthlessly suppressed with many executions. Then the scene changed forever. The German strategy of unrestricted submarine warfare, borne out of desperation to try to starve Britain out of a war which they were stubbornly refusing to lose in France, served only one purpose. The USA was to join the war. President Wilson had done all he could to maintain his country's isolationist stance, but such a war at sea was a war on all mankind and the sleeping giant was awakened. Now it was only a matter of time before the men and materiel of the USA would start to arrive in France. It was badly needed, as on the Eastern Front the internal decay and ultimate collapse of tsarist Russia had begun and troops began to throw down their arms. The communists saw the chance of revolution in this archaic and anarchic country.

In the meantime, the British were expected to continue to apply pressure to the Germans. The French were consolidating under their new hero, Marshal Petain (the 'hero' of Verdun), and so Haig once more devised another major offensive to try to force a hole in the German front through which his forces could flow. In June 1917, it was Ypres and Passchendaele – two names that live in infamy alongside the most murderous of all battles. A quarter of a million British troops struggled through the rain, mud, blood and stench of the fields around them to gain but a few miles. Again, they failed to break though.

For the line officers the situation was clear. There was no solution through brute force, and a seemingly overwhelming barrage of artillery, followed by close infantry support, was certainly not the answer. The cemeteries of Flanders held well over a million men who could testify to that. How far and yet how short a distance we had come since those first opening shots fired by the Norfolk's when they first met the German troops advancing through Belgium on 24 August 1914. It must have seemed very tempting for Jack to speak out at this senseless waste of life and good men. After all he had a reputation for this, running back to his youth, together with an unorthodox style – where had these traits gone? Perhaps his obligation to lead his men from his new position as a senior officer showed him that difficult decisions were, indeed, the privilege of rank. Equally, the British Establishment, of which he was now a part, expected loyalty in return for the rewards of rank and status that had been given him. For the time being he gave it.

Another smaller scale assault had been planned for the Cambrai sector. The date of the attack had been set for 20 November. Central to this was the introduction of a new weapon designed to win the war: the Mark One tank. The Allied troops in this sector were faced by German positions that had been dug and created over years – an almost impregnable wall of defences as part of the so-called 'Hindenburg Line', after the senior commander in that sector (the future Field Marshal Hindenburg who was to become Chancellor of Germany and eventually hand over power to Adolf Hitler, a corporal in Cambrai at that time).

Some two years previously Colonel Fuller had suggested a plan to use the tank in a raid. It had failed, due to the fact that the tank had been used as an individual free-roaming weapon. This time they were to be used in a group to punch a gap in the enemy line and then exploit it – a forerunner of the tactics employed by the Germans in the Second World War. General Julian Byng of 4ht Army Corp proposed the plan to Haig. The attack on Cambrai was to be a small raid with the objective being 'to destroy the enemy's personnel and guns, to demoralize and disorganize him and not to capture ground'.

The whole assault was to take eight to twelve hours in total, with nine battalions of tanks and three divisions of infantry. Initially Haig was not impressed with the idea as his focus was on Passchendaele, but eventually Byng was given approval for his 'raid'. It is important that we fully grasp the intention at Cambrai, because perversely it was the tactical limitations placed on this assault which prevented it from becoming the total breakthrough everyone sought. When it was clear it was becoming more of a success than anyone had anticipated, it also became clear the resources needed to exploit this were not there.

Given the clear limitations of aim, there was no need for the staff officers behind the lines to prepare for a major development of the attack with reserves and further waves of troops. The plan was to attack on a very concentrated front of only 5 miles between the Canal du Nord and St Quentin canal. The town of Cambrai would then be encircled and Bourlon Ridge captured. The entire tank corps (soon to be renamed the Royal Tank Regiment) was to be deployed with 216 tanks in the initial advance, with a further 96 in reserve. The whole was to be supported by fourteen squadrons from the Royal Flying Corps (later, with the Royal Naval Air Service, to form the Royal Air Force). Although not an enthusiast for the plan, Haig could see that new tactics were going to be deployed here by Byng. This meant the coordinated use of aircraft (to cover the noise of the advance of the tanks), together with infantry and tanks advancing together. In this sense, the Cambrai plan was new for the time and a forerunner of the Second World War, with mixed arm interaction. Byng was optimistic of success – not so some of his senior officers. For example, General Harper, commanding the 51st Highland Division, did not even trust the machine gun (having tried to hold up its introduction into the British army), let alone the tank. Harper's view was that the plan was: 'a fantastic and most unmilitary scheme'.

Whilst all the planning and discussions had been taking place, the men at the Front continued their daily war of survival. The heat of the August sun of 1917 had given way to the mists and frosty early mornings of October and November. The relationship between Lucas and one of his battalion commanders – Lieutenant Colonel Jack Sherwood Kelly DSO, CMG – was as close and yet as combustible as ever, as another letter from Lucas to Poppy indicates: 'France, August 17th 1917: I have been having awful rows with him the last week because it was his turn to stay behind and not go into the show with his battalion – as you know him now you can realise the trouble.'[11]

Again, here is a useful insight into man management, of which Lucas was probably a wonderful exponent – well ahead, in terms of leadership, of many of his peers. It would have been so easy, indeed so common for a senior officer, when faced by the fury and rows aimed at him by a lieutenant colonel, to simply reprimand him and send him down the line – almost certainly relieving him of his command. This is exactly what was to happen to Jack in 1919 when he was not managed by Lucas. He was, we can say with some certainty, extraordinarily lucky that Lucas was his brigade commander, as such displays of fury and 'awful rows' would simply not have been tolerated by anyone else. It is a measure of the high regard that Lucas had for Jack that he stayed in the front lines at all. Of course, it is also obvious that all Jack wanted to do was fight. Like a growling and barking dog who sees an intruder in his garden, he was furious that he could not be let off the leash – but he soon would be.

Lucas' accounts to Poppy continued: 'France, October 23rd 1917: Am on a joy ride tomorrow with Col Kelly and another CO. France, November 15th 1917: Just back from the theater and dinner with Col Kelly.'[12] So, for the senior officers at brigade level, it was possible to leave the lines, grab a driver and visit civilization well behind the lines. Meanwhile, as Lucas and Jack took a brief respite from the horrors of the trenches and the possibility of death at any moment, the plan was to go ahead. General Byng briefed his divisional major generals, who in turn briefed their brigadiers – Brigadier General Lucas being one – who in turn briefed the colonels commanding their battalions, who in turn briefed the majors and captains commanding their companies, who in turn briefed their platoon and section commanders, who in turn explained to the men in the mud how they were once more going to advance into German machine-gun fire and 'make a push' that would create turmoil in the German lines. On no account was it to be an attack to win the war or even to take ground. One wonders if this was effectively communicated to Jack.

On the morning of the 17 November, Jack was ordered to move his battalion up from Basseux to their FUP (Forming Up Point) by the 19th, as the regimental diary recorded: 'Marching through Gouzeaucourt early in the morning, the Inniskillings had a dramatic hint of the nature of the surprise being prepared for the enemy. The village was quiet but the houses contained no sleeping soldiers, instead they sheltered tanks.'

The task of 29th Division was to act in support of the 12th, 20th and 6th divisions who had 'brown' and 'blue' lines to reach in the first two days. If they achieved these objectives then the 29th was to move through their lines and press on to reach the 'red' lines, which were the final objectives, and then hold them until reinforced. It was not intended or envisaged that they would break through. For Jack's battalion this meant moving up in close support of the 2/SWB, whose objectives were the Marcoing Copse and the vital crossing points over the Canal du Nord. If these could be taken then the advance into the German rear and Cambrai itself was possible, and utter confusion could be inflicted on the German lines.

In their usual fashion the German commanders were well-informed before the attack began. Their spy network was far better than in the Second World War and they knew the date of the attack, the direction and the units involved. The attack was heralded by the equally usual noise and bustle of men coming into the front lines and the increased activity.

The actual attack began on the very cold and damp morning of 20 November 1917. The men were awakened and moved into lines – both front and coming up the rear communication and support trenches around 3.00am ready for the 6.00am start. Tired, cold and scared, they stirred and rubbed their eyes, trying to awaken their minds to the fact that they could be dead or dying within three hours. They looked at each other – some with the dead eyes of those beyond caring and some wide-eyed and frightened at the prospect of losing a life they had not yet fully lived. Their hated muddy holes now seemed like five-star hotels into which they wished they could return and hide, but there was nowhere to go but up the line. Sergeants and sergeant majors did what they were paid to do – a bit of humour, a bit of nagging, a bit of fatherly advice and a bit of barking under their breath. Their familiar voices were more often than not the key to discipline and the containment of fear. The cold, wet sludge on their feet as they walked over wooden boards trodden on by thousands of men before them who would not return, like a rite of passage into hell. Even with a commanding officer like Jack walking up and down the lines, offering encouragement and with just a woollen scarf around his neck, men still wet themselves, soiled themselves or threw up whilst they waited. Did

Jack spare a thought for Dora back in the Rubens Hotel in London? Perhaps he did – just before he drew his service revolver and barked out the orders through the ear-splitting din to his men.

Then it erupted. As the men blew warm air into frozen hands, they jumped out of their skin as, at 6.00am precisely, 1,003 guns opened fire. With a noise like the thundercrack of a volcano finally blowing its top, thousands of shells fell onto German lines all around Cambrai and the two canals, telling the Germans that within minutes the infantry would be on their way towards them. The German troops knew how to cope. Although many died being blown into irredeemable pieces by direct hits, far more ran deep into dark, damp tunnels underground, where only collapsing walls and dugouts could threaten them and bury them in black, cold and forgotten tombs. The artillery in fact helped shelter the Germans far more than kill them, as the shells tore up the ground, mixed it with mud, and filled the area with huge shell holes that the advancing men and tanks would now have to cross. As the smoke and noise of the shelling did its work, so too did the cold thick mists coming off the water from the canals. A scene from a cold Dante's *Inferno* began to unfold onto the landscape in front of Jack's battalion.

Jack would have been an inspiration – this was what he did best. He gave off that innate confidence and certainty (only found in a natural leader) that this was not only going to be a successful attack, but also that they would all survive. Final checks to weapons, safety catches off, fixing of cold steel bayonets – almost the last order the men would hear – and then coming up behind them the brand-new sound of the squeak and creak of steel tracks of the tanks struggling through the mud.

The roar and acrid, gaseous smell of the tanks just added to the confusion in the men's heads. There were already so many noises from the bowels of hell all around them whilst they waited for the one sound they did not wish to hear – that of the officers' whistles. As the tanks passed by their engines puffed out their acid smoke to add to the carnage of battle. Then the whistles blew and the men shouted and charged up and out of their trenches all along the line. As one battalion after another came up and filled the places where others had been standing, they too took their turn running through the bodies of those smashed in front of them. Initially the attack went well, very well. The Royal Flying Corps did their stuff overhead and the tanks rolled through and past the front lines over pre-arranged routes, and on into the first German lines. The German troops had no choice but to either be crushed by the tanks or run. As Captain D. G. Browne reflected in 1920:

> The immediate onset of the tanks was inevitably overwhelming. The German outposts, dazed or annihilated by the sudden deluge of shells were overrun in an instant. The triple belts of barbed wire were crossed as if

they had been belts of nettles and 350 pathways were cleared then for the infantry. The defenders of the line running panic stricken, casting away arms and equipment . . . over the whole southern half of the battlefield the defence had collapsed and this area was virtually cleared by midday.[13]

The initial assaults therefore went incredibly well, far better than anyone expected. The only place where the attack faltered was in front of the 51st Highland Division, where by all accounts the sceptical General Harper had instructed his infantry to hold back from close support with the tanks. This meant that once the tanks had passed the German lines some German infantry simply set up their machine guns again and took on the advancing infantry as normal, whilst the tanks continued on alone and were cut off and destroyed from behind. Thus the 51st Division stalled at its first objective – the village of Flesquières – and forty tanks were lost in this sector. However, elsewhere the advance and shock of the tanks was going well and by mid-morning many of the first- and second-line objectives had been reached. By the evening an advance of 8km had been secured – the men had achieved more in one day than in the entire three-month Battle of Passchendaele (Third Battle of Ypres).

The Inniskillings were ordered up into the line to the village of Villers-Plouich, which they reached at around 6.45am. On the way, close artillery fire started to fall too close and actually on their leading troops (possibly because Jack was whipping his men along at a fair old pace), and their first casualties were absorbed. With the news that the blue lines had also been taken the entire 29th Division was quickly activated to exploit the gaps and ordered forward to advance through the troops in front of them. All three brigades advanced on their map bearings in arrowhead formations, walking through mangled rusty barbed wire with body parts draped from them, through mud mixed with blood and on into the German lines, where many dead and dying men in both sorts of uniforms could be seen, and then past many of the tanks that had broken down. Around 180 tanks were lost on that first day across the 5-mile front, of which 65 had been destroyed by German guns and over 70 had broken down, but they had done their job well. As if by a stroke of fate, it was the 87 Brigade that was ordered to take the divisional point of the arrowhead. Within that brigade Lieutenant Colonel Jack Sherwood Kelly DSO, CMG and his battalion were ordered to lead the way for the whole division. It is clear why they were chosen. As the commander of the brigade, Lucas knew the best man for the job was Jack, and his battalion, with some equally well-trained, courageous and determined Irishmen.

By 10.30am Jack's leading company of 150 men had come up behind the 2/SWB (who had lost a significant number of men to get to this point). They had passed clumps of SWB tending to wounds, and bodies sprawled around them as they arrived, and knew they were now in range of German machine guns and sniper rifle fire. This was the same 2/SWB that had been decimated the year before on the Somme. Jack made contact with the CO of the Borderers and then took on the forward move. He ordered his line companies to move quickly towards the enemy rear lines and dugouts. They had been moving steadily forward now for two hours, and by 11.30, they were over the Escaut River within sight of the main Canal du Nord. Through the mud, smoke, mist and gunfire it was possible to see the crossing places and icy cold water, which was the objective, some 50yd away. The little bridge over the canal was vital, and as the regimental history records:

> When the canal crossings had been secured, the Inniskillings were to cross the canal and, with the help of the tanks, seize their allotted position of the red line and consolidate. This portion east of the main road to Cambrai was just beyond the ridge of Masnieres and was part of the Rumilly system of trenches of the Hindenburg Line.[14]

The Germans had run back to the other side of the canal bank and had already set up their machine guns in some ruined farmhouses on the eastern edge of Masnières, and in the banks overlooking the Ecluse de Bracheux lock over the canal. The battalion started taking casualties as the fire grew more intense. It was immediately clear to Jack that to press on meant pushing his men into unrelenting machine-gun and artillery fire, but to halt meant not only would the battalion advance stop, but also that of the Newfoundland Regiment, which was also trying to cross the canal. They were stalled in mud, smoke, cold, wet craters full of wounded and wet men, and the question was what to do next. At that moment, a tank appeared and started to engage the German guns. Three companies of the SWB managed to cross the canal over a small bridge 400yd to the west of the lock. A gap of a few minutes saw the Inniskillings arrive to cross and yet another German machine gun opened up, pinning them down and separating them from the SWB on the other side of the canal.

Keeping the momentum of the advance going was vital. It was now around 1.00pm and if the battalion was to get over that bridge, Jack knew that it had to happen now. Rather than ordering one of his men to do it, he ran over to his right, under German rifle fire, to another nearby tank, and ordered them to fire on the Germans on his flank. Then, as if to taunt the Germans, he ran back through the mud and water to his leading company, and ordered his officers and their men to follow him over the bridge. They could see the grey helmets of the German soldiers just above the sandbags opposite them, and through the steam and mist of their guns chattering as they spluttered bullets towards them. With dozens of hobnailed boots thumping on the wooden bridge, bullets whizzing past their heads and wounded and dead bodies slumping like sacks of coal to the ground, they screamed and swore with eyes bulging from rage and fear as they stormed over the bridge, charged up the bank of the canal and crashed over and into the machine-gun position. This is where his men were good at what they did. The Germans in the pits were slaughtered to the man – Jack himself shooting three men dead. The rest of the battalion then followed and joined them on the other side, panting and heaving from their packs with steam rising up from the heat of their uniforms. Jack had survived and yet again led from the front, when a single bullet fired at him could have ended his life.

By 2.30pm Jack was sending runners back to Brigade Headquarters to inform them that the bridge was secure and the rest of the brigade could now follow. Pausing for breath, Jack now looked to his front to see that the ground ran upwards and away from the canal for about 2,000yd, to a small ridge running across their front. The Germans had used this rear area as storage for ammunition and gun-pits, so the whole area ahead of them looked pockmarked and dangerous. The November mists were swirling around both Irishmen and Germans, swallowing them all up. Jack never hesitated, his blood was up and he was in his element. He quickly called his company commanders together and told them the battalion was going up that slope to take the German trench line on the ridge. With two companies in front in extended line and two following behind, they soon came under rifle and machine-gun fire from the ridge, and his 900 or so men starting taking casualties. The platoons rushed forward under covering fire and Jack's men made another 500yd before beginning to stall, not just because of the fire coming down on them, but also because of the mud clagging their boots and now rusty barbed wire that was strewn indiscriminately around the holes. The chaos of the battlefield, disorientation and fear played their parts, perhaps men shot their own comrades by accident, rifles jammed, men screamed, sergeants screamed and the dead were silent as they fell and never moved again. Jack's officers were shouting in their English accents and his NCOs were swearing in their broad Irish accents, but it wasn't enough. Once more Jack ran up from the rear to the left flank of his unit and at the very front, facing 30yd of thick barbed wire. Once he was seen by his men he shouted to get the cutters working. All around him men became heroes and followed his lead (this is true leadership), as they did their part and died to help their comrades break through the wire. One of his officers stood up and mounted a Lewis gun on the shoulders of a sergeant and started firing back to get a better angle on the German lines . . . and then fell back dead, shot through the head. Now that was a man who deserved a medal.

An anonymous document at TNA pays tribute to Jack Kelly in this action. Possibly written by one of his officers, it describes how, once a channel had been cut, it was the giant colonel who rose and shouted 'Charge!' – and his men followed him up the last 100yd of the slope. It was Jack who was first into the German trench, and he that grappled in hand-to-hand fighting – a rare example for any colonel commanding a battalion at any time. But then he was no ordinary colonel.

Those Germans who stayed to fight were over-run and either shot or bayonetted – including three German officers. The rest ran to the next lines to the rear. The RIF had taken the slope (or part of it) and to their left the 2/SWB arrived following Jack's second charge.

Now this is where perhaps the battalion should have stopped. They were already far in advance of where they had expected to be, and the aim of the attack had been to support, not lead an advance to break through completely. But it wasn't enough for Jack. If he had had an army behind him, he would have carried on to Berlin. The same unsigned document describes how:

> Col Kelly then consolidated his position and, during the whole of the time that this work was in progress, he walked up and down the battalion front, encouraging his tired men and inspiring them to fresh efforts. In doing so he was always under the heaviest fire, but he seemed to be absolutely careless of his own safety in regard for the safety of his men. He showed such contempt for the German fire that he never attempted to take cover, and frequently picked up rifles to fire at the enemy.

Having decided he was not going to stop, the battalion – less some 150 casualties – advanced again. But the fire now was heavy, including German artillery, so he decided to stop for his men to rest and dig in, in the German positions, on the ridge. As he looked to his right all he could see were German positions, as they had advanced almost too far. The 88 Brigade had got over the canal, but no further, whilst to his left he could see the 86 Brigade also digging in. Behind him lay the remnants of the 2/SWB. In that morning action the Inniskilling Fusiliers had lost 141 other ranks and 6 officers. Most of his casualties were men killed cutting through the wire. As he gazed back down the slope from where they had come, he could see over forty of his men dead or wounded around the wire. A further five men were missing – blown apart by the German shelling as they approached the ridge. Jack sent forty-six German prisoners to the rear, along with five German officers and five machine guns, whilst around eighty Germans lay dead in various parts of the battlefield.

For five days Jack's battalion waited on the ridge, whilst the rear commander decided what to do about the battle they were unexpectedly winning. They could see the towers of Cambrai in front of them, about 2 miles away, as they lay there tending wounds, cuts from the wire, cleaning mud from their faces, uniforms and rifles, and covering their dead comrades and friends. But it still was not enough for Jack. He was sure the line could be broken with a big push and Cambrai taken, but this was not to be. The pause gave the Germans time to regroup. More lives were lost, more telegrams written home to families and more grief amongst the officers and men.

Back home in London and across Britain, church bells rang out and newspapers celebrated what was of course claimed to be a marvellous victory – but the reality was very different. As B. H. Liddell Hart pointed out, the Third Army, within whose sector Cambrai lay, had only six divisions available for the attack and no reserve, because a breakthrough was not expected. For those five days Jack and the rest of the 29th Division sat exposed to increasingly heavy gunfire and lost many men who had made it through the first day of the attack. Jack, as always, had acted on instinct – he had driven his men forward, quite willingly accepting the dangers, because he could see an opportunity. Further back behind the lines the senior commanders could not. Paradoxically, it was the reverse of most of the First World War, where commanders had thrown men forward in hopeless attacks on impregnable positions, when the men in the field could see it was pointless. But they had done their duty never-the-less. This time it was the men that could see an opportunity and the senior commanders could not.

General Ludendorff fully expected his lines to be broken by the British at any moment after 29 November, and issued instructions for a general retreat. The official German account states that, 'a wide gap remained open for many hours completely unoccupied between Masnieres and Crevecoeur'. Had Allied troops and tanks moved up during the night, who knows how the course of the entire war might have changed at that point. Instead, Jack and his men remained in the lines alone for five days and the Germans saw a miraculous opportunity to save what seemed like a desperate situation. Five German divisions moved into the area over the next twenty-four hours, and a further six started to move there.

By 25 November, 1/Inniskilling needed a rest and the 1/Essex came up to relieve them and a changeover was affected during that evening. The Inniskillings began moving to the rear lines of the 29th divisional sector. It was increasingly apparent to many officers that in front of them the Germans were preparing a massive build-up of forces. The warning signs were everywhere. General Snow, commanding VII Corps, was even able to announce the date and location of the attack, whilst General Jeudwine of 55th Division, supported this view. He cited a list of collaborative evidence as a serious warning to his superiors, such as very active enemy artillery zeroing in on previously ignored targets, as a precursor to heavy bombardment, vastly increased enemy air reconnaissance and air attacks on rear troop concentrations. Yet, incredibly, all this seemed to make no impression until it was too late. On 30 November, only ten days after reeling under the first day of the Allied attack on Cambrai, the Germans unleashed their own offensive. Their recovery had been born out of necessity, whilst their success was as a result of mistakes by the British High Command. Without adequate reserves or preparation for the obvious, British troops were forced back to their original position. The fact that the Germans did not break through altogether, was again in part due to the experience, courage and determination of the 29th Division:

[They] held fast our positions intact and organized and made a defensive flank to link up with the units on their right, which had fallen back. On November 30th the attack came to its lines and nine assaults, four of them heavy ones, were repelled. The front held by the Division was now double in length, though casualties had cut its strength by half. It was desirable to shorten the line a little by withdrawing the line to west of Masnieres, a post, which was now surrounded on three sides. The canal crossings were still held.

However, by 3 December, Haig ordered a withdrawal back to the original start lines. All the efforts of the 29th Division and losses of 45,000 casualties across the sector had been in vain. So it was that the British press back home once more had to leap into acrobatic convolutions – the failure at Cambrai became eclipsed by the gallant defence with headlines such as: 'HOW THE GERMANS MASSED TWENTY DIVISIONS AGAINST THE SHARP BRITISH SALIENT AND TEMPORARILY FORCED OUR LINE'. A bungled attack became a celebration of stoic defence. Byng even blamed the men, not the staff officers: 'I attribute the reason for the local successes on the part of the enemy to one cause and one cause alone, namely the lack of training on the part of junior officers and NCOs and men.'

The fact that any experienced officer, NCO or man had already been killed in previous pointless battles planned by men such as Byng, was not seen as the root of this deficiency. All of this was of course of no help to the men now buried in shallow graves in the cold and wet ground around the crossing points of the canal. They had given their all and followed Jack forward in faith and courage. Jack too had given his all. Lucas wrote to Poppy: 'France November 29th 1917: This is very confidential but I hope Col Kelly will shortly get a VC.'

Five days in the wet and bitter November cold, the smoke, mist and, most of all, the emotional strain of first the attack and then holding on to their positions, had taken its toll on Jack and he collapsed. His lungs had given way to the cold and pneumonia, aggravated by the enduring effects of the gas attack he had suffered the previous spring. On 4 December Jack was sent down the lines once again, back to Treport Hospital, and Lucas handed the battalion over to Major J.R.C. Dent. He wrote to his fiancée: 'France December 7th 1917: Poor old Col Kelly has had a temporary collapse after the dreadful strain of the last fortnight and has gone off to hospital somewhere.'

The next day Lucas managed to get away from the front – it is a measure of his regard for Jack that he wrote the following in one of his most revealing passages to Poppy:

France December 8th 1917: I am motoring miles to the seaside to see Col Kelly, to make quite certain he goes home and has a good rest instead of trying to come straight back to his Battn and breaking down again. I shall have quite a lot of trouble with him as he does not appreciate rest cures . . . We shall both be real pleased if Jack does get his VC <u>but he may not</u>. If ones name is put on the list of divisional commanders it means very little as there are probably at least 50 other names, and only about one vacancy a month.

So, we can deduce a number of things from this. Lucas emphasizes the fighting character of Jack, which was simply irrepressible. He was already being called the bravest man in the British army, well before his exploits at Cambrai, and here his commanding officer drives miles to force him away from the front lines to actually stop him fighting! It is also revealing that there was a VC quota: in order to maintain the elite nature of the VC, even if one's exploits merited the award, many never received it. Similar to the honours system of today, there was a lot of politics involved as to who actually received the medal and those who did not, regardless of merit.

That same unsigned document at TNA concluded with this paragraph:

The success with which the battalion advanced was due chiefly to his brilliant leadership; for the British soldier will always follow a brave leader to the ends of the earth . . . Unfortunately, the physical strain to which he was subjected on that day and during the full fortnight of severe fighting that followed, proved too much for him, and, much against his will, he was sent to hospital. But it would probably be rash for the Germans to hope that he will stay there long . . .

Jack already brought with him to the Inniskillings a huge reputation for bravery, courage and a reckless and relentless fighting ability. His action at Cambrai was therefore entirely in keeping with his growing reputation as 'The bravest man in the British army'. It may have been partly this that caused Lucas to go to the strenuous efforts he did. Jack was no ordinary officer. Staying overnight after seeing Jack, and two days before Jack's daughter Angela was born, Lucas wrote once more: 'France December 9th 1917: I didn't get back till late from Treport, where Col Kelly is in hospital; it was a very cold day, with driving rain, an open car, about 60 miles each way. Lady Murray who runs the hospital gave us a very good lunch.' And again: 'France December 16th 1917: Col Kelly has not started home yet, and is not likely to for a week yet, but is going on strong.' That same day Jack was transported by train once more, back to England, arriving in London on 17 December.

Back to London: Christmas, 1917
Once again Nellie was there to welcome Jack home to the London Hospital and to

her Cranley Gardens home, as he convalesced over the Christmas period. Her love for Jack superseded any doubts that either she or her family had for his commitment to her or the marriage. Visitors to the hospital over December included Major J. S. Felix, who had shared a glass of Madeira with Jack and Nellie in happier times. Felix had also, at times, been as close to Nellie as anyone. One piece of news that awaited Jack was that six days prior to his arrival back in London, Dora had given birth to their daughter, Angela Margaret. We know nothing of how Jack responded to the birth of his child or when or how he managed the relationship with Dora. Did he leave hospital to live with Dora and the baby? Did he leave Dora in the hands of her family? Did he retreat to Reigate and his aunt? Did he tell Nellie – or did she somehow already know? Also in December, another piece of news arrived, this time brought to him by Major Felix. The envelope contained a letter from the War Office, informing Jack that he had been recommended and immediately confirmed for the award of the Victoria Cross, for his actions on 20 November. Only a few months before, Jack had told Nellie that the only way he would leave the army was to win the Victoria Cross. Half said in jest, Jack had now done what he said he needed to do. In early January, the newspapers carried reports of Jack's bravery and on 11 January 1918, the *London Gazette* carried the news of the award, along with a further eighteen winners of the VC. The citation read:

> John Sherwood Kelly CMG, DSO Major (Acting Lt. Col) Norfolk Regiment commanding a battalion of The Royal Inniskilling Fusiliers. For most conspicuous bravery and fearless leading when a party of men of another unit detailed to cover the passage of the Canal by his battalion were held up on the near side of the canal by heavy rifle fire directed at the bridge. Lt. Col Sherwood Kelly at once ordered covering fire and personally led the leading company of his battalion across the canal, and after crossing, reconnoitered under heavy rifle and machine gun fire the high ground held by the enemy. The left flank of his battalion advancing to the assault of this objective was held up by a thick belt of wire, whereupon he crossed to that flank, and with a Lewis Gun team, forced his way under heavy fire through obstacles, got the gun into position on the far side and covered the advance of his battalion through the wire, thereby enabling them to capture the position. Later he personally led a charge against some pits from which a heavy fire was being directed on his men, captured the pits together with five machine guns and 46 prisoners, and killed a large number of the enemy. The great gallantry displayed by this officer throughout the day inspired the greatest confidence in his men and it was mainly due to his example and devotion to duty that his battalion was enabled to capture and hold their objective.[15]

Whatever judgments can be made about Jack – his fiery temper, his clashes with authority and his stubbornness – one cannot argue with his courage in the face of overwhelming odds. On that day in November, Jack, his body already beaten and bruised by serious wounds that had only just healed, threw himself at an enemy determined to kill him – not once, but numerous times, as if to taunt death. His men saw a hero, a giant of a man who pushed them on to victory and was always there at the very front, ready to die for them and their cause.

Far greater in stature than the DSO, the award of the VC was a major event in anyone's life and those close to him would have shared in his recognition. Searching for Dora at this time reveals no clues as to where she fitted into his life now. Indeed, Lucas, in a rare reference to Nellie, wrote to Poppy: 'France January 4th 1918: I'm sure Col Kelly's wife isn't with him.'

Perhaps Jack was with Dora at the Rubens, but nevertheless it was still Nellie that made all the arrangements for the award ceremony, and ensured that as many members of Jack's family that could be found were invited. Nellie also organized an after-ceremony reception at Cranley Gardens, where members of her own family, including her mother, would be present. Was she standing by the man who had just had a child with another woman, and may even have been living with her only a few minutes away from her own home? Who could imagine anyone doing this and why would she? Yet it seems that Jack was indeed still able to rely on Nellie acting as his wife, despite everything that was going on. Nellie is really the heroine to Jack's hero in this story.

Jack was recovered enough to travel in early January 1918. Lucas wrote to Poppy:

France January 11th 1918: If you don't go up to town to see Sherwood Kelly I bet he will turn up at Widdecombe unexpectedly someday without the least warning.

France January 13th 1918: Sherwood Kelly has got his VC, as you knew yesterday. I am glad I hope it will quiet him down a bit now, and that he will stay at home a bit and have a good rest.

For the next six months there was to be no mention of Jack in Lucas' letters – he was still in command of the brigade and Jack was on a new path. Meanwhile, on 23 January 1918, outside Buckingham Palace, friends and family waited for Jack and Nellie to emerge into the cold grey air of a typical London morning – ten days after his 38th birthday and five weeks after the birth of Angela. At 11.15 they came out and walked across the gravel in front of the palace. In the photograph we have of the very moment that Jack joined three of his brothers with Nellie beside him, we see the biggest smile from the man that we have on record. There is no Dora, no Angela, but there he is holding the medal and box high for all to see. We can only imagine what thoughts ran through his head – both on a superficial but also a deeper level. Perhaps these moments and this day was the high point of his life. Right back in the Boer War as a teenager he had dreamt of a Victoria Cross, and now he was holding his own. Was it really about taking on the world and proving it wrong? Or was it about showing his father and family that he could take the world on and stand tall? Or maybe it was the cause – any cause – that spurred him on? In an earlier age Jack would have been a soldier of fortune, a man that other men would follow or that more unscrupulous men would use for their own ends . . . This is what was going to happen the following year.

For the next few months and whilst the war was still in full flow, Jack was returned to the nominal role in the Norfolk Regiment and he would never serve with the RIF again. He had attended a medical board on 27 February 1918, which in all likelihood recommended he withdraw from active service. Despite closer ties once more with Nellie, he was still listed as resident at 'The Hotel Rubens' – possibly with Dora and Angela. We will never know. What we do know is that by March 1918, Dora had moved to Paignton in Devon – probably to be with family that she had in the area. On 2 April 1918, Angela was baptized at St John Baptist Church in Paignton by the Revd Arthur Fuller. Again, we do not know if Jack was present – or even invited. Given the backing Jack had received from Nellie since his return from the Western Front, it is a fair assumption that his relationship with Dora had become more distant, especially in the face of the onslaught of London parties and social gatherings that would have surrounded the status of the new national hero. We can only guess what correspondence might have passed between Jack and Dora – indeed we do not know for sure how much they even saw of each other. It is possible that by now Dora realized she had lost Jack – if indeed she really had him in the first place.

South Africa Again and Brighter Stars

Perhaps to rest and recuperate or perhaps to escape from the emotional dilemma that he had created, Jack wrote to his superiors to ask permission to return to South Africa for another recruiting tour. He was acquainted with General Botha, an old friend from South Africa and now Prime Minister of the Union of South Africa. It is very likely that the South African press, whether pro-British or nationalist, had been reporting on Jack's heroic exploits and, given that he had been back to South Africa in 1916, he was invited back again. According to Jack (in a letter written later in February 1920 when he was resident at the Rubens Hotel): 'I undertook a recruiting tour at the request of the late General Botha' (Botha having died in August 1919). Botha had apparently offered to fund Jack's journey and he set off once more as the conquering hero, leaving Nellie, Dora and Angela behind during the summer of 1918.

Whilst he was touring Jack also met General J. B. M. Hertzog, leader of the pro-nationalist party, and they got on well (perhaps too well for the British section in South Africa). As we know, Jack seemed to have the gift of either finding conflict and getting involved – or creating it where there was none. Touring the Eastern Cape, Jack arrived in East London in May 1918 ostensibly to whip up more support for the war in France and swell the recruiting numbers – especially of Dutch South Africans who were being encouraged to go to France and rid their homeland of the Germans who had been there in occupation since 1914. Accordingly, Jack seems to have at one and the same time got a taste for the stage and speech-making, whilst also managing to offend many of those listening. It is safe to say his early attempts at speech-making were likely to be of the rabble-rousing style, and complaints were made to the British Consulate. Such complaints about Jack reached as far as Sierra Leone a few weeks later, where Major General Thompson (then commanding British troops in West Africa) later made this astute observation back to the War Office in London:

I think the Army Council should be in possession of the facts gathered by me in my recent visit to South Africa, that Lt. Colonel Kelly during his stay in South Africa more or less identified himself with the Nationalist party and with Mr Hertzog in particular. He further made an injudicious speech at a recruiting meeting and altogether got into a bad odour with the English Section and I believe his leave was curtailed by Brigadier-General Martyn CMG who is now at home.

Maj. Gen. C. W. Thompson

The most likely interpretation is that Jack, with his new Victoria Cross and other medals, felt invulnerable, strong, potent and important. If we pause for a moment to consider what he had been through by the age of 38, we can but wonder how he must have felt. He was still learning about life, but had seen so much of death. He had wanted fame and fortune, but now how to use it? He was aware that perhaps his military career was coming to an end and was wondering what to do next . . . why not politics? It is worth noting at this point, that in the background of Jack's life in London, there had been an increasing number of contacts with some very wealthy South African businessmen. Not only was his aunt married to the media entrepreneur Arthur Hamilton (of Margery Hall in Reigate), but through Hamilton, Jack was well acquainted with a series of other serious players on the political stage in London. Maybe he had harboured a desire to launch himself onto the political stage at some point and now was the time.

Back on a stage that he recognized, he was now one of the most decorated South Africans in its history. He had been invited to stand up tall, show his chest and he was ready to do it. Unfortunately Jack was, at this time, out of his depth when it came to making speeches, and a novice in the sensitivities and balance of South African politics. In order to be successful, Jack probably said what he thought would win the day and gather the most positive reaction. It was only later that he realized what he had done and had to back-track, as Brigadier General A. Martyn CB CMG later wrote from his home in Exmouth in March 1919:

> Kelly apparently made some injudicious remarks in his addresses. I saw the account of one in the local press – and at once communicated with him referring to the instructions in the K. R., with reference to soldiers mixing themselves up in political meetings etc. He then returned to Cape Town and I spoke to him on the matter. He assured me that he had not meant politics by any remark he had made, and after considerable conversation I was quite satisfied that his remarks were made in the excitement of the moment and that his educational attainments in my opinion did not suit him to making speeches, as he made statements which he considers harmless and not political which in a country like South Africa are at once seized on by the opposite political parties and turned to their own advantage. Lieut. Col. Kelly was, he informed me, a friend of Gen. Hertzog before the war and he certainly was on good terms with him on their visit to South Africa.

As with Lucas back on the Somme, it was all about how one handled Jack when there was a problem. Again, like Lucas, General Martyn clearly had a gentle but firm and non-judgmental approach, and this worked with Jack. The result was the following epilogue from the general:

> No more loyal or gallant officer in my opinion is serving in H. M. Army, but also in my opinion he is not suitable for 'speech making' in a country like South Africa and if I had been asked I should have said so. After the East London meeting and my telegram referred to above, Lieut. Col. Kelly came to Cape Town and I was fortunately able to get him a passage at once to England . . .[16]

Having been extricated and learnt from this experience, a gentle trip home in the sun might have been wise, but it was not to be. Leaving Cape Town on 6 June 1918 to return home, Jack was, perhaps ill-advisedly, put in command of the newly recruited South African troops on board HMS *City of Karachi*. En route, perhaps with that recently inflated ego that had developed, Jack fell out explosively with the troops on board. Whether it was the VC or whether Jack really was something of a martinet – a real paradox if ever there was one – Jack apparently called the troops on board 'damned South Africans' with bad discipline. One example of this was a reported case of a young lieutenant caught by Jack with an NCO in his cabin smoking. Jack saw this as a dreadful breach of discipline and the mark of 'an undisciplined rabble'. Arriving in Sierra Leone, another major general had another Jack-instigated mess to sort out. Major General Thompson had to call an enquiry into complaints wired over by a Lieutenant Baxter and a Major King. At the end of the hearing the general recorded: 'although I did not suppose an entente cordiale was established yet I was fully under the impression that the matter was settled, that all parties were satisfied and that no further trouble would arise on the voyage'.

Arriving home at the end of June, Jack reconnected with his new political friends and relayed his experiences of the situation in South Africa. He was, it seems, keen to build a political career to replace the military one that he saw diminishing as the war came to an end. He must also have reconnected with Dora for at least a short while, as Lucas, still writing every day to Poppy, commented: 'France July 19th 1918: Sherwood Kelly is staying at the Redcliffe Hotel in Paignton, S Devon. He has been recruiting in S. Africa and brought back 1129 recruits with him. His official address is Hotel Rubens London: so perhaps he is up to no good at Paignton.'

Clearly Jack had kept his affair and his new child with Dora secret for well over a year, as Lucas had no idea what he was doing in Paignton. He was, however, savvy enough to know from past experience what Jack was potentially doing. In fact, instead of having more good times with head-turning ladies, it seems he was spending time with Dora and Angela – perhaps one of the few or only periods he would spend with Angela for the rest of her life. Sadly, she would be too young to even remember them. Three days later Lucas recorded in his penultimate reference to Jack: 'France July 21st 1918: Got a letter from J. Sherwood Kelly again and a lot of S. African newspapers with reports of his recruiting speeches, he seems to have hit a lot of people on the raw, and made them feel uncomfortable judging by the reports.'

The matter rumbled on and the South African High Commissioner pressed for an apology. In March 1919, a Horse Guards' minute recorded: 'I think it is clear that Lieut. Col. Kelly is an officer whose tact is not on a par with his gallantry and I have no doubt he used forcible language. I suggest he should be so informed (the censure being of a mild description) and the High Commissioner be told that suitable action has been taken.'[17] This judgment on Jack's character was prophetic. Within four months of this being written, Jack had left to fight in North Russia, fallen foul of the entire High Command there and was locking horns with Churchill in a very gallant stand, completely lacking in any form of tact. He saw his life as just beginning – perhaps something he felt every morning as he woke up – with a whole new adventure about to begin.

Chapter 7

The Russian Revolution, 1917–19

'The habit of gambling contrary to reasonable calculations is a military vice which, as the pages of history reveal, has ruined more armies than any other cause.'

Captain Sir Basil Liddell Hart, 1944

Although 1917 was another year of costly failure for all sides on the Western Front, it was also the year that signalled the beginning of the end of the war. This was due to two major events of great political and military significance – the entry of the USA into the war and the collapse of Russia into revolution.

In April 1917 the USA entered the war on the Allied side. After a painful and long hesitation, the military and economic might of the USA was to prove decisive. It would take some months for the men and materiel to reach the muddy battlefields of France, but the German High Command recognized the inevitability of their fate, unless the war could be won in France quickly. So, they looked east to Russia.

From the very start of the war in 1914, the Allies relied on splitting the German and Austrian armies over two fronts. After all it was the tsar who had escalated the conflict in his demands over Serbian neutrality, and so it was only right that he put his armies into the field in the East to play their part, whilst the British and French acted to protect Belgium. After initial successes, the Russian armies were beaten by Hindenburg and Ludendorff's attacks in early 1915. As the war went on through 1916 and into 1917, hardships and privations in Russia increased and the dangers of internal collapse grew. Although able to place 6 million men in the field at the start of the war, many of these men were poorly equipped and even more poorly fed. Ineffective command and poor supplies created mutiny, both amongst the army and the navy during the winter of 1917, and the communist soviets fed on this discontent. The tsar became ever more distant and unable to control events, nor did he fully appreciate and understand the new social movements growing in the urban cities. The growth of socialism was not just new to Russia. The new political power that came with the need for labour created a new working class with its own political agenda and ambitions. The European brotherhood of socialism may have been new, but it was there, and events in Russia became the focus of attention for British politicians, every bit as much as the fate of their armies in France. One politician watched with more horror than most – Churchill.

The first serious disturbances began in January 1917. Whilst Jack was at home in Cranley Gardens nursing his chest wound, Moscow and Petrograd fell under the weight of sustained Bolshevik unrest and blood ran in the streets. By March 1917 the riots had spread and the local authorities ran for their lives as the troops they had sent to crush the soviets joined them instead. Difficulty in finding loyal troops and generals was now a harsh fact of life for the White or royal and loyal Russians.

All the Allied powers felt the same: alarm at the loss of Russia from the war effort and equal alarm that revolution might spread to their own workers and encourage supporters of communism and Bolshevism. It was clear that the rise of Labour brought about by industrialization was changing the political landscape, but it was also evident that the explosion in Russia was due to the economic hardships of four years of war. It might not have been as bad in Britain, but it was still bad. Food shortages, long casualty lists, anger at the authority and incompetence of the Establishment, diminishing morale and the growing militancy of the unions and Labour Party, all raised the spectre of social unrest at home before the Germans could be defeated. Was the British monarchy under threat too? Opinions were divided in the Cabinet led by Lloyd George, who, having defected from the Liberal party along with many supporters, had succeeded Asquith as prime minister in 1916. No one really knew at this stage what was going on in Russia, who was loyal and what the tsar could do to re-establish his authority.

There was nothing new in the threat of Bolshevism in Russia. Europe had watched as revolution broke out in 1905 – and done nothing. What were they going to do now? In March 1917, it was clear that the tsar had been deposed and chaos set in across this vast nation. The best form of information came from British businessmen and the many roving 'missions' that we had in Russia – a cover for open spying. Many large stocks were held in Russia, and British investment in coal, wood and other raw materials was significant, hence they made a lot of noise and asked what was to be done. The moral dilemma for the British government and the royal family was what to do to help Tsar Nicholas, his wife the tsarina and their family? Could they be rescued? Could they be bought by ransom? Could they be released by diplomatic means? The answer was undoubtedly yes on all three counts, so which did the British government try?

There were experts on the situation in Russia. As Robert Jackson pointed out, men such as Colonel Alfred Knox (later General Knox) had informed the British government as early as 1914 that the Russian army could collapse at any time.[1] His views were rated very highly by many, including Churchill, whose eyes were always clearly focussed on the socialist menace both at home and abroad. Whenever possible, Churchill had used his position as First Lord of the Admiralty to send ammunition, guns and supplies to North Russia to help support the tsar and his armies – a massive liability if they should fall into the wrong hands. R. H. Bruce Lockhart was another roving emissary to the tsar and warned in 1915 and 1916 of the way events were turning. Thus, it might be supposed that we had a plan to support the tsar – King George V's cousin and a loyal friend of Britain. More recently, however, new research has shown a gradual distancing of Britain, her government and her king from support for Tsar Nicholas. The king knew full well what was happening, as recorded in his diary: 'March 13th 1917: Bad news from Russia, practically a revolution has broken out in Petrograd and some of the Guards regiments have mutinied against their officers. This rising is against the government and not the Tsar.' Trotsky stated it more clearly when he said that 'Neither at the front nor in the rear was there to be found a Brigade or a regiment ready to fight for Nicholas II'.[2]

After an initial period of shock, the British government seemed to drift in different directions about what could and should be done. The issues over entanglement in the affairs of another nation raised their ugly head. Whilst indecision and division developed, communism had a chance to grow and establish itself unchecked by intervention from the Allies. George V continued to do what he could to support his cousin and clear his conscience, as he wrote in a telegram to Tsar Nicholas on 19 March: 'Events of last week have deeply distressed me. My thoughts are constantly with you and I shall remain your true and devoted friend as you know I have been in the past.' Nicholas never received this or any other telegram ever again from George V – not because they were intercepted by Bolshevik guards, or because the location of the tsar was unknown, but because they were stopped by Lloyd George.[3]

By degrees, Lloyd George had come into the fold of the non-interventionists in the Cabinet – those who also saw a certain justice in what was happening in Russia: 'the revolution whereby the Russian people have placed their destinies on the sure foundation of freedom is the greatest service which they have yet made to the cause for which the allied peoples have been fighting since 1914. It reveals the fundamental truth that this war is at bottom a struggle for Popular Government as for liberty.[4] In this short sentence we see some of the mastery of Lloyd George, the Welsh wizard. At a stroke support for the tsar was jettisoned and a play for the support for the votes of the new British working class was made in an attempt to bring them closer to the Liberal Party. The tsar was alone as far as Britain was concerned – although not quite. There were others in the coalition Cabinet who were appalled at such sentiments. Some saw Bolshevism as a threat to all democracies, not the saviour. Churchill was not alone in wanting to 'strangle Bolshevism at birth', but how to avoid the prime minister and the wrath of the socialist movement in this country? That was the problem now. Lloyd George would stick to his dictate that: 'It was not our duty to settle the political order of Russia.'[5]

Even more surprising than the government's desertion of the tsar was the fact that George V also withdrew from an active policy of trying to save his cousin. Recent research has now established that during the spring and early summer of 1917 a series of high-level meetings were held to discuss the tsar's future. Although an ally, a relation of the British royal family and a staunch friend of Britain, a decision was taken to distance British interests from the internal affairs of Russia – despite the protests of Churchill and others. The plan to send a warship to collect the tsar and his family – discussed with Alexander Kerensky, the then more moderate leader of the Russian Provisional Government – was shelved, even though Kerensky would have been glad to have been rid of the tsar. A series of increasingly pointed and sharp letters were exchanged between Lord Stamfordham (the king's private secretary), Arthur Balfour (the British Foreign Secretary) and Sir George Buchanan (the British representative in Petrograd). It is clear that over these weeks George V became conflicted in his desire to save Nicholas and his family. Phrases such as 'concern at the dangers of the voyage' (as if this was more dangerous than being placed in the hands of the Bolsheviks!), and 'general grounds of expediency' betray the search for any moral excuse for what might turn out to be condemning Nicholas to his death.

Explanations of this complete volte-face have also become clearer as historians uncover more archival evidence and place them against the political and social backcloth of the time. There was, for example, a real threat of socialist unrest growing in Britain in 1917. The strike rate was increasing, and dissatisfaction with the war, the losses and the shortages aided this. How would the public react to the arrival of the tsar and his family, saved from the clutches of the Russian working classes by the government? In addition, the royal family, as now and always, was acutely aware of the need to manage its own PR campaign very carefully. Avoiding placing the royal family in the public eye for the wrong reasons, but at the same time maintaining the lustre of monarchy and divine right, has always been the balancing act waged as a private strategy against public opinion. One such move on 17 July 1917, was formally to change the name of the royal family from Hanover to Windsor. Without the war, the changing attitude of the public towards all things German and increasing alarm at attacks from 'radicals and extremists', this would never have happened. At the same time the Battenbergs changed their family name to Mountbatten. The new socialist menace had established itself as a real threat in the psyche of the Establishment and political classes. Left isolated and marooned by all the Allied powers, the tsar and his young and beautiful family were doomed. What has often been referred to as 'this shabby affair' even surprised and shocked the Russians: 'With tears in his eyes scarcely able to control his emotions Sir George [Buchanan] informed the Russian Minister of Foreign Affairs of the British Governments final refusal to give refuge to the former Emperor of Russia . . . I can say definitely that this refusal was due exclusively to considerations of internal British politics.'[6]

And so it was that the 'true and devoted friend' that was George V deserted Nicholas in the face of threats to his own position from his own people. We will never know what Nicholas told his family. In 1992 the bodies of Nicholas and his family did actually reach Britain, but only for forensic examination to determine in what order they were shot, had their bodies cut up, dumped in acid and buried. Lloyd George would no doubt have stood by his words that this was a moral price worth paying, in the struggle for 'popular liberty' in Russia.

The story did not quite end there. After the war, and partly due to Jack's developing role in highlighting British policy in Russia, storms of denial over the role of Britain in the murder of the tsar followed. One such aspect involved Meriel Buchanan, daughter of Sir George, who, after his death, stated that her father had falsified his memoirs to protect the king's honour (and to save his pension, which Lloyd George had threatened would be stopped if he told the truth).

Thus, it is clear that not only were there divisions on the Russian question at the highest levels within the Cabinet of Lloyd George, there were also men who would stop at nothing to prevent Britain's involvement. Certainly, Lloyd George would have none of it.

At almost the same time as General Byng was formulating the finishing touches for the Third Army's role in the attack on Cambrai in October 1917, the Russian Revolution was about to explode into a new and decisive phase. Up to this point the Bolsheviks had played a relatively minor part in national events. Successive provisional governments came and went but failed to make any real progress, despite high ideals and promises. Others had, on the other hand, been biding their time and watching. Vladimir Lenin could have been a student of Chinese military general Sun Tzu who, over 2,000 years ago, said: 'I have heard of military operations that were clumsy but swift, but I have never seen one that was skillful and lasted a long time. It is never beneficial to a nation to have a military operation continue for a long time.'[7]

For Lenin, the successful takeover of power by the Bolsheviks depended on timing. With groups all around central government posturing for control, the Bolsheviks were able to build their resources and support all over Russia, and most importantly, amongst the army and navy. Like Hitler would do twenty years later, Lenin watched, planned and waited so that his campaign was swift and ruthless. In the eye of the storm was Kerensky, trying to patch-up what he could from the chaos around him and contain the revolutionary ferment:

'What do they expect of me?' He shouted at Raymond Robbins, an American ostensibly working for the Red Cross but actually a member of the American Intelligence Service. 'Half the time I'm forced to talk Western European Liberalism to satisfy the allies and the rest of the time I have to talk Russian Slavic Socialism to keep myself alive!'[8]

Kerensky was the first leader to feel the pressure of outside influence. Key to the Allied interest in Russia was the question of whether they would then maintain forces in the field against the German and Austro-Hungarian armies. A close second was what the various governments were going to do to safeguard Western financial interests, loans and investments in Russia, from the revolutionaries. Allied prospects of victory were now assured once the Americans arrived in sufficient numbers, but this depended on keeping the war going on two fronts. Lloyd George may have publicly denounced intervention in the hope that his high-minded form of democratic liberalism would appeal to his known disaffected masses, but the reality, of course, was that Britain had been intervening in the affairs of Russia ever since the Crimea.

Well before 1914 Western businessmen had been investing huge sums in what today would be called the emerging markets – imperial or tsarist Russia being one of the largest. As Michael Sayers and Albert Kahn pointed out as long ago as 1946, men such as Herbert Hoover had private interests in no fewer than eleven Russian oil companies, and in 1912 he had joined with the British multi-millionaire Leslie Urquhart to form three timber and mineral companies in the Urals and Siberia.[9] Growth was dramatic as production costs were so low. Russo-Asiatic shares rose from $16.25 in 1913 to $47.50 by 1914 alone, and Western banks owned shares in numerous coal and silver mines, railroads, oil refineries and oil fields, all purchased at rock-bottom prices from the economically crippled tsarist regime – oil that today has created hundreds of billionaires. Like vultures over a body not quite dead, the Western powers watched and waited for a weakness that would allow further advantage – either economic or political. The tsarist regime owed vast sums in national debts to the Americans and to many European powers, and these powers also depended on trade with Russia for future economic growth themselves. All this was threatened by a Bolshevik takeover of power. During 1917 instructions went out to buy as many banks as possible. This high-risk strategy could only be explained by the fact that they hoped, via economic exploitation, to take control of the Russian state once the tsarist regime had gone forever and the Bolshevik menace had been eliminated – leaving their economic stranglehold over the entire nation: 'if the Bolsheviks could now be ousted by military intervention, Britain would have virtual control of the entire economy of White Russia.'[10]

During the remaining months of 1917 and on into 1918, Lloyd George monitored events and played his dangerous game of political roulette, balancing the potential dangers and opportunities in handling the growing socialist movement in Britain, with the equally dangerous game of supporting the supposed growth of liberty in Russia. His aim was to control the outcome to the huge economic advantage of British business – much of which supported his party. Thus, non-intervention in a political sense did not mean non-intervention economically. Somewhere lost in this higher-stakes game was the tsar and his family, whose future remained uncertain over the months ahead and through the winter of 1917–18.

During the summer of 1917 the Russian army disintegrated. It had never been a unified fighting force but rather an amalgam of widely differing standards of unit, fattened by whole corps of ethnic troops, swelling ranks by numbers not quality. With the propaganda of the Bolsheviks permeating every thought of the ordinary soldier, confusion reigned and loyalties waned. A rapid disintegration left senior commanders either dead or having to rely on their reputation to keep the loyalty of their men. Men such as generals Kornilov and Brusilov stood firm, and loyal troops gravitated to loyal commanders and continued the fight against the Germans. Others deserted in their thousands and drifted into the arms of the Bolsheviks.

Throughout these days the Germans prospered, their divisions exploiting the holes that opened up in front of them. The depth of desperation of loyal officers even saw them attack the German lines alone and face certain death. Lenin and his senior aides had been planning, watching, preparing and amassing their forces. By October, Lenin judged that the time was right to strike. And then ten days that shook the world began: 'Consolidate your keenest energy, save up your extra strength, keep your form concealed and your plans secret, being unfathomable to enemies, waiting for a vulnerable gap to advance upon.'

After the overthrow of Kerensky, Lenin immediately moved to end the war with Germany, ordering General Dukhonin to begin negotiations for an armistice. He refused and was later shot. But talks did begin at Brest-Litovsk in December 1917 and suddenly the worst fears of the Allied powers became reality. They were no longer talking to Kerensky, but Lenin and his soviets, and the question now was what to do. If Lloyd George thought for a moment that his support for 'popular democracy' would be a vote winner with the Bolsheviks in power, he was wrong. He now had the reaction of the British Right, businessmen and the Conservative middle class to deal with. Direct military intervention was not possible. There were no spare troops in the spring of 1918 and the German final offensive of the war was coming. Only the Americans or possibly the ever-watchful Japanese could help, thus the policy of defensive intervention began to develop. Lenin played his own double and triple games. He knew that the longer the Germans could keep up the fight, the more time he would have to win his own, and establish the revolution permanently in Russia. The negotiations at Brest-Litovsk therefore dragged on, with the Germans becoming more impatient by the day. It also soon became evident that a further problem was looming. The Allied powers, especially Britain, had been helping Russia stay in the war by sending huge amounts of guns, ammunition and stores to key Russian ports. In the Far East Japan now moved to recover these from Vladivostok. The British, however, chose to await events and left their vast caches in Archangel, intact for now.

As Jack walked out of Buckingham Palace on that cold misty London morning in January 1918, in another world far away, the forces opposed to Bolshevism in Russia began to concentrate in various parts of Russia to try to restore the monarchy and the old order. To the far south General Kaledin deployed his loyal forces in the Don River and the British government now had to work out which side they were on. According to Robert Jackson this was not a decision to make now. Instead, in traditional and well-practised diplomatic style, the government supported both. As Bruce Lockhart recalled later:

On New Year's Day [1918] I was back at the offices of the War Cabinet. A scheme was being evolved. It was certain that I was to return to Russia almost at once. In what capacity I was not told. Three days later all my doubts were put at rest. I was to go to Russia as head of a special mission to establish unofficial relations with the Bolsheviks . . . My instructions were of the vaguest. I was to have no authority. If the Bolsheviks would give me the necessary diplomatic privileges without being recognized by the British government we would make a similar concession to Litvinoff whom the Bolsheviks had already appointed Soviet Ambassador in London.[11]

As Jack contemplated his future in that spring of 1918, the snow was falling across London in what was now the fifth year of the worst war in history. Lloyd George was also wondering how to survive the year and battled to use his wizard powers to the full to satisfy everyone. A few hundred miles to the west the Germans had also done their own pondering, but they were now on the move and had finally lost their patience with Lenin, striking out in major offensives in North Russia. Within weeks the Bolsheviks had crumbled. Humiliating negotiation followed to buy the Germans off, resulting in huge swathes of Russian territory being ceded to them. On 3 March the Treaty of Brest-Litovsk was finally signed. The Germans, not over-bothered about the legitimacy of those signing on behalf of the Russian people, had already decided that it mattered not whether it was a Russian communist or a member of the Russian royal family that signed – as long as someone did. Immediately after, the German divisions on the Eastern Front received their marching orders to head West, and Ludendorff's 'Friedensturm' offensive began on the Western Front on 21 March 1918.

Under pressure all along the front to absorb these final and desperate German attacks, it is not surprising that the Bolsheviks now tried to take advantage of Allied distraction. Suddenly the massive stores in the North Russian ports became one of the keys to the success of the revolution, as Lenin could arm his revolutionary guards and soviets with fresh guns and ammunition in endless supply. Rear Admiral Kemp was in command of the small British presence around Murmansk, and was responsible for protecting convoys entering or leaving Murmansk. On 13 February 1918, he had already asked for a force of 6,000 men to guard the stores and warehouses, which were being progressively looted by the local soviets. He could not afford to fire a shot for fear of sparking an incident on Russian soil. His request was denied, but he did land 130 Royal Marines from his ships to reinforce the still loyal local tsarist troops. In Britain, this news began to permeate into the newspapers. The Foreign Office was, of course, on the surface, appalled, whilst the First Lord of the Admiralty, Sir Eric Geddes, was supportive. General Knox went much further and called for 5,000 men to defend Murmansk and 15,000 men for Archangel.[12] Such calls were not new, as Brinkley points out:

> an allied conference met in Paris on December 22nd 1917 to consider a special memorandum by The British Foreign Office. This memorandum, formulated largely by Lord Milner, stressed the necessity of keeping the Eastern Front active by every means possible . . . it recommended especially the further development of relations with General Alekseev and the Don Cossacks but also suggested the need for a more active allied policy in the Ukraine.[13]

As an aside to all this we can note that Lord Alfred Milner, who had been such a significant figure in South Africa during the Boer Wars, and whose actions impacted on the life of Jack, was still very active and very much a part of the support for Lloyd George. He was again about to influence the life of Jack and others – as they were pawns in a great game played in the corridors of power. Thus, on the surface Lloyd George preached non-intervention and support for 'popular democracy' (whatever that meant in Russia at that time or any time), whilst behind the scenes tremendous pressure built for increased action to either support the loyal White Armies in crushing the Bolsheviks and thus preserving Britain's economic interests in Russia, or the complete opposite – working with the Bolsheviks – depending on how events unfolded. A great game indeed, where the lives of men were simply useful in achieving a political, not moral, end. According to Sayers and Kahn, Sir Samuel Hoare (Chief of the British Intelligence Service in Russia) had already recommended that the British and French governments back a coup led by General Kornilov, that would at once 'keep Russia in the war, suppress the revolution and protect Anglo-French financial stakes in Russia.'[14]

Nor could Lloyd George complain that he was not extremely well-informed about events in Russia. In early 1918, Captain S. G. Reilly had arrived in Russia as a member of the British Secret Service. He worked with and extended the spy rings across Russia and could boast 'sealed Red Army orders were being read in London before they were being opened in Moscow'. Reilly was also able to draw on large sums of money to finance his operations. Quite clearly, had he and his closest advisors wanted to, Lloyd George could have extinguished the Bolshevik threat as Churchill had wanted to do: 'at birth'. As he played with the fate of millions – indeed the entire world – Lloyd George could see three distinct results in Russia. Firstly, with mass peasant support (possibly armed with British stores in the north), increasing organization and bloodthirsty executions, Lenin was on the verge of winning complete power. This would lead to the destruction of capitalism and democracy inside Russia, as a precursor to extending communism outside Russia. Secondly, it was possible that Russia (as happened in the 1980s) could simply disintegrate. Already in 1917 and 1918 a number of areas had declared their independence. Thirdly, the Allies could actively and openly support the loyal army commanders and divisions spread across Russia, release arms to them and even send Allied troops to challenge and ultimately crush the passionate but ill-equipped Bolshevik units.

Writing in the 1930s, Lloyd George was clear that British aims were simple and always had been. These were to 'prevent military stores at Murmansk, Archangel and Vladivostok falling into enemy hands and to succour the Czech-Slovak troops in the Urals and enable them to reconstitute an anti-German front . . . or to withdraw safely and join the allied forces in the west'.[15]

Unfortunately for Lloyd George, his attempts at sanitizing both the degree of already extant British involvement and intervention, as he waited to see which side would win, or his efforts to minimize his aims were unconvincing to the judgment of history. Writing in 1958, E. M. Halliday in his excellent book *The Ignorant Armies* (which Jack was soon to join) saw the agreement to occupy the northern ports of Russia as the preliminary to bridgeheads for a campaign of action. Any commander fighting a war on foreign soil needs bridgeheads, and normally they have to be gained at tremendous cost in lives. But the Allies had three massive ports already in their hands should they decide to use them. These ports also had all the stores needed to support an entire army if it were landed. Halliday went much further in identifying more penetrating and far-reaching motives:

one of them officially admitted, the other was officially concealed – although it was widely known to exist. The first was a desire to strike down through north Russia from Archangel to the Trans-Siberian railroad, 400 miles to the south and there effect a junction with the Czechs, who in the meantime were to have fought their way westward along that railroad until they reached at least as far as the City of Viatka. This would have posed a new and formidable allied threat to Germany in the East. The second was the hope that this maneuver, or military events subsequent to it, might happily coincide with a complete overthrow of the communist government, thus removing a nasty threat to world security and to civilization.[16]

Around Lloyd George and behind closed doors there was no sympathy for 'popular democracy' or respect for the Bolsheviks. To many this was simply political rubbish, designed to keep Lloyd George, his party and his cronies, in power. Indeed, one of the Cabinet's closest advisors, General Knox, had already suggested at least 500 men be sent to Archangel. In a 1917 conversation his longer term motives were clear:

Knox: 'I am not interested in stabilizing Kerensky and his government. It is incompetent and inefficient and worthless.'

Robbins: 'Well General, you were with Korninlov.'

Knox: (In great anger and shouting) 'The only thing in Russia today is a military dictatorship. These people have got to have the whip hand over them!'

Robbins: 'General, you may get a dictatorship of a very different character.'

Knox: 'You mean this Trotsky-Lenin-Bolshevik stuff – this soap box stuff?'

Robbins: 'Yes, that is what I mean.'

Knox: 'Robbins, you are not a military man. You do not know anything about military affairs. Military men know what to do with this kind of stuff. We stand them up and shoot them!'

So not much ambiguity there about what Knox – and no doubt many, if not the majority including Churchill – felt needed to be done in Russia. With the volunteer and loyal army of General Denikin to the south, the Czech and Slovak armies to the west, and a strong Allied force in the north (at least the size of a division), it was at this moment possible to snuff out the Bolshevik Revolution as soon as the war in the west had been won. The key problem was how to get Lloyd George to support this strategy and how to unite both the Cabinet and British public behind the scheme.

Chapter 8

Intervention and Court Martial, 1919

'No good turn goes unpunished.'
Anon.

Throughout the summer of 1918, Jack was back in Suffolk where he had been posted to train new volunteers coming through the ranks of the 12th Service Battalion of the Norfolk's. After the momentous days of Gallipoli, accolades, the adulation of his countrymen in South Africa and fighting on the Somme, culminating in his Victoria Cross, this was a frustrating time for him. Added to his lack of fulfilment were the two women in his life – each with their own hold over him and each causing him emotional turmoil.

The last four years had given Jack a reason for existence, a cause, a whole social network, rank, authority, respect, excitement, glory and challenge. It had also given him a wife and a home amongst one of the most respected families in London, the heady romance of a love affair and, of course, a child. However, it is a fair bet that he would have preferred to face yet more German bullets, gas and the hell of the Somme, than his new existence and the mundane routine of a training major for recruits. Every day became a struggle and every hour a reminder of his inactivity in stark contrast to his adventures of previous months. On 23 September, as the war was drawing to its close, Jack was asked to take over command of the 12th (S) Battalion from Major M. E. Barclay. At that time, the battalion was in reserve around Ploegsteert, and this is where Jack ended this particular war on 11 November, with the signing of the armistice.

Just as he had been in 1902 and again in 1906, Jack was at war with himself, hard (if not impossible) to live with, fractious, frustrated and explosive. Not surprisingly his relationships with both Nellie and Dora suffered and they hardly saw him. When he was fighting and just on leave he was predictable and jovial, fun and good company. Almost a template of 'Paddy' Blair Mayne of the SAS in the Second World War, when he was away from conflict with nothing to do or feeling unwanted, Jack was unpredictable, and with dramatic changes of mood and temper, was no respecter of people or rank. After the VC celebrations in January 1918, and an article in the *Ladies Field* in April 1918, in which Jack and

Nellie were featured as the epitome of style and marital bliss (with Dora safely hidden in the background in South Devon), by the autumn it was clear that Jack had had enough of his marriage. Within a year Nellie was finally forced into filing for a divorce from a man she adored. His sense of indestructibility was so strong that he could not see the emotional need for anyone alongside him, and his beleaguered state of mind meant that no one could get near to him – not even Dora or Angela. Modern psychology teaches us that men, especially, become driven in order to feel valued, but also to vent a rage that they cannot control in any other way. They become disinterested in what may happen to them and have nothing except anger to drive them along. This, coupled with an Irish temperament, and we have a complex man difficult to love, who did not know how to love either himself or others. By late 1918 he was in a vastly different place emotionally than when he entered it in 1914. He had changed and the world had changed around him. No doubt he sought any relief and opportunity to break the stranglehold of boredom and the cumulative emotional tension that must have affected him.

It was to be events in Russia that changed Jack's world again and began to take centre stage over the Western Front. In April 1918, the tsar and his family had been moved from Siberia, where they had been held captive for the previous six months, to Ekaterinburg in the Ural Mountains. This remote place was to become their cemetery, as on 17 July the tsar and his beautiful family were shot, bayoneted, burned in sulphuric acid and buried. The tsarist regime had ended.

Over the next few months the Bolsheviks murdered tens of thousands more and their Red Army divisions began to take shape and become increasingly formidable. Such a strengthening of the Bolshevik grip over Russia did not go unnoticed. During May 1918, Major General F. C. Poole was appointed as commander of British forces in North Russia. At this time 560 men were dispatched to Archangel and a further 600 to Murmansk, to guard and defend the stores there and prevent them from falling into Bolshevik hands. Leon Trotsky was enraged by these actions, which to him looked like an invasion of Russian territory. Red Army units surrounded the ports as best they could. French and American troops were also earmarked to defend stores in the East – like vultures waiting for the Russian Bolshevik bear to fall and be devoured by Western imperialist ambitions. Any pretence that the British were in fact trying to work with the Bolsheviks was blown apart on 31 July 1918, when Admiral Kemp organized a coup in the city of Archangel, expelling the Bolshevik Soviet in charge of the town. With the tsarist imperial flag flying over the town hall, backed by the small but well-equipped force, a British bridgehead in Russia with enormous stockpiles of ammunition and guns was ready and waiting for either expansion into Russia or withdrawal. There was therefore already an active support from the British army for the White Russians, despite what Lloyd George might have protested.

General Poole had just over 2,000 men to guard an area 6 times the size of England. In November 1918 units of the Royal Sussex and Green Howards regiments also arrived in Murmansk, just in time to experience the severities of a Russian winter. Huge snowdrifts, average temperatures of -30 °C, and constant patrolling deep into Bolshevik territory took their toll. On the surface, these small numbers of reinforcements were being sent to guard the stores intended for the White Army troops now fighting for a dead regime. However, they were increasingly advancing inland, up to 350 miles in fact, probing and pushing at the Red Army, which was not yet strong enough in the area to push back. But the situation was changing and deteriorating on the ground. At the same time on 11 November 1918, the Great War ended on the Western Front and the Bolsheviks launched a massive attack on the Dvina River in North Russia against troops of the Royal Scots. A desperate action followed, including a personal charge by Sergeant Salmons, who: 'Charged into the middle of the enemy ranks, firing a Lewis gun from the hip until he collapsed, his body torn by bullets and bayonet thrusts, in the middle of a heap of dead and dying Bolsheviks.'[1] After the attack had been beaten off, nineteen infantrymen of the Royal Scots had been killed and thirty-four wounded. Similar actions took place throughout the coming months.

The British troops now serving in the Murmansk area had reached sizeable proportions and had been divided into 236 and 237 brigades commanded by brigadiers Turner and Price respectively. In October, a new commander at Archangel had been appointed in Major General Edmund Ironside. The 38-year-old Ironside had been commanding a brigade in France when he was hurriedly promoted and sent to Russia. In the Archangel sector, however, there were fewer regular British units, although those that were there were being ordered deep into hostile territory, largely advancing down the Dvina River. Apart from the conditions and shortages of supplies, the Red Army was also increasingly flexing its muscles with heavy attacks in January in the Shenkursk region 400 miles to the south of Archangel. After the privations of the severe winter, numerous cases of frostbite and some desperate defensive actions, the troops of Ironside's 'Elope' force waited for a decision to be made on their future. Until then, Ironside brought his units back into a defensive perimeter around Archangel. After all the war had, by February 1919, been over for more than three months and so the German threat to the supplies had been removed.

Whilst the future was being pondered, Ironside was developing his own unique leadership style in Archangel. He was not a Lucas and his methods were regimental and by the book and destined to clash with Jack in the future. One incident is worthy of note. In early December, a group of locally recruited men supposedly loyal to the tsarist regime mutinied and barricaded themselves into a barracks block, hoping to start a coup that would see the whole of Archangel rise up and throw the British out. It did not develop as they hoped, and thirteen men were rounded up and court-martialled by Ironside. They were sentenced to death and according to Ironside's later account of this and subsequent events at Archangel, they were reprieved and given life sentences. However, more recent research proves that they were in fact lined up and shot in the back of the neck – and Ironside signed the death warrants. Amongst other things this tells us that Ironside was willing to re-write history. He had his own reasons for doing this and we should not try to judge what these were, but his willingness is a key pointer in this story.

Opinions over Russia were in turmoil and Lloyd George had done nothing to clarify a situation that he hoped to bend to his advantage, whatever the outcome. The option now open to him had crystallized into a withdrawal of all troops immediately, the destruction of stores and the internal affairs of Russia left to Russia. After all, the German threat to the stores had gone, so why remain? If Lloyd George really did want popular democracy to rule regardless of British strategic, economic or political interests, then that was the obvious answer. Significant financial and business interests were at stake and, just as today, they dictated responses.

Alternatively, a limited ring of defences could protect the stores until they could be handed over to White Russian units. This was supporting the old legitimacy of Russia and the forces encouraged by the British and French to fight Bolshevism. Men such as Balfour and Milner, always with an eye on the prize that fate might gift them, favoured this. In other words, continue to watch and wait whilst protecting the stores by force if need be.

There was a third option being aggressively advocated by the new Secretary for War appointed in 1919 – Churchill. Churchill had never disguised his hatred of Bolshevism. In April 1918, he had written about using Czech troops against the Bolsheviks rather than the Germans. For Churchill, Lenin was like 'a plague bacillus' with the 'foul baboonery of Bolshevism' being something to be destroyed not watched whilst it festered and spread. In later life Churchill reflected that the tsarist regime had almost survived: 'With victory in her grasp she fell upon the earth, devoured alive, like Herod of old, by worms'. Little doubt then about what Churchill advocated. In December 1918 he demanded that, 'the allies intervene thoroughly with large forces, abundantly supplied with mechanical devices'. He was not alone, but he did not have the support of the prime minister. However, this was hardly necessary for someone like Churchill. Early on in his new role he sent out a 'Secret and Urgent' request for information from field commanders, enquiring how they felt their men would react if they were ordered to fight in Russia against the Bolsheviks. Their response left no room for doubt: 'they would parade for service overseas with the exception of Russia'.[2] In fact, the situation was deteriorating as many units began to grumble as they waited to be allowed to return home. There were even mutinous signs from British regiments and the fear that Bolshevism was spreading like a virus, with agitators already at work in Britain, was a very real one. Therefore, if using well-equipped and experienced troops was the best way of ensuring Bolshevism and therefore communism was crushed, Churchill would have to find them without ordering the army to do it directly.

In his study of Churchill, Sir Robert Rhodes James identifies some of his key characteristics that were evident back in 1914 and 1915: a single-minded determination to get a plan through despite the odds, once his mind was made up – just like Jack. Churchill balanced an uncertain Cabinet and an equally uncertain prime minister with consummate ease. A blustering warship on the surface, a silent torpedo under it. His opening salvoes in December 1918 of 'thorough intervention' and 'large forces' had been transformed into 'messages of defiance' and 'material support' by February 1919. He was working towards the same end but by different means. He was well aware that Lloyd George, indeed no party, was now able to operate independently of the reaction of the new British Labour movement. He may not have liked it but he could deal with it. Churchill's tactical appreciation of the political battlefield was impressive, and as he played the moral servant of government on the one hand, he exploited the weaknesses he was creating on the other. Churchill could see that the cabinet was racked by indecision on what action to take, but equally desperate for the Communist revolution to fail: 'The downfall of Bolshevism was universally desired in the British Cabinet. Ministers hoped that this could be achieved with British material assistance but without the need to intervene militarily.'

Lloyd George was also away in France as he worked on the treaty being discussed at Versailles that would punish Germans and ensure that this had been the war to end all wars. Such absence coupled with indecision gave Churchill the opening he needed. 'In these conditions of drift and irresolution, the Prime Minister frequently absent and biding his time, there was a good opportunity for a single-minded man to carry his views considerably further than would have been the case in more normal conditions.'[3]

As historian Sir Martin Gilbert has pointed out, Churchill may have had strong views about what needed to be done in Russia, but he had not been in a position to do much about it until 10 January 1919, when he was appointed Minister of War in Lloyd George's newly elected government. The newspapers were already closely monitoring events, and only the week before Churchill took up his new role the *Daily Express* commented:

> We are sorry for the Russians, but they must fight it out amongst themselves. Great Britain is already the policeman of half the world. It will not and cannot be the policeman of all Europe. We want to return to industry and to restore the ravages of war. We want to see our sons home again. In fact we want peace. The frozen plains of Eastern Europe are not worth the bones of a single British Grenadier.[4]

Completely unphased, during February and March 1919, Churchill worked tirelessly to achieve two objectives. On the one hand, he wanted to convince his colleagues and the prime minister that Britain must play a more active role in defeating Bolshevism, without being seen to interfere in the internal affairs of Russia. On the other, he had to find a way of increasing the military power of the British army in North Russia – without ordering the army to do it. His solution was to call for volunteers to go to Russia in a Russian Relief Force to bring back the men already out there – and then order these new forces into the heartland of Russia and to Moscow itself. A bold, daring and dangerous plan, but full of hope and dash which appealed to both those around him in power, but also to the men who volunteered their goodwill and patriotism for a cause presented so brilliantly. As such, Jack requested a command and was given one. In April 1919, he was appointed as commanding officer of 2nd Battalion The Hampshire Regiment (2/Hampshires) – a regular battalion too, but one being expanded with volunteers for service in Russia. It was just what he needed as two divorces began to unfold around him.

Two Divorces

For two years, Jack had led a nomadic existence and could be found between his aunt's home in Reigate (where many a meeting of political ambitions was held), the Rubens Hotel with Dora, and then any number of other hotels and addresses, including a flat in Windsor. By the spring of 1919 Dora was still resident in the West Country, but working in London as she had enlisted in the Women's Royal Naval Service the previous 14 November. Listed as a driver, we can assume she wanted to do more in support of the war effort, whilst still trying to discover what Jack's real intentions were. Interestingly, she was also now listed as living at the Royal Court Hotel and no longer the Rubens. If Dora had any doubts that Jack would settle with her permanently, these evaporated in April 1919 when he was able to announce he was back in regular service and would be going overseas again. How the news affected Dora we shall never know, but there is a document that lists her immediate discharge from the WRNS on the grounds of 'Urgency & Consideration', dated 17 April. It may be that she now left London permanently, knowing Jack was not going to be there. Before Jack left, however, there were the matters of two divorces – both of which were of his making.

Left with probably little option, Nellie at last heeded the advice of her brother and family: the famous VC hero of only a year before was now being cited as a difficult, if not impossible, man to live with, for whom 'the old fascinations' had returned within months of marriage. But she still loved him, amid the turmoil of knowing of the affair with Dora and her child with Jack. We can be reasonably sure that for Jack, however, the matter was a pretty open and shut case. Jack had never easily adjusted to married life. He was a free spirit and quite a selfish one, who now had other things on his mind as command of the 2/Hampshires called him away. Dora possibly still hoped that once he had got Russia out of his system and was divorced from Nellie, they could at last be together as a family. It seems unlikely that it was a coincidence, but Nellie began her divorce from Jack in April 1919 and in the following month – May – Dora began hers from her estranged husband James. Could it be that Jack and Dora had indeed planned to be together at last?

The divorce case in London for Nellie was a messy affair. Though undefended (as Jack was not there), the media were of course interested in the famous VC's private life, and the story was carried in just about every national and regional newspaper. The case was not helped by the fact that Jack had ignored an order for 'restitution of conjugal rights' which had been granted for Nellie some time before, in response to the prolonged period that he had lived apart from Nellie since 1916. In addition, there were some salacious headlines such as: 'Col. Sherwood-Kelly's Visit to the Seaside'. The clerk from the Sackville Hotel in Bexhill-on-Sea produced the visitors' book of the hotel, which contained the entry: 'Colonel and Mrs Sherwood-Kelly, Hotel Rubens, London – British.' Nellie confirmed that she had never been to Bexhill or that hotel and that she recognized the handwriting of her husband. Further, a maid from the hotel said that when she recognized Colonel Sherwood Kelly at the lawyers' offices, as the gentleman who had stayed at the hotel with a lady, he laughed out loud and said to her, 'You have had a jolly fine joy-ride!' – to which the court erupted with laughter. The judge granted the divorce petition and Jack, who was on board his ship bound for North Russia, was ordered to pay costs.

Dora, on the other hand, was able to rely on the loving support of James – her husband of six years and with whom she had never lived – and his determination that the matter would be handled quietly and sensitively, if at all possible. Their court case also reached the newspapers, but on a much smaller scale. The headlines of the *Glasgow Herald* read: 'Strange Story of Married Life – Lived Together Once in Five Years – Scottish Army Officer's Action'. The case was heard in Edinburgh on 31 May 1919, and Dora was variously named as Cameron, Aitken or Ogilvy and her address was given as the Royal Court Hotel, London (and not the Rubens). The grounds were infidelity. James explained that they had hardly lived together – indeed only for twelve days when he was on leave in 1916. He further explained that they then met in March 1918, when Dora told him about her affair and that she confessed that she had a child and showed him the birth certificate. The petition for divorce was granted in Dora's absence. As a postscript, the reporter for one newspaper made the passing comment that the plight of unhappy relations between army men and their wives was continuing. Worthy of further research, it is an overlooked aspect of war and especially the Great War. Massive strains were placed on emotional relationships and without doubt contributed to many break-ups, stressful attachments and worse. Today of course we are increasingly familiar with PTSD and the psychological impact of battle on men's minds. In the period 1914–18 this was unheard of, and men were still expected to absorb the dramatic and shocking scenes of war without any after-effects. Of course, there were substantial effects and no support, so unsurprisingly these emotional and psychological collapses were also felt by those closest to them.

Four days after the hearing, James wrote to Dora on 3 June 1919:

Euston Hotel, London

My Dear Dora,
You are now FREE. The case came off in Edinburgh on Saturday 31st and was fairly short and went well. My counsel wrote to all the leading Scotch papers and asked them to either ignore the case or if they had to notice it to leave out all the facts and reasons. I enclose you a cutting from the 'Glasgow Herald'. I think you will agree with me that it does not give any encouragement to those people who live by gossip and scandal. The case had to be given against you as you didn't defend – and so far as the notices in the newspapers go it might have been 'because you refused to live in Scotland' or any of the many reasons one can get a divorce in Scotch law so long as one waits four years.

<u>You know</u> I didn't want to do this but it only adds to my regrets over the whole of the last four years. I hope you will permit me to write to you occasionally and let me know if you do – whether you have changed your name so I do not commit any "faux pas" by addressing you wrong. I am on my way to pick up this sloop and will then go to Ireland in her. You will be surprised to hear that I have got to hate Argyllish and the people therein and have joined an Expedition which a fellow is starting from Vancouver to prospect in The South Sea Islands. I believe the natives there tie up wonderful pearls with strings and give away for a 2/6d pocket knife. Excuse my dirty thumb marks on the paper but my hands are rather 'piggy' as I have just come off the train. Forgive me for having 'crashed' the earlier part of your life – if I had only been less young and weak it would never have happened – it took me a few years to learn that home influence can sometimes ruin one's life. Goodbye baby – we shall meet again – but where or when.
Yours ever
Jim

Interpretation of what sort of man James Cameron was is left to the reader. Dora was to receive another letter, this time from Jack, and the contrast between the two men could not be more stark. Hidden away amongst the mass of military papers is the following written to Dora, three months later, when Jack was in North Russia:

2nd Hampshire Regt.
26th July, 1919

Dear Old Girl,
Your letter of the 9th inst received last evening – You could not have been in love with me when it was written – one of your hate moods – Eh! Any way I am training myself to realise that you are never likely to wish to marry me – Wise Girl – Yes I received your other two letters – I envy you your freedom – anyway I hope soon to join those ranks – I am glad you like the plates etc. I sent you – I have eight films in all – I long to see my Babe, news of her acts as a tonic on me –
– Jonnie

OAS Mrs Cameron
Dunkerry Lodge
Minehead
Somerset

Give my Babe a huge hug and kiss from me[5]

So here it was, evidence that Dora had left James but was not rushing into the arms of Jack either. Possibly wary and hurt from many desertions by Jack in the past, Jack is aware that Dora is angry with him – one of her 'hate moods' – and there is a strong possibility she will not marry him. Dora had seen her young and quite innocent world turned upside down since 1916, and the past three years must have felt like a blur of experiences and emotions. Just when Jack was getting divorced and could have moved to be with her and settle down to family life, cutting the grass and playing in the nursery, he announced he was leaving for Russia. Perhaps she knew all along that he could never settle, and once Angela had been born, her mother's instincts to protect herself and her child took over. She chose to remain free for now. Interestingly, Jack spells 'baby' phonetically as 'babe' – this is not the first piece of evidence that Jack's levels of literacy were perhaps minimal and is an important pointer for the future of this story.

At the age of 39 Jack was still a young man, but physically he had treated his body severely. The seven wounds on his frame hurt every day, as did his chest from the effects of both gas in 1915 and the bullet wound of 1916. But he was perhaps at his prime of self-confidence – not to say arrogance and determination to fight. As an Ulsterman, we can safely appreciate that he was always open to the suggestion of a fight. If there was not one going on that he could join, then he would create one. If we are in any doubt about his bloody-mindedness towards Nellie, one only needs to remember that in the very same month that Nellie was going through the public agony of a divorce from a man whom she had idolized, the same man was already volunteering and preparing to travel to Russia as part of Churchill's 'Volunteer Relief Force' the very next month. No quiet contemplation of the hurt he had caused or any attempt, it seems, to support and make amends to either Nellie or Dora. Instead, he was packing his bags, cleaning his uniform and marching to a station to pick up where he had left off a year before.

The Invasion of Russia – Through the Side Door
Having been persuaded that formal and open action was impossible and that the army would not follow, Churchill pressed on with his reserve plan. He has therefore been correctly judged by historians as the architect of intervention in Russia at this time. In possibly the most recent detailed book to be published on Churchill's role in this whole episode in 2006, Clifford Kinvig states unequivocally that: 'Despite tremendous losses in World War One, a considerable force landed in Russia in 1918/1919 under the auspices of Winston Churchill. The aim was to influence the military and political outcome of the Russian Revolution'.[6]

Lloyd George knew full well that Churchill wanted a full-scale war against the Bolsheviks, but could not have his way. Lloyd George was also well aware of Churchill's already highly suspect reputation as a man who would rashly support potentially disastrous military enterprises – as both Antwerp and Gallipoli had shown (and Norway in 1940 would demonstrate again). The debate dogged Cabinet discussions until 4 March 1919, when at last the decision was taken to evacuate all British troops from North Russia by June. For Churchill, this was a disaster. Not at all used to not having his own way and convinced that this decision was wrong, Churchill swung into action with the idea of sending out a relief force even larger than the one that was already out there, to bring it back! Whilst they were there of course, it might be possible to either provoke a war or even get as far as Moscow and overthrow the Bolsheviks. As Minister of War he was in the key position to force the pace and issue orders to the commanders that he had appointed. Churchill was playing a dangerous game, but as Oscar Wilde once so aptly put it, when he could have been referring to Churchill: 'In matters of grave importance, style not sincerity, is the vital thing'.[7]

Thus, a relief force of volunteers was called for with the aim of supporting the White Russian Army (or what was left of it) and bringing back the men from North Russia who had been out there alone for nearly a year. The tone was set for 'relief' and 'rescue', but it was 'intervention' by any other name. Churchill was no fool – but neither were those who monitored his political career. Responding to the decision to evacuate all troops from Russia, the *Daily Express* again warned: 'Even with this undertaking given by the government to do the sensible thing, we must watch Mr Churchill carefully. There is too much of the warlord about him'.

By January 1919 the general demobilization of the British army was well under way, and this applied to the battle-hardened and weary 29th Division like any other. The KOSB and 2/Hampshires had met in a final football match just prior to arriving back in barracks in Aldershot, and then watching after a few weeks the regiments and battalions break up forever. The War Office had decided to keep a small cadre of men from each regiment as training troops, as new recruits joined up. These were the most experienced and battle- trained men from each battalion. The 2/Hampshires soon received news of the situation in Russia. It was presented to the men as a new enterprise, driven by Churchill's persuasive energy, to support the weak and overstretched British units trying to both guard the munitions and help the rightful government against the evil revolutionaries. Who would not be stirred by such propaganda, as demonstrated by the regimental diary of the Hampshire's: 'Operations had been continued to assist those "White" Russians who were friendly to the Allies, but the troops originally sent out were mostly units of "low category" men including many due for demobilization, and early in 1919 it was decided to relieve them with Regulars'.

They of course had no idea of the reality of the situation they were travelling to. Ironside was attempting to hold lines that were over-extended. He was reliant on his own troops whose morale was dropping by the day, many of whom were sympathetic to the cause of the working Russian Bolshevik and whose fighting quality was very variable. It was of course a mess – civil wars always are – and no one was ever certain who was on what side and who could be relied upon. He was also using an aggregation of other nationalities on whom they also could not rely. At the same time, it was not clear whether Ironside was fighting to protect the stores or to help the White Russians in their war – the consequences were potentially disastrous as he wavered between the two, not knowing whether he was supposed to be actively fighting the Bolsheviks alongside the White Russian units, or simply holding the line until relieved and withdrawn. In fact, Ironside had done a superb job in establishing a rapport with local leaders in a complex political situation, with fear of collapse and confusion daily infecting every action. Equally he had put a command together that was effective. What he did not have were clear orders, as Churchill awaited events in Britain to see if circumstances could be changed to suit his purpose. The men in Russia, therefore, were just pawns in another of his politico/strategic games. The local Russians were by now, of course, dependent on the British and had put their faith in them for both protection and support. Churchill's speech in the House of Commons on 3 March reached Ironside on 8 March, and although it gave at least some clarity to Ironside that he was there for a good reason, the worlds of the soldier and the politician were still poles apart. In a master stroke of wordsmith genius, Churchill was now seeking to build support for those who had put their trust in Britain – a superbly deft tactic to play on the conscience of the British press:

> Further, we have incurred heavy commitments towards the people of those districts who have espoused our cause, and to the Russian forces fighting with us. It has been the custom of this country to pay particular attention to matters of this kind and always to endeavour, to the best of our ability, to do our duty by those who have put their trust in us and who have run into danger in consequence of action which we have advised them to take.[8]

Churchill provided a cause for supportive forces to rally around. There were Czechs, Poles, Fins and even Americans ready to fight against the Bolsheviks. As well as inspiring anti-Bolshevik forces, Churchill could claim that the relief force would hold faith with their Russian allies. This was, of course, contrary to what the Cabinet had stated it would do or had agreed the relief force was for.

On 25 April, Ironside received a package from Churchill. Interestingly, in his memoirs, Ironside admits that the package contained no orders – even though at the Cabinet meeting on 4 March an explicit decision had been made to withdraw. Ironside, perhaps trying to validate his part in history, stated that, 'Though I was still left without instructions, I had now a better idea of what was going on in Russia and could see what was in the minds of The General Staff'.[9] Given that the package had come from Churchill and that it was over six weeks since a decision had been made to withdraw, the question remains why there were no explicit orders on preparing to withdraw? Why was the commander in the field left to assume what he was to do? Had Churchill not issued any orders as he was hoping that there was still some way for the existing troops and the relief force about to arrive to be able to crush the Bolshevik Revolution? It was all about timing. If Churchill could keep the existing army in the field and reinforce it with 8,000 fresh and experienced troops, whilst the White Russians prepared for their spring offensive, then there was still a chance. If they withdrew then there was not – but this could not be committed to paper. Even more deftly, as only the surest of politicians would know how to do, responsibility for the increasingly offensive operations against the Bolsheviks would shift from Churchill and onto Ironside.

Thus, for men for whom the army was their life and fighting their reason to exist, possibly with no family to return to, this was a rescue operation to bring back British troops under threat – it was not an invasion. There were also those in the army who hated what communism represented: the opposite of the 'popular democracy' that Lloyd George professed to be unfolding in Russia. By March, Churchill had got his way. He had prepared the ground well and kept open the objectives of action – only one of which was to bring back the men stranded in Russia. Indeed, deliberate ambiguity was a key ploy and Churchill had no problem in getting his volunteers. The public call for volunteers took place on 8 April and within hours over sixty men had signed up. Posters went up for the RRF and the newspapers carried patriotic reports of scenes in recruiting offices, where men only just recently released from duty queued up in lines, as the *Daily Mail* reported: 'The fighting spirit of the old army is aflame. Yesterday hundreds of veterans of The Great War were crowding Great Scotland Yard, Whitehall [where Jack turned up that very day], to join the North Russian Relief Force.'

On the whole, it was only senior men and officers who turned up – mostly career soldiers with a long service history, ideal men for such a force. Jack was, of course, one of the first, having followed developments in the newspapers and in conversations with his pals in the bar at the Authors' Club, where he spent most evenings. The men, of course, were being lied to. They had no idea, in Kinvig's words, that they were actually being sent out to push the political and military situation into a favourable position for Churchill. Former officers who were now unemployed could now be found serving as corporals. One naval officer noted, when part of the relief force arrived, 'They are all volunteers, and any quantity of ex-officers in the ranks, colonels etc galore; fellows wearing DSOs and MCs in private's uniform. I have never seen a finer crowd of men anywhere.'[10]

But we should not be fooled. Many of these men were not volunteers at all. New evidence has been uncovered to show that, in defiance of government policy, Churchill made sure men were ordered to North Russia. Officers like Jack, who had no desire to finish fighting wars or return home, may well have volunteered. Equally, some men whose service had run out or who had been demobilized and also did not wish to return home (due, for example, to their wives having left them for other men), also volunteered. But the average soldier just wanted to go home. He had survived the war and done his bit and that was enough. But it was not to be.

In his bundles of letters, photographs and diaries left to his family, Private Stanley Berrett of the Wiltshire Regiment had quite a lot to say about the whole saga of the Russian campaign, including about Lieutenant Colonel Jack Kelly VC, DSO, CMG, who was to be his new commanding officer. Stanley Berrett was perhaps typical of the men whose lives were affected by Churchill's next gamble. Like all gamblers, Churchill found it very hard, if not impossible, to kick his habit – that of interfering in military matters, treating them as if they were simply political or business deals to be done, regardless of what happened to the men in between. Stanley was a regular soldier. He had joined the army in February 1915 and for seven years he served with the Wiltshire Regiment and the Royal Engineers as a trained signaller. He fought and survived Ypres and Arras and was wounded on the Somme in 1916. He spent a month in hospital before being posted back to France, where he also survived the German spring offensive which ended the war in November 1918. Stanley's brother Tom also served with the Wiltshire Regiment but was killed on 1 September 1917, about 8km from where Stanley was, although neither knew the other's whereabouts. Stanley and his family had more than done their service and he deserved to go home. His was one of tens of thousands of similar stories that were irrelevant to those in power, grinding out political careers regardless of the cost to others.

Stanley kept a diary and had a strong memory, and so it was that before his death he wrote down his experiences. It was very unusual and rare for a private soldier to do this, and an invaluable addition to our understanding of these events and how they impacted on the lives of ordinary soldiers. Unlike the generals, Stanley had no time, need or interest to doctor his memoirs and accounts – what he saw was how it was.

It is Stanley's grandson, Richard Berrett, who commented in 2010: 'My grandfather was always angry, well into his 80s, about two things: Firstly he had NOT volunteered to go to Russia and neither had his pals. Secondly how his Colonel was treated.' In his diary Stanley states:

> In 1918 when the armistice was about we had to parade and were asked 'how long have you to do?' As I had joined in 1915 I had four to do so I was one of the bunch for Russia. They said we were volunteers but that was a load of squit. Anyway, we went to England for severe training and away to Archangel on the SS Stephen.

Evidence of the fact that men had been ordered to go, instead of the great propaganda exercise that this was some sort of military crusade, is hard to find. But Stanley tells us that he was one of the 8,000 men who had been 'recruited' – double the size Churchill had expected and a mix of men who had been ordered to go and others who had answered the call for volunteers. The anger that Stanley felt all his life about having been called a volunteer, was no doubt shared by the other 200 or so men from his regiment who were also unable to return home, but instead ordered to North Russia.

Two brigades were formed under two explosive and relatively young brigadiers – G. W. St George Grogan and L. W. de Vere Sadleir-Jackson. What was to become the 2/Hampshires was in fact an amalgam of men from many regular regiments. Although the headquarters company was made up of Hampshire's and there were officers from the regiment spread throughout, there were also volunteers from the Somerset Light Infantry, the Dorset Regiment and Wiltshire's, and their commanding officer was to be none other than Jack. This was to be Jack's fifth and final regimental link – he had come a long way on his five-year journey through the ranks of the KEH, the Norfolk's, the KOSB, the RIF and now the Hampshire's.

The battalion was attached to Grogan's Brigade. In April, officers and men were ordered to assemble at Crowborough Barracks, to the south of Tunbridge Wells in East Sussex. This was where Stanley and his mates would have arrived by train and first met their new CO – the man being called 'The bravest man in the British army'. The newly formed battalion had around two weeks to fit itself out, drill and get to know the commanding officer. The barracks, according to Stanley, were not a happy place. Canadian troops had been based there previously and were so frustrated about waiting for their demobilization that they vandalized the camp and discipline broke down. According to Stanley's recollections, maybe thirty or so different regiments were represented, so welding the whole into a fighting unit was the challenge for Jack and his new officers. This was exactly what he needed to take his mind off Nellie and the divorce case (running at exactly the same time in London), and Dora's, which was also imminent.

The battalion was formed into four companies – W (Hampshire), X (Somerset), Y (Dorset) and Z (Wiltshire). Alongside supporting units of a Light Trench Mortar Battery, a unit from the Machine Gun Corps and Army Service Corps and some Ox and Bucks Light Infantry, the whole was named 238 Special Brigade for the North Russian Relief Force or NRRF. Churchill was especially keen to stress that these were units of relief – to bring home men and materiel now at risk from falling into the hands of the Bolsheviks. Jack reported to Brigadier General Grogan DSO, CMG, VC of the Worcestershire Regiment.

The newspapers played the game, as they were drip-fed with lies by the government. *The Times* was clear that the NRRF was composed entirely of volunteers. Like a modern-day crusade, these were men to be painted as heroes, making further sacrifices for the nation, risking all in the cause and so on. In other words, the propaganda of four years of war was continuing – what we could call the new phenomenon of 'fake news' today, is in fact an age-old method of public control. Research and books written on the subject up to the 1990s maintained the lie that Ironside published in his memoirs in 1953. In his account *Archangel 1918–1919* (and as Stanley's grandson pointed out to me), Ironside maintained that none of Grogan's Brigade 'had any service in the war as they had been too young to go out to France'. He went on to further lie that 'there had been a rush to get posted when once their destination was given out'. All of this now flies in the face of the evidence. Even contemporary photographs of the men involved show a remarkable number with overseas service stripes and wound stripes, not to mention medal ribbons – not bad for men who, according to Ironside, had been too young to fight. Even parliamentary debates in 1919 had covered instances of soldiers in uniform being arrested for refusing to embark at ports such as Southampton, when they were finally told they were headed for North Russia. Finally unearthing primary evidence, such as the diaries of men like Stanley, only confirms just how widespread the dissatisfaction was amongst the men. This was to become even worse once they realized that they were not in fact even a relief force – but an invasion force. There were growing claims that this was a step too far, interfering in the affairs of another nation, capitalist right-wing conservatism attempting to pervert the working man – but this was all rather 'back page' . . . unless a spark could be found to ignite national indignation.

On 9 May, 238 Special Brigade went on parade for an inspection by General Sir Henry Rawlinson. Having done their field training on the dry scrub and yellow heather of Crowborough Common (presumably thought to be close to the landscape of the North Russian steppe), the battalion was issued with the white 'Polar Star' cloth badge of the NRRF, which they sewed onto their upper arm. Moving in haste to Tilbury Docks by rail on 13 May, another Churchill escapade was about to begin, based more on his impetuosity than reality and with the customary lack of planning, direction, aim and support. Had the men been more aware of Antwerp and Gallipoli they might have realized this. Their ship, the SS *Stephen*, left on the evening of the 15th, rounded the North Cape on the 19th and, after a short stop at Murmansk, arrived at Archangel on 21 May. A week later, on the 27th, Captain Alan Lendrum MC and Bar landed and his association with his old commanding officer from Cambrai days was rekindled. Lendrum had not only regained his rank but also two Military Cross decorations. He too had volunteered for the NRRF.

The mood on board was by all accounts one of excitement, noise and incident as the men who had come together felt rather special – they were after all on a new adventure, despite the fact many did not want to be there. On board with his battalion there was an opportunity for Jack to meet old acquaintances and make new ones too. One remarkable photograph survives showing Jack on board the troop ship together with five fellow VC winners:

> Lieutenant Colonel D. G. Johnson VC, DSO, MC of the South Wales Borderers.
> The Brigade Commander Brigadier General G. W. St George Grogan VC, CMG, DSO and Bar from the Worcestershire Regiment.
> Captain A. C. T. White VC, MC from the Yorkshire Regiment.
> Lieutenant M. Moore VC from the Hampshire Regiment.
> Lieutenant A. M. Toye VC, MC from the Middlesex Regiment.

These men, who had already offered everything, including their lives, in the past four years, were now giving even more on this operation. There is a sense of missionary zeal in this particular group photograph, and it is almost certain that they felt in the vanguard of something far greater that was unfolding. After all, there was scarcely a need for six winners of the Victoria Cross to travel to Russia with a further 8,000 men to help the withdrawal of fewer than 3,000 men. Maybe they were not as ignorant as some historians would like to see them. Churchill must have been delighted when he saw the quality of men going to carry out his plan. Whilst Lloyd George was clear that a military solution was not being employed, Churchill was doing exactly that. News was reaching London every day of the excesses of the Red Terror, with assassinations, murders and executions commonplace. Churchill once told his constituents at Dundee: 'Civilization is being completely extinguished over gigantic areas, while Bolsheviks hop and caper like troops of ferocious baboons amid the ruins of cities and the corpses of their victims'. Although one day he would sit alongside Stalin, he was never to change his views on the Bolsheviks.

On arrival, the SS *Stephen* waited for some ice to clear before disembarking the troops. Unlike the Baltic Sea, North Russia was just coming into a hot, sticky, insect-ridden spring. Some days offered frost-covered ground, whilst others sticky mud, as the countryside started to wake up after winter. The port was ablaze with activity and colour as the ships steamed in, and there was great cheering and anticipation. They arrived like victors awaiting their laurels, even though the wider conflict in Russia was not that far away and getting closer every day. As soon as they were down the gangplanks, commanders were quickly briefed on the situation, warned of the unreliability of supposedly loyal Russian troops and the known dispositions of the local Red Army Bolshevik forces surrounding them. Ironside, in his recollections of the events, reinforced his contention that: 'the men and officers were all volunteers who had been specially chosen for their physical fitness and experience of fighting . . .' – that was certainly true of the commanding officer of the 2/Hampshires. Early on, Ironside had a taste of exactly what had arrived when he inspected the Hampshire's:

> As I was talking to The Hampshires telling them what they were likely to meet and how important to destroy Bolshevism (!), I heard a sort of running commentary coming from behind me. 'Good for you! That's the stuff to give them!' It came from the C.O. of the battalion. I signalled to him to stop with my hand. I thought that I was unconventional to stand anything, but this was more than I could tolerate. He was a man who had fought all through the late war with great distinction, rising from Lieutenant to Lieut. Colonel. He was not a regular officer but he had been specially chosen for his fighting experience. It was difficult to know how to deal with the incident. It takes all kinds to make a fighting army, and fighting officers had been hard to find with us. I said no more but told Grogan of the incident, telling him to watch this CO carefully. I don't think he was the man to command a battalion of young regular soldiers.[11]

What are we to make of this? On one level, it was just Jack's enthusiasm for the coming fight that exuded from him. He was merely supporting and endorsing

Ironside's words openly, as he addressed the troops. To another commander it would have meant nothing more than the exuberance of exactly the sort of fighting man he needed. But to Ironside it was effrontery to speak when he was speaking. It is interesting that Ironside even mentions this minor episode – until one realizes the clashes between them that were to follow. Interesting too that Ironside felt Jack unfit to command a roughly thrown together battalion of men, when he had already successfully commanded experienced front-line battalions in both Gallipoli and on the Somme. Both these facts are skilfully omitted from his description of Jack, as is the fact that Jack was a holder of the Victoria Cross. Clearly Ironside felt challenged by this larger than life heroic but colonial figure, confident and brusque, heady with the command of another battalion and another war to be fought. If Ironside was not up to the task of working with him, then he would have to work without him – his warning to Grogan being a signal that any occasion to remove Jack from command should be used. Within hours, then, Jack was a marked man as far as Ironside was concerned. His men, on the other hand, seemed to relish Jack's leadership style – Stanley recalling him as 'a good CO'. Anyone with even a semblance of a military background will recognize that such praise, though brief, does not come easily from a soldier under command.

Soon Jack and the Hampshire's were loaded onto barges ready to be sent up the wide and flat River Dwina to Berezniki. Jack quickly started to make some unconventional decisions in the face of unconventional battle conditions. The risk of coming under fire as they slowly took the battalion up these open and undefended rivers was very real. So, Jack ordered the Hampshire's to put all their Lewis and mounted machine guns on each side of the flat-bottomed barges. Pointed outwards, these barges thus became modern day men-of-war, able to machine-gun out-of-existence anyone opening fire on them. Quite remarkably, the Regimental Museum of the Hampshire Regiment contains a photograph album of pictures of what are referred to as 'Kelly's Mystery Ships'. In another Jack can be seen standing tall, and a little thinner already, amongst his men in the heat, flies and mosquitoes of a North Russian mud flat. The men were packed into the boats like sardines in a can and accompanied in a flotilla by seaplanes, Royal Navy gunboats and RAF aircraft. All in all, a small invasion force. Unorthodox and not in the army manual, but undoubtedly effective. Jack was already aware that his men were outnumbered, outgunned and could easily be outflanked as they pressed on into the interior of Russia, not sure if they were still protecting the stores, bringing back the men already out there or being asked to destroy Bolshevism on the quiet.

The strategic excuse for this 200-mile inland incursion was to join up with another brigade of British 'volunteers' led by Brigadier Sadlier-Jackson, and then to attack Kotlas, thus protecting Archangel from attack as the stores and men were withdrawn. By 5 June, Jack was taking his men off the barges and taking over command of an area from the 339th United States Infantry, as they were pulling out. The American citizens were completely unaware that their men were even out there, however, this theatre of war was now becoming a solely British affair. By the 12 June Jack was back doing what he knew best. Although he had plenty of junior officers who should have been doing the patrolling of the area to work out what lay in front and to the side of them (there was after all no front line as in France), Jack set the tone himself and led patrols deep into the woods around them. He was doing what his men already knew, showing he feared nothing and couldn't wait to get to grips with fighting this new enemy. On 12 June, the Hampshire's diary records: 'The C.O. took out No. One platoon of W Company and ran into a Bolo patrol in a neutral village. Two of the enemy were killed and one wounded. The C.O. killed one man in personal conflict.'[12]

Not content with killing his first Bolshevik, Jack then took out another patrol on the 16 June: 'The C.O. took out 9 platoon on an all-day reconnaissance of the route to Troitskoye. Marched 35 miles in 17 hours.' This was a huge patrol and would have exhausted even the fittest troops. Jack was trying to obtain all the information he could of the surrounding geography, especially the area around Troitskoye, towards which the battalion would be moving if ordered further forward. Indeed, his aggressive soldiering had already been praised with Grogan writing to Jack: 'The GOC wishes personally to thank you on the very gallant way you led the patrol on June 13th, 1919 which resulted in you killing three of the enemy at great personal risk to yourself. The information obtained by you was very valuable and the result of your encounter cannot but increase the morale of our men.'

What was dawning on Jack, however, was the vastness of the country and the minuscule size of the British forces now deep inside Russian territory. They were not large enough to help the White Russians in any meaningful way, to win the war against a Bolshevik enemy that had really already won their revolution. Equally they were not numerous enough to take on the Bolsheviks – poorly equipped and unreliable as they were. Simply put, 8,000 men was not enough to enter and conquer Moscow for Churchill. Thus, whilst Ironside still made plans for aggressive local actions and continued to plan actions in support of the local White Russian forces (all completely at odds with the avowed policy of Lloyd George and the government), Jack could see that there was no plan either to withdraw or invade. The whole thing seemed pointless. Men were being worked hard, bitten to death by mosquitos, and being sacrificed in the hope that the White Russians would somehow win victory and British forces would be there to support them – and of course protect and exploit the raw materials so heavily invested in by British businesses. There were numerous stories of the treachery of so-called friendly or White Russian forces, who gladly took the uniforms and weapons offered by the British and then at night simply ran over to the Bolshevik lines. There was news of British officers being murdered by their troops. Indeed, on the

20 June, the very day Jack was ordered to attack, a serious mutiny occurred at Onega, a small town on the White Sea coast and 100 miles back towards Archangel. Two White Russian battalions killed their officers and deserted with their weapons. Jack felt the whole area was a mess, populated by savage and untrustworthy people, and his men were being wasted. Against this background he was ordered to prepare an attack on Troitskoye.

Partly to boost flagging Russian morale and partly attempting to link up with Russian forces further to the east, Ironside endorsed a plan for the 19/20 June whereby the so-called 3rd Russian Rifles – British trained and officered White Russian troops – would launch an attack on the villages of Topsa and Troitskoye, whilst Jack took two companies of the Hampshire's on a 9-mile trek through the stifling heat, horse flies, swamp and forests to appear behind the Bolshevik forces at the same time. One of the officers serving with the 3rd Russian Rifles was Lendrum, formally of 1/RIF. He told Jack that the whole force was unreliable and that it was likely he would be led forward and then deserted, specifically with the purpose of leaving his battalion stranded and then annihilated.

In his preparations for the attack, Jack dragged his fit and experienced battalion on the march between 12.30am and 4.00am along tracks, through streams and across marshes which he knew well (he had after all already walked 35 miles around it recently, further straining his gas-damaged lungs). The regimental diary of the Hampshire's confirms that the route up to Troitskoye was awful and that the battalion had to cross two large marshes with swarms of mosquitos, first unpacking their sixty mules and then manhandling their heavy equipment, before going back to get the mules. At any moment, they could have been ambushed and surrounded.

Arriving at their FUP, the battalion started to come under fire from the Bolsheviks at 4.45am. They had learnt that Troitskoye, far from being held by a small force of Bolsheviks, had in fact been reinforced in order to try to trap the British force, which they also knew was coming towards them. The fire coming at the battalion was greater than one would have expected from a small unit, so they were already exposed with a very difficult route out if they became surrounded, and with absolutely no support behind them. Jack also found and complained later that communication lines with the brigade did not work. Jack ordered Y company to emerge from the woods at 4.45am, under cover of mortars and the machine guns that they had lugged up the tracks and through the marshes. After a few hours exchanging fire, Jack could see nothing of the expected White Russian advance nearby, and had sustained fifteen casualties (including the young Captain D. T. Gorman MC – buried at Archangel – who had been wounded five times serving in France, and Sergeant Batten, who had seventeen years' regular service and was now killed 118 miles inland from Archangel in the marshes of North Russia). Indeed, it must have been heart-breaking for Jack to see Captain Gorman, shot in the stomach, dragged for hours through 'that awful forest' only to die sixteen hours later in Topsa. After six hours, he received reports that Bolshevik patrols were working their way around his rear. This, together with no news of the Russian attack on Topsa, made Jack remember the warning from Lendrum and curse the local White Russians who had failed to turn up, and indeed his own senior officers who had sent them there. He decided to extract the battalion whilst he still could, rather than risk being completely cut off and surrounded, as the regimental diary recorded:

> It was obvious that if the Russians failed (the attack at Topsa) our position would be most precarious, as if a withdrawal were necessitated, we should have to march 18 miles through enemy country. Added to this was the fact that if we sustained heavy casualties we should not be able to evacuate them. The uncertainty of the situation undoubtedly weighed heavily on the CO especially as we were encountering more opposition than we had been led to expect. In addition the Bolo's were working round our flanks in the most alarming manner and our position was becoming somewhat critical.[13]

So just a few days before the Treaty of Versailles was about to be signed in France on 28 June, the next war in Russia was in full flow. The news of the Hampshire's withdrawal seems to have been understood by Grogan without difficulty as the result of a sound decision by the CO on the ground, but it did not sit at all easily with Ironside, who was subjected to a series of complaints sent through to him of Jack's open criticism of his leadership. The final straw came when in late July Jack was ordered to carry out a raid on Bolshevik blockhouses (bunkers defended by machine guns) under cover of gas. He quickly wrote a letter to Brigadier General Turner, the GOC of this area of the front, bypassing Grogan, saying that the attack would serve no purpose and his men would needlessly be killed in trying to impress the local but unreliable White Russian forces. However, his tone was apparently high-handed: 'if the proposed operation is left to my discretion I shall not carry it out. I am continuing to make all preparations in case you order me to carry out the raid . . .'.

> Attacked at 04.45. At 10.30 as no news was heard or seen of 3rd N. R. Rifles on our right who were attacking Topsa and the enemy who were fighting very well nearly surrounded us, the C.O. decided to withdraw from the position we had reached round Troitskoye village. After having withdrawn about two miles news was heard that the 3rd N. R. Rifles had taken their objectives and Topsa so we marched into Topsa via the woods to the south.

It was almost unthinkable that 'the bravest man in the British army', who had recently killed Bolshevik soldiers and led fighting patrols, should have lost his head through cowardice, and yet that was to be the upshot of the judgement made by his high command. Jack's actions at Troitskoye were less to do with being frightened or 'having lost his head' (as Ironside was to claim later), but more to do with practical considerations on the ground and his concluding that further maximum effort to support the Russians was pointless. Frequently Jack could foresee positions where the whole battalion would be cut off and murdered – and there were no supporting or reliable units nearby to assist them if they had been surrounded. These were actions in keeping with a man unafraid of making decisions, not someone afraid of the enemy. They were also the product of his creeping certainty that this whole affair was a mess and being badly handled, and the actions of a man who, as we have seen, put the safety of his men above everything else – as was his way. Ordering men to their deaths was something he was used to doing, but to senseless deaths he was not.

Little by little Jack was single-handedly opposing the high command in Russia, and Ironside would have no more second-guessing of his orders. He was a marked man it would seem. Jack had already seen at first hand, however, that he and his men were being used. He had decided that the campaign in Russia was a pointless waste of men and resources. Whilst he had the best interests of his men at heart, he was in danger of crossing the line in a manner which the British army could never tolerate. Indeed, at his later court martial, although none of his senior officers in the battalion complained about his decisions and attitudes, there was a statement from Lieutenant G. E. Hill, an Intelligence Officer. In it he stated that on the route back from Troitskoye, Jack was openly complaining about the senior commanders in North Russia and the Russians themselves:

Archangel
17th September 1919

Sir,
I have the honour to report that on the night of the 19th/20th June 1919 in the capacity of Intelligence Officer, I accompanied the Column commanded by Lieut. Colonel Sherwood Kelly V.C., from KURGOMEN round the enemy flank to TROITSA with the object of capturing the latter. During the march I was with Lieut. Colonel Sherwood Kelly at the head of the column and heard him continuously making remarks in a loud voice about the command in North Russia such as the following: 'You cannot expect the show we are going on to succeed when we are commanded by a lot of people with no service like all these people out here. We will have to go through with this show, but it is no damn good. It is all very well for

those damn people who sit on the ruddy backsides behind and run the show to tell us the Russians are going to fight, but I know they are not and we shall have to do the whole thing.'

Later in the day, when the Column was resting after the operation, I heard Lieut. Colonel Sherwood Kelly say to his men: 'It is the Brigadier's fault that this show has failed but what can you expect, the man is only a very junior Major' or words to that effect. Owing to the length of time that has elapsed since events took place, I cannot repeat Lieut. Colonel Sherwood Kelly's words verbatim, but I can definitely state that both before and after the operation, Lieut. Colonel Sherwood Kelly's remarks to his men ridiculing his superiors, and especially Brigadier General Graham, were almost continuous and drew forth laughter from the men in the ranks.

I have the honour to be,
Sir,
Your obedient servant[14]

Although Ironside was not aware of the specifics, he was increasingly informed of Jack's open criticism. For Ironside the issue was not how to discipline Jack but how to dress this matter up in a way that flagged up Jack as the main reason for failure, rather than Churchill's vacillation and duplicity, Ironside's own indecision and average performance as a commander, the hopelessness of the strategic situation and the massive problems of trying to work with loyal but disrupted White Russian units. Thus, Ironside painted a picture of a man totally inept and who panicked, as he recorded in his diary:

Russian attack [on Troitskoye] was a complete success. Over 500 prisoners taken and 100 dead were counted on the position. Unfortunately The Hampshires failed to take any part in the fight. Had they obeyed orders the result would have been an overwhelming success. The story was this. They duly arrived at their appointed position some minutes before the zero hour, after a march of nine miles through the forest. They laid a cable behind them as they went and were all the time in communication with brigade headquarters. Just before the attack commenced some twenty or thirty of the enemy were seen coming up from their rear towards their front, apparently quite unaware of enemy troops being behind their line. The C.O. considered that he was being outflanked and withdrew his men some distance along the path by which he had come. He neither engaged the enemy party which he thought was outflanking him nor informed the brigade of what he was doing. Later he withdrew to his starting point without making any attempt to join in the fight which had then started.

When I interviewed the C.O. the next day he could not explain why he had acted as he had. He had obviously lost his head, thinking he had overshot his position and gone too far forward. It was a clear case of disobedience of orders, aggravated by the fact that he could have communicated with his superior at any moment. The effect of the non-cooperation of the British troops had a grave effect upon the Russians just at the very moment when they needed an overwhelming success to raise their morale. Had the CO been a regular officer I should certainly had him court martialled. He had fought brilliantly through the war and now appeared to me to be worn out with the responsibility of having had to act in an isolated position. To put an end to the unfortunate incident I withdrew the battalion from the line, sending the CO down to base with orders that he should be sent home for demobilization.

Interpretation of events is the key role of the historian, not judgment – that is for others to decide. When we assess what Ironside said in his account one could make the following interpretations:

Firstly, that Ironside included this event at all in his account was a deliberate attempt to put his side of the story and blacken Jack's name after his subsequent but not consequent court martial. He even adjusted the facts – he stated that the battalion only had to advance 9 miles, when the regimental history clearly states it was more than double this. Ironside also states the battalion made no effort to engage the enemy – so what then of the twelve to fifteen casualties, including the deaths of Captain Gorman MC and Sergeant Batten?

Secondly, it is clear that Ironside had already marked Jack as insubordinate from the moment they met, and a clash could only have been avoided if Jack ignored every passion and resolute thought in his body. Jack had become more intemperate than ever and had the confidence of a man who had commanded two front-line regular battalions in the war.

Thirdly, to say that Jack was worn out with responsibility of leading in an exposed position ignores the fact that he had been in this pointless position before, at Cambrai and elsewhere, where after terrible sacrifice by his men, they waited for relief and support for two days before being asked to withdraw. He had no wish to repeat that experience with the lives of his men in North Russia, of all places, where there was absolutely no chance of support. He was not worn out with responsibility at all, he was simply unwilling to order brave men to die as a morale-building exercise for unreliable Russian units, to no doubt then be told to withdraw again. Ironside ignored the detail of the operational aspects, whereas Jack, on the ground, surrounded by unreliable Russian units, could sense that they were wasting lives.

Fourthly, anyone who knew Jack would know that he was one of the last people on the planet with whom to have a face-to-face meeting. The probability is that there was a huge row between the 6ft 4in mountain of man that was Jack and the far more politically aware Ironside, where Jack told him exactly what he thought of both the campaign itself (as he could now see it) and the conduct of operations. Jack was happy to kill Bolsheviks, but not in some weak, half-hearted way, or in a demonstration for morale-boosting purposes. Where were the orders for a full assault? Where were the men needed to do the job properly? Why was this whole thing being done on a shoestring, with no one in Britain aware that a war was being fought – 'a shameful, illegitimate little war'? Indeed, anyone who could write that Jack was unable to explain why he acted as he did clearly was a liar. If there was one man in the entire British army more than able and willing to speak his mind, it was Jack. What is more likely is that such were the tirade of insults poured onto Ironside, that he could not even begin to record these in his memoirs without some of the mud sticking.

Fifthly, if Ironside had indeed threatened him with a court martial had he been a regular officer, this would have touched a raw nerve. Jack would have told him not to worry about that and demanded a court martial – indeed dared Ironside to do it. When Ironside pulled back from making this whole affair public, Jack made it happen anyway. Deep down there would have been a resentment that he was regarded as a colonial and had never been treated like a regular officer. If a regular officer would have been court-martialled then so should he. Jack was not dealing with Lucas in the 29th Division any more, but was face to face with the Establishment. The kamikaze side of Jack's personality surfaced easily again.

Sixthly, rather like many a public-school headmaster of any age, Ironside had decided early on that Jack was trouble, a 'bad hat', and was having none of it. The high-handed and arrogant way in which he ignored the facts surrounding the attack on Troitskoye was breathtaking, but typical of a man who had already decided the fate of the individual in front of him. With the war over there was no longer a need to tolerate such obstinacy or disrespect. Ironside's account was not only at odds with Jack's version but also totally contradictory to the regimental history (often very unbiased accounts put together from a range of sources).

Finally, Ironside may have wished to try to paint Jack as a man who had lost his head and was out of his depth – but he had picked the wrong target. Ironside was not only wrong to lie in his account of the action . . . if he thought Jack was 'worn out' he had another thing coming. All he had done was inflame the rage of an outrageous temper and provide Jack with yet another battle.

There is also a considerable amount of other primary evidence to suggest that Jack had done nothing wrong except challenge Ironside's authority. The Archangel War Diary for 20 June stated: 'Enemy morale by no means low and were forewarned of attack by deserter from 4th North Russian Rifles.' In his excellent study of this whole episode, Kinvig also cites an extract from a letter from one of Jack's subalterns, a young lieutenant and VC winner himself, who said:

they gave us a very warm time but our own better shooting told heavily. However we were nearly surrounded and cut off so, fagged out as we were – we had to retreat at 9.30 am in the blazing heat, no rest, little food. My platoon was the last to leave, the enemy had worked up to within seventy yards, covering us with very heavy fire the whole time. We just got out and had to trek right back over our old trail, and we got back to TOPSA at 12 midnight.[15]

Kinvig also relates the comment of one Hampshire's sergeant, who said of Jack: 'He said he is not going to get any more of his men or officers killed for the sake of this ******country.'

Finally, in Jack's complete defence, we hear from Major Allfrey, of the companion brigade, with his opinion of the Hampshire's attack: 'In my opinion, and also Col. Davies's, the show is tactically wrong . . . After five years of war good troops ought never to be placed in such a rotten predicament by some damn fool of a muddle-headed broken-down old regular soldier' (this, we can assume, being a reference to Brigadier General Graham, who had planned the attack on Troitska).

In almost every respect, the operations in North Russia were a disaster – a Churchillian masterpiece. There was evidence of dissatisfaction everywhere. Supplies for the men had to be transported over massive distances – hundreds of miles. Mule trains were attacked and food and supplies stolen, there were no fresh fruit or vegetables, and soldiers even cooked grass to try to make some sort of soup. The swamp lands of the Dwina River were almost impossible to navigate, let alone pin down an enemy. Finally, of course, there was the unreliability and viciousness of their Russian hosts – if they were not even prepared to fight then why should they? The anger in the ranks of the 238 Brigade grew: they wanted to go home and they were not doing what they were told was needed. Where was the withdrawal they were supposed to be facilitating as a relief force? Censorship was introduced to prevent letters going home, complaining about the campaign. Even those letters that did get through early on, took seven weeks to get home. Jack, however, decided to take steps to complain even more vociferously – maybe a lack of judgement, maybe a rush of blood to that temperamental head or maybe a genuine determination that an injustice was being done. Already at loggerheads with Ironside and receiving calming words from Grogan, trying to keep him on side, on 26 July (the same day he took over command of the important Railway Front at Obozerskaya, from White Russian, Colonel Akutin) he wrote a letter to Mr E. E. Janson. Mr Janson was a wealthy South African mine owner, of Eaton Square in London. In his letter Jack criticized the management and direction of the campaign in Russia. He stated that the British soldiers who had volunteered were not actually pulling out at all, but fighting 400 miles inland, supporting local

White Russian forces in the war against the Bolsheviks – explosive stuff given the attitude of much of the British public, the trades unions and the press:

2nd Hampshire Regiment
26th July 1919

My Dear Jan
The position out here is, from a military point of view very critical – If the papers would publish the true state of affairs and cease advertising Ironside, who is weak and not fit for the job, (we have lost all confidence in him) it would be a good thing – He – Ironside, has posed as the saviour of North Russia and will stick at nothing to save his face now that things have turned out contrary to expectation – For instance one reads such trash as 'Ironsides Confidence Justified'. Well the Russian Battalion to which that referred (Dyer's Btn) mutinied, murdered 12 officers 6 of whom were British and two companies joined the Bolo's – along with the M.G.C. of the 4th North R. Rifles – Another advert is – 'A Hercules in Khaki and builder of an Anti-Bolshevik Army' – well the whole of the Onega front 4,000 Russians trained and armed and clothed by Ironside have all gone over to the Bolo's killing or capturing all British Officers with them – We are here, on railway front, sent from Pinega, to quell mutiny of Russian troops – You can make what use you like of this letter and it is your duty in the interests of the British here to expose the show.

Love to you both – Jonnie.

OAS
E.W. Janson Esq
11 Eaton Mansions
Eton Square, London[16]

Jack knew full well that his letters may not get through the army censor, so just to be certain one got through (or indeed hit the censor's eye), he added the following to his second letter to Dora on the same day:

The position out here at present is <u>very serious</u> – it is time things were correctly reported in the papers – Since last I wrote we have been moved from the Pinega front to the Vologda Railway front – some 200 miles from Pinega – The whole of the Russians on the Onega front 4,000 in all have joined the Bolsheviks murdering or capturing <u>all</u> the British Officers with them – The Russian troops <u>everywhere</u> are turning against us – So much for Ironside's Anti-Bolshevik Army – The whole show is one huge advert for him – It is time some strong reliable man was sent out – We have lost all confidence in Ironside and are sick of reading the lying statements of what he is supposed to be doing.

It is worth noting that amongst Jack's circle of friends were people such as Janson and Hamilton – South Africans of great wealth. To what extent Jack was seen as one of them, or perhaps a pawn of some kind, is now relevant. Neither letter made it through the censors. Instead in early August they were opened by the censor in England who immediately realized what he had in his hands. Jack later claimed that he had written the letters knowing that they would be opened, giving him an opportunity to tell the public of this 'useless, aimless and ill-managed campaign' and that he was 'determined to get back by some means or other to England'. Within days Ironside had been informed and was in a rage. Brigadier Turner was asked for a report on Jack. He stated openly that, 'He is a hot headed and quarrelsome man who has rows with practically everyone with whom he has come into contact'. Turner however went on to say, 'He has a fine smart well-drilled battalion and his men like him, but I do not consider he is suitable for command of a regular battalion under the present conditions' – in other words he was a good soldier, strong leader of men, well-liked and courageous – but he spoke his mind and did not toe the line. The current conflict, with its political overtones, could not depend on his support and he could not be prevented from speaking out against the orders being given. In truth Turner was right in that men like Jack had been a necessity during the war, but in peacetime he would have been very unlikely to have either risen as high in rank as he had or commanded a regular battalion.

This explosive situation smouldered on throughout July and early August and caused problems for the officers around him. Grogan seems to have been understanding of Jack's actions at Troitskoye, but found Jack's single-handed challenge to the authority of GHQ staff irritating. At one point Jack had told Grogan over the telephone that the whole affair was a shambles, and that if he was a party to all this he needed his head tested! Later, at his subsequent court martial, Jack even admitted:

I did in fact make myself thoroughly unpopular at GHQ. So much so that General Grogan said to me that it would be a source of the greatest satisfaction on the part of General Ironside's staff if I was sent home. However on every occasion I have come into contact with the staff my motives have been a very real concern for the well being of the officers and men.

Jack thought that he had an implicit agreement with Ironside not to take the matter further with General Sir Henry Rawlinson, who was now the Commander-in-Chief in North Russia. During August, the Hampshire's had little to do, but Jack continued in command, with his junior officers well aware of what had happened. However, Ironside either did not make such an undertaking with Jack or went back on his word and wrote to Rawlinson, pointing out that he thought Jack had lost his head, had not recovered from his wounds received in 1916, and should be sent home in disgrace. On 15 August Jack was sitting at his desk in his command tent when his signal officer brought in a message from Ironside, stating that he had discussed the matter with General Rawlinson, and it had been agreed that Jack was to be removed from his command on 18 August, and sent home, as recorded by Brigadier General Turner:

On the 18th August, under instructions from GHQ, Colonel Kelly was relieved of his Command.

Except for the above mentioned incident [where Jack had made changes to front line dispositions without consulting Turner] during the time Colonel Kelly has been with me no difficulty or question has arisen between us; our relations have been most cordial, and to the best of my belief he has loyally supported me in every way, and as Colonel Kelly was thoroughly conversant with my plans for withdrawal, I deprecated his removal so soon before it was likely the plans might have to be set in force.

The battalion under his command was in a thoroughly efficient state and well disciplined . . .

Jack was enraged beyond control. The whole Russian affair was enough to make his blood boil in its waste of time and men, but the explosive point was the attack on his honour and character which he was not prepared to allow to happen. Jack now chose to expose the whole affair to the British people, partly to warn them about what was going on – a war on Bolshevism, not a withdrawal – but also to expose those in command over him who had ganged together to destroy his reputation. Maybe his temper now got the better of him. This was to be a personal war between Jack and the whole British Establishment. He packed his bags and said his goodbyes – both to his officers in the battalion and his men. He had not been relieved of command ever before in his life, and the level of injustice he felt was unbearable to a proud man. Walking out and off the jetty to his boat home, he resolved that he was not going to let Ironside, Rawlinson, Grogan, and especially Churchill, get away with what he saw as the gross manipulation of both the British public and the men who had volunteered to go to Russia.

It is at this point that it is just possible the hero had become frayed around the edges – perhaps even deeper than that. Carrying the epithet 'the bravest man in the British army' created quite an expectation – an expectation of himself that is. It could also be that a hard life, four years of war with five quite serious wounds, service in some tough conditions in Gallipoli, France and now North Russia, and the emotional pressures he had created for himself back home with Nellie and Dora, had worn out this colossus.

North Russia had become a sort of melting pot or collection point for the soldiers of fortune and the soldiers from the 'mental hell' created by the Great War. Jack was not alone in having been immersed for too long in the struggle of mud and blood, that a return to normal life after the armistice was just too much of a shock. Maybe this was a hidden reason for avoiding commitment to both Nellie and Dora. The Russian episode created an opportunity to delay the inevitable and to prolong the adrenalin, the desire for the company of men and the need for conflict. We can't assume that everyone was sane at this time and saw matters in context. The written word, especially in the hands of the amateur writer, can only go so far to portray the personal stresses, mental conflicts, nightmares, need for immersion in uniform that conflict provided. There was also the structure of the army, a routine created by the system which avoided the need to make one's own decisions. There was the team spirit and the uncomplicated nature of life – they fought and they either lived or died. It was impossible to appreciate what some of the younger officers and men around them had been through, and totally farcical to judge their actions by any normal peacetime standards. Actions by men such as Jack in peacetime were a reflection of the hangover of wartime into their everyday lives. Had the Russian episode been a national matter of life or death then Jack's outburst at commanding officers might have been absorbed – but Russia was a show, a stage play, and Jack had only just come to see this.

Yet another holder of the Victoria Cross who volunteered for the Russian expedition was Charles Hudson VC, CB, DSO, MC. He shared similar experiences to Jack and all those who had been through and survived the worst the war could offer. His own life was fascinating and he had attended Sandhurst (though did not complete the course), worked on Ceylon tea plantations and returned home due to the outbreak of war. He served like Jack as a temporary lieutenant colonel in the Sherwood Foresters, and by the age of 26 he had been awarded an MC, a DSO with Bar and the Victoria Cross. Although he died in 1959, Hudson's memoirs were published privately in 1992. Within these is a reference to a 'newly arrived Colonel' whom he obviously met more than once whilst in Russia. Although he does not mention Jack by name it could only have been him. The new man was boisterous and overbearing in manner but, he says, 'good company'. However, it is in his description of touring some blockhouses with this colonel that he revealed that, to his way of thinking, the man's nerve had completely gone. 'Even a light shell some distance away caused him to shake with fear and turn white'. This is a revelation. If it was Jack (and there's a strong possibility that it was), then to his men he maintained the bravado expected of him – or he expected of himself. In private he was broken, his nerve had gone. Anyone who has suffered stress or emotional collapse and anxiety will know that when it strikes there is no defence. The human body has many defences, but when stress and anxiety takes over – perhaps through years of attrition, years of being what one is not, years of pretending to be indestructible – then the defences become as thin as rice paper and there is little cure. Was this Jack in the summer of 1919? Nerves broken and putting up a pretence. That is not to say he withdrew his men from the fight through cowardice – he was still leading patrols and killing the enemy by hand – but he was fighting to stay afloat and possibly his decision-making lost all sense of direction, hence the letters which in this sense endorse Ironside's view of Jack.

We may recall here that when Jack was 14 years old, he had seen his father take on the colossus that was Cecil Rhodes, when he disagreed fundamentally with the injustice of the Glen Grey Act of 1894. Perhaps, as Jack sat in his cabin on board ship, he recalled how his father had agonized over what to do, but ultimately decided to ruin his own career and reputation and make this matter public. He'd ended up writing to the Cape newspapers, calling out Rhodes and telling the people the truth and displaying the injustice for all to see. Perhaps Jack sat in his cabin and cried that his military career was over and that justice needed to be done. In any event, on board his six-day journey home across the North Sea, Jack, in exactly the same way his father had done, wrote a letter to the *Daily Express* – the newspaper that had been so keen to watch Churchill's plans in North Russia – stating: 'I ask you, Sir, to publish this letter so that people in England may know the truth about the situation in Archangel and may be able to take steps to right it.'

On Saturday, 6 September 1919, Lieutenant Colonel Jack Sherwood Kelly suddenly became a household name, as his letter and photograph were splashed across the front pages of the *Daily Express*. If it was notoriety he wanted, he had it. If it was justice he craved, he was to be disappointed.

'Archangel Scandal Exposed'
'Duplicity of Churchill Policy in Russia'
'The Public Humbugged'
'Famous VC appeals to the Nation'

Such were the headlines that greeted Churchill, the Cabinet, Lloyd George and the officers of the General Staff that weekend. Jack had done a good job. It was a cutting, no-holds-barred attack on both British policy in North Russia, and the way in which operations were being carried out. As such, he was attacking and criticizing both Churchill and Ironside. He said he had volunteered for the Relief Force in the sincere belief that relief was urgently needed, in order to make possible the withdrawal of low category troops in the last stage of exhaustion due to fierce fighting amongst the rigours of an Arctic winter. But he went on:

> I was reluctantly but inevitably drawn to the following conclusion: That the troops of the Relief Force which we were told had been sent out for purely defensive purposes, were being used for offensive purposes on a large scale and far into the interior, in furtherance of some ambitious plan of campaign the nature of which we were not allowed to know. My personal experience of those operations was that they were not even well conducted and they were not calculated to benefit in a military or any other sense a sound and practical British policy in Russia. They only entailed useless loss and suffering in troops that had already made great sacrifices in the Great War.

Not content with those broadsides, Jack vented his spleen on the 'much vaunted "loyal Russian Army", composed largely of Bolshevik prisoners dressed khaki' and the 'puppet government set up by us in Archangel . . .'.

The reaction of the British press and the trades union movement was electric. Here at last was clear evidence, placed before everyone, of what they had feared. Churchill's plans to, at the very least, wait and see what would happen in Russia, and, at most, to use the relief force to actively fight alongside the White Russians, were exposed. Immediately there was a dramatic reaction and activity in the House of Commons. Meanwhile, Jack had arrived back in London and unpacked – probably at the Rubens Hotel near Victoria, which was again to be his home for the next few months.

We do not know how Nellie was reacting to all this, but just to have him home was probably enough. With this new conflict to fight, he was at least in good spirits! With the game exposed so effectively, Churchill began to prepare his ground to survive the storm. Lloyd George could see that such a scandal could do enormous damage and that Jack had unleashed a demon that could engulf the whole government. The next few days saw constant reports, anger and criticism throughout the press. Pressure increased on the government, Churchill and the War Office. Standing where he liked to be – alone – Jack received a letter from the War Office on 13 September, coinciding with a statement from Churchill in the House of Commons the previous evening. Clearly Churchill had held several meetings to plan the best way out of this mess, and decided to use eloquence and military justice, rather than answer Jack's charges in any detail. Of course, Jack did not realize what he was up against now. He was used to face-to-face combat, either with words or bullets, but Churchill's weapons of subtle insinuation were used at a distance and with the authority of one who knew how to escape from almost any situation. The key section of Churchill's statement read:

To add to the difficulties of such an operation in its most critical phase, by inspiring the enemy, or disarming the Russian national forces or by spreading despondency among our troops, is wrong and unpatriotic. In a military officer such conduct is a grave offence. In this connection attention must be drawn particularly to the statements which have been published purporting to emanate from Lt. Colonel Sherwood-Kelly.

Suddenly, deftly and without effort, Churchill had evaded Jack's initial challenge on the matter of what was happening in Russia itself, and turned the matter into questioning Jack's character, patriotism and role in undermining the morale of British troops in North Russia. The goalposts were moving fast and Jack could now sense that he was in a game where the rules were made by others. The statement continued: 'This officer was, on 16th August, removed from his command at Archangel and sent back to England by General Rawlinson for a serious offence under the Army Act. General Rawlinson has reported that he refrained from trial by court martial only on account of his gallant fighting record.' Again, the words were chosen carefully to imply that Rawlinson had been sensitive to Jack, who clearly had been guilty of some grave but unspecified offence. To the general reader and to Jack this could have meant anything – cowardice, inciting the troops to mutiny or treason being the most obvious. The statement concluded: 'He has now been alleged to have committed an offence of a different character against King's regulations in regard to which disciplinary action must take its course'.

Jack was out of his depth and drowning rapidly. His violent temper, coupled with his deep-rooted problems with authority, had become confused with a genuine frustration at the waste of British lives in a futile campaign in Russia, which he felt he and his men had been duped into volunteering for. But the issue was now about challenging and taking on the government to protect his honour and this, as is so often the case, saw discretion fly out of the window in favour of valour. Like a drowning man, he clutched at every straw. The day before the War Office statement was published, Jack sent a letter to Mr Thomas MP (who was due to speak at the Trades Union Congress in Glasgow on 13 September) about the whole scandalous Russian affair. On the same morning that he received his letter from the War Office, Jack wrote a second letter to the *Daily Express*. Why did he do this? Undoubtedly, because he knew he needed support. The army would not help him, his colleagues had, he felt, deserted him and the Conservative and Liberal parties would disavow him. Though far from being a socialist, Jack knew that the voice of the unions would be a loud one in his favour. But there may just be another possible explanation. We have already seen how Jack, through his relationship with his aunt and contacts of Dora, was acquainted with men of considerable wealth and power. Jack had already appealed to one of them. If you were going to write to complain about the campaign in Russia, would you write to a South African mining magnate? Why him? – unless the target was less Russia and perhaps more Churchill? Two other aspects are worthy of note at this point. Firstly, Jack was simply unable to have written the letters directly – his vocabulary, as we know, was limited and ripe and his educational background had not equipped him to write such penetrating narrative and at such length. Letters that survive from Jack from 1922 and 1923 are written phonetically, and simply bear no resemblance to the author of these letters to the press. Secondly, at his funeral in 1931, there were very few people present. However, one person that was there was a Mr Basil Clarke.

Born in 1879 in Altringham, Basil Clarke had never intended to be a journalist but had hoped for a career in music. By chance he started work for the *Manchester Guardian* where he saw he had a talent. By 1915 the *Daily Mail* had employed him to travel around the neutral countries of Europe to better understand their intentions. By January 1916 he had really made a name for himself by accusing the government of failing to enforce the blockade of Germany and his fame became global. He left the *Daily Mail* and during 1916 was on the Somme writing accounts of what he saw there. As such he became a leading figure in journalism for the troops. By 1917 he was at the Ministry of Reconstruction and it was here he developed an interest in public relations and propaganda. Indeed, he pioneered an approach to public relations that was totally new and which he called 'propaganda by news' – the practice of influencing the news agenda through the selection of which news to release. He believed that it is facts that will influence public opinion, and not propaganda, so they should be presented as plainly as possible, rather than trying to add negatives to the text which distorts the facts. In an age today of 'fake news' we can see that Clarke was totally correct. So why was Clarke attending Jack's funeral in 1931? Of course, there could be a completely ordinary explanation, but it is possible that these explosive letters of 1919 were in fact agreed by Jack but written by someone else on his behalf – perhaps by Clarke. The motivations for Clarke would have been practising his later philosophy of influencing public opinion and government through facts, and this was an ideal opportunity for him to hone his craft. Clarke was already a stinging critic of Churchill, and wrote of Churchill whilst Secretary of State for War (January 1919– February 1921) that: 'he (Churchill) was an expensive luxury . . . because of his adventurism and poor judgement and it was difficult to understand how he had held onto office except through social and political influence'. But the third piece of the jigsaw that brings Clarke into the frame for writing these letters 'from Jack' is that he was well-acquainted with Sir Frederick Hamilton – husband to Jack's aunt, but also a newspaper giant of the time.

Thus, on 13 September, *The Times* and the *Daily Express* carried a second letter, probably written by Clarke, as well as a report on Mr Thomas' speech at the TUC:

'COL. SHERWOOD-KELLY'S REPLY TO MR. CHURCHILL'S
  CHARGES'
'WHAT HIS "SERIOUS OFFENCE" WAS'
'The only way of calling public attention to the Russian Scandal'
'DEMAND FOR A COURT MARTIAL'

The second and longer letter splashed across the front pages of the national press took a giant stride further than ever before, naming all the senior military officers who had been involved in the arguments and obvious deceptions in Russia. The letter stated that he (Jack) had not intended to rush into print, but he had been given no alternative. Now it was his personal honour that was at stake. It further stated that Churchill's wording was deliberately distorted (in this he was of course correct) and could have meant anything. The letter carried a series of explanations of his conduct, which he claimed to have always been founded on protecting his men in what he saw as a pointless strategy, where they were being used and killed for a plan initiated by Churchill against the wishes and knowledge of the British people. Jack published letters he had received from Grogan and his letters of concern to Turner. Jack then explained what the so-called 'serious offence' was (which were letters home to his friends) – not cowardice as Churchill and the War Office were trying to imply. Jack also went on to produce a telegram from Turner sent to Rawlinson just before he met with Jack on 16 August:

'15.8.19 Presume this officer (Kelly) is only required temporarily at Archangel. I do not wish to lose his services at this juncture. Things are now working quite smoothly.'

This was the same Turner who had previously commented that Jack was not suited to the command of a battalion at this time. Clearly Turner did not consider that Jack deserved to be relieved of command, even if Ironside had made up his mind that he would be. The rest of the letter then dealt with the duplicity with which Jack felt he had been treated by both Rawlinson and Ironside, saying what they needed to say to his face just to get him on a boat home, then dropping him from command and breaking any promises they had made to give him a new battalion in England. Finally, Jack stated that they had threatened him with a court martial, and that he hoped this second letter would provide one so that he could clear his name. Had he still been serving with his old friend Lucas, maybe he would have received different advice about how he was acting and where it would lead. In the last letter where Jack is mentioned, Lucas wrote:

Germany, Sept 21st 1919: I am very grateful for the paper about Kelly. I was hunting round the 3 battns to try to get a copy when yours turned up.

He is an awful ass because he won't get any good out of it, and little sympathy with the army; he will probably call me as a witness to character if he is tried by court martial.

To Thomas at the TUC, Jack's actions were far more glorious. He sensed that Churchill's timing had been excellent – issuing his denials the day before the congress began, and passing the matter from his own hands and responsibility back to the army for their justice to run its course. Mr Thomas, referring to Jack as 'the gallant Colonel Kelly', went on to say that Jack knew exactly what he was giving up when 'he' wrote his letters – his career and his future – but that he had not expected to give up his honour too. Mr Thomas hoped that the court martial would be in public and that the government would answer the charges against them of duplicity. He also hoped that Parliament would hold its own court martial on Churchill and ensure that the facts were made known to the British public.

The *Daily Express* spent the rest of September attacking Churchill and his 'private war'. Churchill must have felt real venom towards Jack that month – this could have finished Churchill's career. Outbursts of support for Jack and anger against the government were recorded in Liverpool, Newcastle, Nottingham and Glasgow. Meanwhile back in Russia the troops had had enough. There had already been mutinies – in October 1918 a section of the Royal Scots had refused to take part in what they saw as a badly planned attack on Kuluga. In February 1919, the 13th Yorkshire Regiment had 'gone on strike' and demanded they be withdrawn from Russia, as they had been promised. In August 1919, just as Jack was being sent home, 100 Royal Marines were court-martialled for mutiny, following an ambush in which they were betrayed by White Russian troops. The whole mess was collapsing and Churchill stood exposed. Only the previous month, on 19 July 1919, Churchill had been emboldened enough to state in a speech at the Anglo-Russian Club that he had full support for active intervention and a fight to the death with Bolshevism – all completely contrary to the government line. For Stanley Berrett and his comrades of the 2/Hampshires, the story was a grim one. They clearly knew that their CO had been removed and this caused a great deal of disquiet – Jack had been a popular CO and obviously been fighting for his men. Stanley recorded the bitterness felt by the men throughout the 2/Hampshires over Jack's treatment and the whole affair: 'we may as well have stayed in England and saved a lot of money because it was no good at all and eventually we had to get out quick'. When the withdrawal took place it was done quickly, and all the stores that were supposed to have been saved were simply left behind, and fell into the hands of the Bolsheviks when Archangel fell soon after. The Oxfordshire & Buckinghamshire regimental history records that their battalion arrived back at Liverpool to a civic reception from the Lord Mayor. This was not to be for Jack's battalion:

When we did get back to the sea we had to board small boats to go out to the big vessel and the Russian in charge of the small boats refused to budge until a gun was pushed into his ribs, they moved then and we got away. After sinking the small boats with machine gun fire we got back to Tilbury but were not allowed to go anywhere. Our badges were taken off our uniforms and we were put straight on a train for Ireland and the rebels.[17]

Anger and outrage on the journey home were running high, and across the United Kingdom unrest was in the air. Indeed, there was a real concern that a socialist revolution could break out here as it had done in Austria and Hungary. A further risk was 800 armed and furious men with strong socialist tendencies who had been used to try to kill fellow workers in Russia. Incarcerating the men and sending them to Ireland confined to barracks would hopefully cool their heels, whilst the 'Jack saga' was dealt with. In fact, Jack never saw his men again. Stanley also recorded that, on the train out of Dublin, the men painted in large white letters on the outside of the carriages: 'Up Kelly and down Churchill'! Back in North Russia the bodies of over 350 British officers and men, mostly from the army and Royal Navy, lay in the swampy and soon-to-be frozen ground, whilst another 219 bodies were never recovered and are recorded on a cryptic memorial in an obscure part of Archangel – hardly where their loved ones expected them to be having survived the Great War. The NRRF had been put together, despite clear instructions to the contrary from the prime minister. The men had been ordered to go and the rest volunteered, having been told it was a relief operation, when in fact it was an invasion. Churchill took no notice of whether, as an invasion force, it had any chance of success, and charged on with another ill-conceived and poorly planned adventure that cost lives. Churchill faced numerous questions in the House, notably on 22 October, where a certain MP, Mr Thomas, was also keen to know what was still going on in Russia and how much the whole episode had cost. Churchill skilfully avoided identifying this figure and was unaware of the number of casualties. He was also unsure whether British warships and troops were still engaged in operations in North Russia. Clearly, he was unaware of quite a lot.

Meanwhile, the now bitter and increasingly nasty battle between Churchill and Jack continued. On 6 October, Jack wrote a third letter to the *Daily Express*, commenting on the news that British troops had all been withdrawn from Archangel. He stated that it was the exposure of Churchill's policy that had speeded up the decision to pull out completely – and he was probably right. As Churchill was fuming at being trumped and was being forced into unpicking his plan, Jack once again became something of a celebrity. Relations with Nellie improved as she and he dodged reporters on their Kensington doorstep. Finally, Jack was ordered to present himself before a court martial on 28 October.

Jack was not in the mood to compromise. He had done what he had done, not because he was opposed to an all-out war against the Bolsheviks, but because of the half-hearted and underhanded way in which it had been planned, and at the needless waste of men's lives. He also felt that the matter had spiralled from an issue over Russia, into accusations about his personal conduct and honour, and this demanded redress. He of course continued to drag Ironside, Rawlinson and Grogan into the enquiry, clearly feeling that their reputations needed bruising as much as his own. They, of course, kept silent on the whole matter throughout. Predictably the army closed ranks and had to disavow what Jack had done, but equally predictably they did not want to make Jack a martyr. He had, after all, a superb fighting record. What he had said about Churchill's Russian policy was true, so what was desired was to brush him under the carpet as quickly and as quietly as possible. Jack's own defence ended with his stating:

What is my responsibility? I was a volunteer and went to Russia because I was led to believe that the small British force that spent the winter there was in great peril. We were told that this was a defensive measure and that we were being sent to rescue the lives of our comrades whose position was hopeless.

I went determined to do my best. Ninety percent of my battalion consisted of officers and men who had served their King and Country throughout the great war and I felt they had the right to live and that their lives were too valuable to sacrifice, besides the money that was being squandered and the politicians responsible for the waste of those British lives in the Russian scandal should be brought to trial.

I have carried out my duty to the best of my skill and ability. Loyalty to the Throne is with me a paramount ideal. I have sacrificed everything to carry those ideals into action. I have nothing left but a soldier's honour so I plead with you to believe that the action I took was to protect my men's lives against needless sacrifice and to save the country from squandering wealth she could ill afford. I leave this matter in your hands hoping you will remember my past services to my King and Country.

Jack watched as the court martial acted fast in hearing the accusations and defence and then handing down its sentence – a severe reprimand – the lightest that a court martial could confer. Churchill, of course, was nowhere and everywhere. Did Jack feel vindicated? We do not know. We do know that, despite everything, Nellie was with him in court, as were many reporters. Did he affect the careers of those officers who had impugned his honour? Well, surprisingly enough, perhaps he did. On his return home from Russia, Ironside, far from having his major general's rank confirmed and being treated like some sort of hero for holding the fort and bringing back the men, was actually reverted in rank back to colonel and on half pension to boot. Subsequently, Ironside's career took him to Inspector General of the Overseas Forces, a post that was dissolved from under him, and he was removed rapidly from his appointment as Chief of the Imperial General Staff when the British army collapsed in May 1940. Did Jack affect the withdrawal from Russia – almost certainly. There would have been many meetings behind closed doors between Churchill and other members of the Cabinet, with the prime minister probably telling him what a bloody headstrong fool he had been (and that now he was up against an even bigger bloody headstrong fool determined to bring him down, but that was not going to be allowed to happen). The men were to be withdrawn from Russia immediately, as all hope of saving Russia from Bolshevism had gone, and Jack, as a critic, was to be neutralized.

There are two footnotes to this whole episode. Lest we be in any doubt as to Churchill's hidden agenda, one is to be found in the pages of *Punch* magazine, or the *London Charivari*, as it was then known. In the edition published on 20 August 1919, on p. 174, a small item appears at the bottom of the page:

After 5 years the famous story of Russian soldiers training in England has come true. At this very moment, one thousand White Russian Army officers are receiving military training at Newmarket. The announcement greatly shocked Captain Wedgewood Benn who thought it a dreadful thing that Russian officers should be trained by us to fight against their own Government. But not so said Mr Churchill. The object was merely to enable them to relieve our own officers and men. The House as a whole was satisfied with this answer.

Secondly, the White Russian Awards, given out after 1919 to all members of the Royal Air Force, Royal Navy and the army, did not include the name of Lieutenant Colonel Jack Sherwood Kelly. His service there went unrecognized and someone somewhere decided on a spiteful deletion of his name from the roll of honour and withheld his medal.

And so, the show went on. As the bodies of British servicemen were buried in North Russia, the total cost of this latest Churchillian adventure was calculated at a staggering £49,631,000. This episode in his life was over, but Churchill was, as we know, to continue his rollercoaster career, leading the nation in the Second World War and wasting the lives of many more servicemen when he repeated the mistakes of Antwerp, Gallipoli and Russia. On a very different stage was Jack, about to try his hand at another challenge – this time in domestic politics where he hoped a new career could take shape.

Chapter 9

At War with Peace, 1919–26

'Work yourself hard, but not as if you were being made a victim and not with any desire for sympathy or admiration. Desire one thing alone – that your actions or inactions alike should be worthy of a life well spent.'

Marcus Aurelius, *Meditations*

The Christmas of 1919 for Jack and Nellie was a strange one. Quite clearly the exertions of the previous few months, both in Russia physically, and mentally and emotionally in London, had drained them both. Despite the unpredictable nature of dealing with Jack's emotional state, the divorce, the pressures of his infidelity, his letters to the press and his uncontrollable rage, from what we can tell Nellie continued to stand by him. It must have taken an extraordinary amount of personal determination and love to overcome what had been years of difficulty coping with and trying to communicate with Jack.

The world around both Nellie and Jack was changing fast. Coming to terms with peace and re-establishing some sort of normal routine of family life presented their own challenges. The post-war world was very different to that of five years previously, and many aspects of society had gone forever. In Jack's world, striving and battling was the norm. Jack had been engulfed by wars of one kind or another his entire life. Conflict was not only a state of mind, but a world without conflict was frightening to a man who was afraid of standing still and being exposed. Maybe he was also frightened of being a father. The challenge of putting aside a uniform and reaching for civilian clothes was as much as he could bear in this new world which he had seen coming, and he longed for something else to happen. For 'the bravest man in the British army', peacetime was potentially his nemesis. Unlike the millions who now longed for peace, anonymity and a hope of return to the world of 1914, Jack was worried about what he would do out of uniform, in a world without danger . . . a world that no longer cared for heroes.

In the period 1920 to 1922, Jack became a rather nomadic figure and is recorded in many different sources as being variously resident at the Rubens Hotel and the Authors' Club in London and at the Deepdene Hotel near Dorking – obviously close to the Hamiltons in Reigate. He was also recorded as living in Windsor, then at Nutfield Cottage in Ascot and two addresses in Bournemouth. His soul was unable to find rest and his determination to cause conflict where there was none was as strong as ever. This was also a period of financial hardship and tough times for Jack – as it was for hundreds of thousands of other returning soldiers.

In February 1920, he was definitely staying at the Rubens Hotel when he wrote on hotel-headed paper on the 2 February to the War Office, complaining about being out of pocket for the recruiting tour to South Africa. Money was in short supply and, in his estimation, it seems the War Office owed him money. But an accounting bureaucrat within the bowels of the department also had a blank space to fill under receipts for money paid out to Jack. It was still pretty easy to touch a nerve with Jack, as his response illustrates:

Hotel Rubens
Buckingham Palace Road SW1

2.2.20

Sir,
I am in receipt of your letter of the 31st January and in reply beg to state that the Secretary for Defence South Africa is mistaken and quite unaware of the conditions under which I undertook a recruiting tour at the request of the late General Botha – it was agreed at the time that I should not be bothered with returns and further pointed out that the allowance was not sufficient to cover my expenses – I was then assured I would have all out of pocket expenses refunded. I would ask the Secretary for Defense SA if he thinks it is possible to travel much on 15/- in SA?

In conclusion, it is quite impossible to furnish a statement at this juncture – it might interest the Secretary for Defence SA to know that I was out of pocket over the tour. I am returning shortly to SA. I am quite prepared to go into the whole question with the Secretary for Defence after arrival there.

I have the honour to be Sir Your obedient servant
J Sherwood Kelly Lt Col.

Having Jack arrive in your office with a full head of steam on a question of money, as above, is not something that many people would relish. How this matter ended we don't know, but it is a fair bet that the whole question was dropped on the grounds of self-preservation by the Secretary for Defence SA.

The Britain that Jack and its citizens had fought for had gone, but not only had the world changed, there were also new dangers. Very real threats spread across Europe as the new political virus of Bolshevism and communism escalated. Those who felt disadvantaged and abused by the Establishment joined the swelling ranks of socialist parties in every country.

Jack's hatred of Bolshevism was very real. He had seen what it meant at first hand and recognized, as Churchill had done, that it meant the end of liberty and the Empire – in fact everything that he stood for. He next saw the challenge of Bolshevism on the very streets of London. Leninism was a new phenomenon, as was disruption of the state, disinformation, fake news – all of which seems part of a new political phenomenon today. A 100 years ago it was, in fact, a well-established form of revolutionary disruption of the established state. Jack had already made it clear in his remonstrations in 1919 that he was happy to crush Bolshevism if the resources and willpower were provided. In the summer of 1919 he was able to show first hand his willingness to sacrifice himself for what he believed.

Grumbling discontent amongst the police force had, by 1918, manifested itself in direct action. For the first time the government witnessed the potential power of the trade unions amongst their own organs of control over the people. In August 1918, a whole series of strikes was called by the National Union of Police and Prison Officers (NUPPO) and the Metropolitan Police went on strike. This had never happened before and the strike and Union were in fact banned by the then Police Commissioner Sir Edward Henry. However, this did not stop a strike from developing across London. The war was not yet over, the Labour party was only reliable for support as long as the war continued, and Union activity was spreading across the country. There were even plenty of Bolshevik agitators working away, leaving fear and rumour in their wake. The demands of NUPPO were simple – a pay increase and better pension rights, but also recognition of the Union. The government panicked and gave into all demands except recognition of the Union. However, NUPPO's membership swelled from 10,000 Metropolitan officers to 50,000 across the country. By the end of 1918 numerous unions were active and by the summer of 1919 there were strikes across Britain.

The two main unions that struck in favour of the Police were the railways and transport workers. London was quickly coming to a standstill and Jack, along with other professionals from law firms, the army, navy, civil service and many sections of London society, came out on the streets and volunteered to keep London working. The working man stood back and watched as the Establishment fought back. It was a remarkable sight. Trams could be seen being pulled down London's streets, not by horses but by men, and buses were being driven by judges, not bus drivers. London was displaying its characteristically robust reaction to being held to ransom. Jack's love for horses was well-known and he volunteered to work as a stableman in the Southern Railway at Blackfriars, as the *Dundee Evening Telegraph* reported on 30 September 1920:

To Save the Horses Lt Col Works As Stable Hand

Lt Col. John 'Jack' Sherwood Kelly VC DSO CMG whose recent revelations with regard to Russia aroused the attention of the whole country is among those who have volunteered to save the railway horses. 'I am working as a stable hand' said Lt Col Sherwood Kelly having found him in the stables of the South East and Chatham Railway at Blackfriars. 'I feed and water the horses and sweep the stables. I am living in the premises and getting my meals at the public house nearby.'

Lt Col Kelly looked stalwart of frame and had hallmarks of a veteran soldier – clad in a loose tweed jacket, open shirt and riding breeches.

Laudable and praiseworthy though his actions were, it was right up Jack's street to be doing something he loved – looking after horses and eating and drinking each evening at the local pub. What a celebrity he must have been. He had also solved his problem of his ongoing need for accommodation. His relationship with Nellie was intact in so far as they spoke to each other, but broken in terms of living together. The company is, in fact, reported as even having offered him pay, but Jack declined to accept and instead asked that an equivalent sum be handed to 'The Waifs and Strays Society' for homeless children.

Because of his reputation for heroism and courage and his notoriety for the Russian affair, Jack was something of a celebrity and as such was invited to many events and parties. In June 1920, he was recorded as attending a garden party at Buckingham Palace and resuming his contact with King George V. They had first met at the VC investiture back in January 1918, where the king and Jack spent some time chatting together about Russia. This was a relationship that was to continue and drew Jack close to the king – close enough to be invited into a very personal role right at the end of his life.

Almost certainly Jack also retained close contacts with Janson, Hamilton and the other wealthy South African businessmen with homes in London and the Shires. He may well have remained close to Basil Clarke. But whatever his hopes and dreams were, 1921 saw his health relapse as the nine or so wounds of various kinds finally coalesced and brought his body to a halt. For any normal man, one lung badly damaged by gas and another torn apart by a shrapnel shell would have meant the rest of their life spent in inactivity, carefully nursing their bodies back to health. Added to these a large hand-sized chunk of muscle and flesh missing from his shoulder blade from the other shrapnel wound, plus the bullet hole in his leg and the ever-present pain from the bullet holes in his body, and the way he had generally exhausted himself, was enough for even Jack's quite super-human physique and psyche and he spent many weeks that year confined to bed and visiting doctors. We know that Jack wrote many times to the War Office, trying, unsuccessfully, to get his pension position reviewed and to get a military job. Either they had nothing for him, or, more likely, he had become a permanent black sheep.

Whatever this post-war wilderness period meant to Jack and however poorly he was feeling, his irrepressible temperament and sense of justice was as strong as ever. Hidden in the National Newspaper Archive is a short but illuminating report in the *Western Times* on 19 July 1921, of a clash (yet another) between Jack and a local taxi driver. The headline read 'Feud Over Taxi Fare' and covered a story that Jack was residing at Lee in London, but travelling in Ilfracombe in a taxi driven by a Mr Charles Mills Burfitt. Apparently, Jack had had words with Mr Burfitt over the cost of the taxi fare and an argument resulted in which Mr Burfitt called Jack 'a waster' (memories of Lucas' words return) and threatened to 'knock his block off'. Jack is reported to have got out of the car, taken off his jacket in full view of everyone in the High Street, and started rolling up his sleeves as a crowd started to gather. In his defence, Jack stated to the newspaper that Mr Burfitt had been cheeky and sarcastic about how hard up Jack was, and unable to pay his fare, to which he admitted he exploded. The matter ended as Mr Burfitt, possibly sensing he would be on the end of a right good thrashing, withdrew, saying he could keep his fare as 'he was obviously hard up'. We can only imagine how Jack must have felt – a proud man from his shoe laces to the top of his head, this must have felt such a humiliation. But he was not alone. Up and down the country wounded men, mentally damaged men, limbless and beaten men faced the hopelessness of the future. Many men would no doubt have succumbed to the pressures of civilian life after all that they had gone through. On 25 November 1918, *The Times* carried a quotation from a speech delivered two days before by Lloyd George. In it Lloyd George had promised that the land must become a 'home fit for heroes'. Fine election stuff, but for Jack and millions of others who could testify, England was never to be that place. Suicide rates for returned soldiers were very high, almost fifteen times the rate before the war, as men were unable to adjust to failed marriages, careers that no longer existed, a society that had changed behind their backs and an England where the codes of valour and service that they had fought for had been eroded. There was no special treatment for a man who woke up every night in a cold sweat because the noise of a car sounded like a shell about to fall on him. There were no special jobs for the thousands of men blinded by gas or who had no legs. They had to fend as best they could. Post Traumatic Stress Disorder affected millions, not just a few, and Jack was no doubt affected in his own way too, though he might possibly not have recognized it (other than the episode referred to in Russia two years before).

Still trying to communicate with Dora, a letter has recently emerged written by Jack, showing how hard their separation had hit him. It reveals a deeper emotional side to Jack than has hitherto been seen. It also reveals that Dora was still writing to him, despite the fact she was already seeing a new man in her life. It is certain that Dora had in fact written to say that their relationship was over. She had been forced to leave London, in effect start a new life as a single mother, and, if at all possible, meet and marry someone whom she could rely on. It is all too easy to be critical of Jack, but love is not always easy and true love was a new and daunting phenomenon for him. He was in France when he wrote:

55 Versailles
May 28, 1922

Dear Woman,
Last night in the train I opened your letter & I am so grieved about your father that I did not send you my sympathy. Please forgive me. I do hope he is better and that you are happy again.

Please, dear woman, let me write down just to say good bye to the only woman I have ever really loved for only you can help me. I would be there any day at any time and will you give me something of yours to keep to remind me, if that were necessary, of all that you meant to me?

Would you also let me know what in all the world you would like best as a wedding present from me. Something that will remind you every day that you are always remembered. I should like to give you a ring if I may, but if there is anything you would like for your house – but it must be something good that you use it . . . It shall be as you wish. If you could put it in a telegram I should be grateful because I want to get it now.

Please forgive the shaky writing but the vibration is bad.

My address is C/o
Dr Gampton
7 Frognal
Findlay Road
London NW3

I am always your unhappy friend
John

Dora is unlikely to have replied. By the time Jack's letter arrived she was married to Thomas and trying to re-start her life. At least Jack had managed to admit the hurt he was feeling and recognized the mistakes he had made. This was quite a step forward for him. But it was too late. Dora was gone and gone for good and he had to get used to the hurt that created in him – a hurt he himself had dished out to others in the past. Four months later, on 30 September 1922, Jack was listed on the cross-Channel ferry leaving Southampton for France. Why he was regularly visiting France we do not know, but on the booking sheet Jack is registered as living at 38 Westbourne Park Road in Bournemouth, which would square with his ongoing separation from Nellie and shortage of funds.

Further evidence of Jack's financial hardship comes within another newspaper report only two months later, dated 20 November 1922 and headed 'Famous VC Unable to Pay His Gas Bill'. Jack finds himself called to the Windsor Magistrates Court for non-payment of his gas bill of £45. Stating that he was both insolvent and in hospital awaiting an operation and could not work due to wounds received during the war, must have made this the lowest point in Jack's life. The magistrate, in consideration of the colonel's war service, adjourned the case for three months – which no doubt gave him time to find the money for the gas bill. But where was Nellie?

If we assume that for around two years, between 1920 and 1922, Jack and Nellie were not seeing each other, that would explain why in 1922 Jack's personal fortunes started to pick up again. By the summer of 1922 Jack had, it seems, returned to a relationship of sorts with Nellie.

In 1991, a newspaper article in Norfolk was published in the *Eastern Daily Press*, carrying some of the material that was then available about Jack's life. Out of the blue, in one of those magical moments of history, I received a telephone call from Mr W. R. Morris, a resident of Bungay in Suffolk. He told me that he had known Jack Kelly in the early 1920s. To do justice to the then 86-year-old Mr Morris, let us allow him to take us verbatim through his memories:

I was born in 1905 and went to London to work in 1921 starting on the 29th September. My first job was as an office boy for a firm of solicitors at Number 4 Lincoln's Inn. The buildings were very grand near Chancery Lane and very old and ornate, I had never seen anything like them. I worked doing all sorts of jobs. I had to keep smart and clean and my collars were taken off every night to be washed and starched before I put them on the same shirt every day – I only had one shirt.

I worked for a Leonard Alfred Lauraine North – he was the only partner at the start but there were many more later. I was paid 12 shillings a week and my main job was to lick stamps and to run errands. In the late part of 1922 I started to see Lt Colonel Kelly come into the offices. He would arrive through the door looking huge. He had a solid face and fixed smile and was a huge man – you couldn't see the light from outside behind him as he came in. He would crack his stick down on the table and say good morning and then started to take off his bowler hat and gloves. He never wore an overcoat no matter what the weather and you could tell he was a military man. He always had a blue or black pin-striped suit, with a white collar and tie and very shiny shoes. He had a thin moustache and looked a very strong and confident man – you wouldn't want to argue with him. If we saw him coming through the window we would all jump to attention taking the micky before he opened the door – but we were very serious when he was in.

He would wait and then his wife would arrive – or sometimes they would arrive together and he would say 'Col and Mrs Sherwood Kelly to see Mr North'. She was immaculately dressed and looked to us like a film star, a yahoo, a stunner. Very tall and thin but very gentle and quiet, they were very different. She had a ton of money.

Mrs Sherwood Kelly would go in to Mr North alone and the Colonel would pace around in the outer office. He sometimes talked to us but it was very brisk. Mr North would write a letter to a firm of Stockbrokers called Forster and Braithwaite at 27 Austin Friars London EC2 and I would be given 2d to run the letter over by hand. Sometimes the letters contained instructions to buy £500 of ICI or Boots The Chemists shares and at other times they would be instructions to sell shares and I would bring back a bankers draft or even notes. This carried on during 1923 and clearly they were a partnership, sometimes buying and sometimes selling, but it was all her money.

We heard about him trying to become an MP in 1923 and read in the newspapers that he had beaten some chap up for being rude to him. That did not surprise us in the least. He was a strong talking man of few words, talked very English but we liked him. But by 1924 they stopped coming in together and he became very aggressive. He would march in, bang his stick down and bark out, 'Sherwood-Kelly for Mr North!' We had heard that he and Mrs Sherwood-Kelly had divorced because Mr North had arranged part of a financial settlement for Col. Kelly. There was no fuss, I think it all went through very smoothly with no names in the press. He would go through and see Mr North himself and all I would do is take letters to sell shares and the money went to Col. Kelly. I was always astonished at the amounts that he took each month – you could buy a very nice house for under £500 in those days. He stopped coming around 1925 but I never saw her again.

Clearly Jack and Nellie were moving closer together once more and for what would be the final period in their lives. Apart from the fact that she was no doubt his financial salvation, we can assume that they had at this time a high level of social status once more as a couple. Jack's health problems would always be there as his body had been so badly damaged by gas and bullets, but even so, the amounts of money being used or traded were considerable.

Nevertheless, despite Nellie clearly being there for him again, Jack maintained contact with Dora. Despite the fact that he had not received a reply to his last letter in May 1922, Jack wrote again in a letter dated 9 January 1923. It seems that he had not seen Angela for some time. He wrote:

119 Old Christchurch Road
Bournemouth

Forgive me for writing, but I <u>implore</u> of you to send me a <u>recent</u> snap of Angela –
    Never a day passes but I think of her – my life is a hell and has been since that letter from you in France saying you were finished with me –
    Don't think me a cad for writing this letter but please grant my request –
    I know you are bound to be happy in your married life and deserve it –
I am still unmarried.

    Johnnie
    Don't think too badly of me. I am hoping for a war with Turkey!!!

Although short, this rare and useful insight into Jack's personality reveals another side to the man which had been largely hidden – his love for Dora and Angela. It seems that Dora had shut him out for good and Jack was suffering the pain of any parent unable to see their own child. Dora had, in fact, become a different woman – she had to be. Throughout their relationship Jack had been an unpredictable partner, seldom there, rarely able to give time to her and even more unlikely to settle down. With her relocation to Devon to give birth to Angela, Dora had left London and Jack behind. Perhaps there was a window when Jack could have made their life work together, but if there was it was a very small one and was not open for long, as Jack disappeared again to Russia at the very moment Dora was getting divorced and had a child. It is likely that her vivacity and sparkle had been overshadowed by the reality of life as a single mother. During 1921 and 1922 she met and was courting Thomas Arthur Codner. A solicitor from Torquay with a nice home in Kingkerswell, Devon, Thomas was reliable to Jack's unreliable and he was a father figure in Jack's absence. In short, he was there for her. Thus, on 30 May 1922, at the registry office in Newton Abbot, Dora Ogilvy Cameron, of Oak Hill, Barton Road, Torquay, and Thomas were married. Thomas was 35 years of age to Dora's 29, and Angela was now a beautiful little girl of nearly 5 years.

    It would appear that Jack's second letter never received a reply, nor did he ever see Dora or Angela again. Interestingly though, only two weeks after Jack's letter to Dora there is a reference to his being a passenger, yet again, on a cross-Channel ferry to France, aboard *The Zeelandia* – again from Southampton, on 25 January

1923, and this time on to Cherbourg. It is a complete assumption that his business there was to meet with Dora and Angela, but he travelled to France at least twice in three months and the letter to Dora was sent in between the two trips. We will probably never know, but it might have been a special time for both of them as they decided finally to part. Perhaps Dora's heart had not yet turned to stone and perhaps Jack's letter had not gone unanswered.

Later generations recall Dora as a quite brittle, if not bitter, woman in her later years. Photographs show Dora as a thoughtful, deep-thinking, mature woman. Looking back one wonders whether she was always angry with Jack, or angry with herself for falling in love with a man such as he was. Maybe her life did not turn out the way she had planned. Angela grew up as the eldest of three children, alongside her sister Primrose and brother Tom, but always wondered who her real father was . . . right up until her death in March 2005. She was never told. Why Dora refused to tell her or whether the matter was ever discussed we will never know. What we know from anecdotal evidence is that Angela always had a striking portrait of a large man in uniform seated on a charger, who she knew was her father. Angela inherited Jack's great love for horses and the outdoors. She also developed a desire to serve – being commissioned into the army just before the outbreak of the Second World War. Angela was married in 1942 but her husband was posted away only six weeks later and they were never to be reunited. And so, there were shadows and images of her father's life within her own. Another inherited trait as the daughter of John 'Jack' Sherwood Kelly was her love for speed and fast cars. Jack himself developed this hobby in the 1920s. Angela took and passed her advanced driving course numerous times, just to prove she could do it.

Dora passed away on Christmas Day 1983 and this left Angela alone – save for her ponies, nephew and nieces. One particular photograph shows a startling similarity between Angela and the face of her father. She was loved by many and perhaps the most poignant epitaph for those searching for parallels with her father, is the fact that she was also described as 'having the common touch' and 'time for everyone no matter their station in life'. Just as her father walked the mud and cold of the trenches and shared a chat and a whiskey with his men only hours before they might all be going to their death, so Angela made everyone feel important. She is recorded as saying: 'everyone has their story to tell, make sure you find time to listen, you may learn something of interest'.

Whether Jack would have made a good father who can tell, but although Jack never met Angela again after 1922, he would have been very proud of the life Angela lived – and the way she lived it.

A New War: 1922–4
It seems one of the more incredible aspects of Jack's life was his determination to go into politics. What drove him to this conclusion, given the way politicians had

ruined his military career, is an open question. Possibly it was because he had already tasted the smell of political battle in 1919 and he could now smell another. Great Britain, as well as Europe, was under enormous threat. Jack and his comrades returned to a country that was far from a home fit for heroes. Quite the opposite – it was now a land of high unemployment, industrial unrest and political change. It was also a nation saddled with huge war debts, with American bankers demanding payback for the enormous wartime loans. There was deflation and prices and wages were falling. In Europe, the threat of Bolshevism was everywhere and political uncertainty affected every country. There was a need to ensure reparations were paid by Germany, and fear over right-wing political reaction to the effects of war such as Mussolini's March on Rome in Italy in 1922 and Adolf Hitler's aborted coup in Munch in 1923.

The political developments and general election of 1922 are a largely forgotten episode in our political history, but it was a pivotal year. It saw the convergence of the old and new worlds: the old world of class control and Empire now facing the new world of emerging post-war fascism, socialism and communism. The war-time coalition led by Lloyd George and the Liberals had worn itself out and there was a widespread feeling that it was time to return to the peacetime politics of not working together. The coalition was ended by the Conservative backbenchers – who went on to set up their all-powerful 1922 Committee, which still exerts such influence today. Lloyd George was forced to resign as prime minister and a general election was called for the 15 November 1922. It was a time of great confusion, both for politicians and the public. The Liberal Party, which had been so dominant for nearly a century, was falling apart. The new Labour Party was on the march and gathering strength at a frightening speed, and the Conservative Party was meandering and lacking leadership. The solid and safe Andrew Bonar Law campaigned as leader on a narrow and rather negative platform – looking at the alternatives, there really was no other option than a Conservative Party government. Indeed, he himself admitted his confusion about the new state of flux and change when he said: 'people hardly know where they are. And I am one of them'. Honest enough but hardly visionary leadership.

Watching all these developments towards the end of 1922 were Jack and Nellie and many others, who felt that maybe the world was changing so much that openings for new men and women were coming. Indeed, the election of 1922 was notable for many reasons: one of which was that it was the first election where the socialist threat really became ominous. Another was that two female MPs were elected – much to the enthusiastic support of Nellie, who was herself becoming a political animal and speaking out. Indeed, the *Folkestone Herald* on 23 April 1921 carried a report of Mrs Sherwood Kelly, wife of the VC hero Lt Colonel Jack Sherwood Kelly, making a speech to the men and women of Folkestone, as she was a leading member of The Primrose League. This league had been set up in the late nineteenth century and had been impressively successful in gaining large numbers of supporters, including many in the wealthy echelons of society. It existed to promote Conservative values – presumably in the face of the challenges that the new socialist menace offered and the decline of the Liberal Party. Nellie would have supported imperial policies to retain the Empire and to fight the socialist menace, and may have shown a new side to her personality which Jack had never seen before. Nellie was to develop her strong views in coming years, and the woman he thought he knew was replaced by a woman he was glad he knew.

The election result was alarming for the Establishment. The Liberal Party split irrevocably. It was the last election that the Liberal Party gained in excess of 100 seats, with one of the casualties being Churchill. Churchill was between parties, uncertain as to whether he was still a Liberal, an independent anti-Bolshevist or, in fact, still a Conservative (the latter being where his political career had started). For Churchill, it was all about getting back into Parliament – more a question of where he could win a seat than who the constituents were or what policies he believed in. Churchill had not had an easy time, having had his appendix removed a few weeks before he needed to campaign, as a national Liberal, for his seat in Dundee. When he did start he was well under par and unable to deflect the heckling and opposition he met with at meetings. After he had come in fourth place, Churchill commented that he left Dundee 'without an office, without a seat, without a party and without an appendix'. This was the fourth time that the lives of Churchill and Jack had come into close orbit and affected each other: the Boer War, Gallipoli, Russia and now both were trying to get elected to Parliament. It was as if their shadows were working in a parallel universe.

The Conservative Party, though successful, bore the internal scars of division and rudderless vision. It was the new Labour Party with their total of 142 seats – including a gain of 45 seats from the Liberals – who really won new dominance on the political stage. With nearly 30 per cent of the vote, the world really was changing and the working man was leading the charge. So it was that over the next twelve months Bonar Law struggled on and then, when illness claimed his career, he was replaced by Stanley Baldwin. The year 1923 became all about winning a new mandate from the people on the clear issue of tariff reform.

It was during the summer of 1923 that Jack became energized once more. His health was recovered and on 22 April 1923 he is listed as arriving back from New York aboard the White Star Line ship *Homeric*. There is no record of Nellie being with him and he is listed as being resident at Brown's Hotel in London – not at Cranley Gardens. Jack even resumed his sporting interest and prowess, as reported in the *Portsmouth Evening News* for 17 August 1923, where Jack was listed as playing in Chichester Cricket week for Mr Leveson-Gower's XI against Priory Park, where Lieutenant Colonel Kelly VC was bowled for Johnstone for 13 (let's hope Jack did not have visions of repeating his performance with his brother Edward all those years ago back in South Africa).

Having increasingly become attracted to a political career, Jack announced his decision to try to become a Member of Parliament. The political context of the period opened up new opportunities for Jack, and there was clearly a job to be done to reunite the people. Jack's connections with political animals such as Janson and Hamilton no doubt helped, as maybe did his relationship with Clarke. But, crucially, it was Nellie's brother William Pomeroy Crawford Greene, who had also survived the war, who first announced he was going to stand for Parliament at the next election as a Conservative candidate. It was possible that William and Nellie also saw a chance to redirect and channel Jack's energy and drive into a political career, thereby saving the relationship and giving Jack direction in his rudderless world. In any event Jack put his name forward to the Conservative Party to stand as a parliamentary candidate and was given Clay Cross in Derbyshire. Churchill also determined to stand again, still as a Liberal, but this time for a seat in Leicester.

Created as a new seat in 1918, there were few harder seats to win in the country, but Jack set about campaigning in this perfect example of a town and area created by the Industrial Revolution. Alongside him on the trail, we find Nellie once more giving her best to the man she continued to love, despite all that had transpired. The need for shares being sold to fund his life ended as they began to work together as a team, with the battle plan of winning hearts and minds in a constituency strongly targeted by the new socialist party.

It was a tough run. Jack had started from nothing as there had been no Conservative candidate standing in Clay Cross before. But in the election of 6 December 1923, Jack pushed the Liberals down into third place and received 4,881 votes (against the 11,939 of Mr Charles Duncan MP for the Labour Party, as expected). It was as though Jack was once again leading his troops into combat and the general election gave him another battlefield on which to fight. The *Derbyshire Times* reported that:

> the result was declared between half past two and three o'clock but owing to a torrential downpour there were few people in the precincts of the schoolyard but the drill hall attached was packed with supporters of the Labour candidate . . . and the presiding officer announced the figures there, the result being greeted with rounds of applause.
>
> Lt. Col. Kelly remarked that he did not think any other constituency in England had been fought cleaner and better, and with less acrimony than at Clay Cross. From start to finish it had been a friendly contest and he congratulated 'Our Member' on his success.
>
> Lt. Col Kelly intimated that he would fight the seat again. He thanked all who had worked magnificently. 'It has been a fine clean fight and I congratulate our MP.'

The paper continues with a further comment of equal interest and the only factual evidence of Nellie's thoughts: 'Mrs Sherwood-Kelly was also anxious to thank the electors. She said, "We have made many staunch friends and we hope to come and live amongst you".'

An Extraordinary Meeting

It was in the run-up to the December 1923 election day that an extraordinary event (referred to previously) took place. Jack was speaking at a rally in Shirebrook, only to notice a woman walk up to Nellie and say that she was the mother of Jack Johnson – as Jack explained to the the *Derbyshire Times*:

> Since 1916 I have been trying to find Johnson. I advertised regularly for several years, made enquiries at the War Office, and also got in touch with The Cornish Miners Association of which I understood Johnson was a member. Last week I went to Shirebrook and while I was speaking a woman went up to my wife and said, 'We feel that your husband belongs to us.' My wife answered, 'I don't quite understand – who are you?' The woman replied, 'My son is Jack Johnson'.

The article continued:

> Johnson was not in the village at the time but an appointment was made for Col Kelly to go to his mother's house last Friday. It was in that way that he again met Jack Johnson. 'There was a good deal of handshaking and I am afraid a few tears' said Col Kelly. 'You can understand my feelings when I tell you that Johnson undoubtedly saved my life. He would not leave me for a moment for 48 hours and tended me as a mother would have done. I feel my campaign in this election has been worthwhile if only for enabling me to show my gratitude to the man to whom I owe so much.'

The 1923 result had been a shock, as in the January of 1924 the only way Parliament could assemble was with the Labour Party holding the balance of power. Ramsay MacDonald became the first Labour prime minister with Liberal support. The right-wing press gasped with disbelief that the Labour miracle could have happened in under twenty years. They called the new socialist leadership a group of 'wild men' and expected Lenin to arrive at any moment. The Annual Register felt that the result of the 1923 election was 'as profound as that associated with the Reform Act of 1832'.

Undaunted, Jack and Nellie returned to London closer than ever before and even more motivated and energized by the challenges of speaking out for what they both believed in. Nellie's brother William had been handed Worcester, which he won easily and remained their Member of Parliament until his retirement in 1945. Jack and Nellie worked together now and supported local political activists in London throughout 1924. They watched as the Conservative Party (under Stanley Baldwin) grew in popularity, whilst the Liberals (under Herbert Asquith) watched as their party disintegrated around them. Both Nellie and Jack spent as much time as they could meeting and greeting local party supporters in and around Clay Cross, and prepared the way for a second run at the seat. Before they could do that, however, it was necessary to be adopted again by the local constituency party.

All of their joint efforts were not in vain. The year 1924 was dominated by MacDonald's efforts in foreign affairs, most notably to try to establish relations with the newly recognized Soviet Union and to build new trade links. In any event confidence motions in the government during September 1924 led to MacDonald calling for a mandate from the British people, and the king agreed to dissolve Parliament pending the third election in three years. The *Derbyshire Times* reported:

Col. Sherwood Kelly VC Adopted by The Conservatives

There was a representative gathering at Clay Cross Drill Hall on Wednesday under the auspices of the Clay Cross Unionist Association. Dr. F. Marriott president of the Association occupied the chair and remarked that Col Sherwood-Kelly made such an excellent impression from one end of the constituency to the other that the Executive of the Association felt that they could not do better than to invite him to come again. In his opinion Col Kelly was the best man to represent the Clay Cross division in the House of Commons. They had to show the Socialists and Bolsheviks that they were up against Englishmen – Englishmen to whom no difficulty was too great to overcome.

Jack had found a new battleground and a new side to himself – speechmaker and political leader. His experience the previous year had encouraged him to believe that he could win this seat and Nellie was there to back him. His enthusiasm had always been one of the key aspects of his inspirational leadership and he was revitalized by the thought of entering Parliament (although Churchill may not have really looked forward to that particular prospect with great enthusiasm).

In one newspaper report headed 'The Red Flag or The Union Jack', Jack gave a masterly performance and we can see just how far his eloquence had developed. Due justice to Jack's energy and fire can only be done by reading the full report:

Col. Sherwood-Kelly was enthusiastically received and at the outset said that they had to decide at this election whether they were to be governed by The Red Flag or The Union Jack. There were a good many English people who did not appreciate what the Union Jack meant abroad. Englishmen always woke up at a crisis and they had reached a crisis today – a crisis brought about by the Communists whom he called 'Sluts'! Are we he asked to be governed by the British House of Commons or from Moscow! Mr Stanley Baldwin and the Conservatives stood four square for God, King and Empire. It was left the Conservatives, as it always was, to retrieve a situation at a crisis. Well they had been awakened and their enemies would wish they had never roused them up! (Cheers and Applause). And now they were awakened all of them would have to put their whole hearts and souls into it to save the Empire. All sorts of promises were made at the last election, but what had been done for the men who won the war – our British Tommies – who are the British workmen, for it was from amongst them that the Tommies were drawn? Everyone knew what he thought of the British Tommy: he had proved it over and over again. The men who won the war saved England, and were going to save England again at this election. (Cheers) The working men realized that they had been gulled at the last election and they were determined not to be gulled again. They had no desire to be governed from Moscow. (Applause) Why should we make a loan to Russia to enable the Bolsheviks to carry on propaganda for the destruction of the British Empire? In Mister Stanley Baldwin we had a fine, sturdy Englishman – not a firebrand – who would save the Empire for us. 'If I get in, and I'm going to get in this time . . .' (The remainder of the sentence was lost in the loud cheering). In thanking the audience for his wonderful reception, the Colonel said that if he was beaten this time he should come again, but there was no such thing as being beaten this time. (Cheers) The solid British working man would be behind the Conservatives in their stand against the menace of Bolshevism and Socialism (Applause).

The motion to adopt Jack was carried unanimously and the hall erupted into a fever of noise, red faces, cheering and back-slapping. Jack, reading and sensing the euphoric temperature of the meeting, concluded the evening by saying that if he were returned for the seat he hoped he would live up to what they expected of him. He also hoped that they realized he meant what he said, and nothing would turn him back from any pledge he made. The applause rang out loud and long and his supporters left thinking that far from Clay Cross being a lost cause to the Conservatives, with Jack leading the charge they had at least a chance of building on the 4,800 votes he had gained in 1923. For Jack and Nellie, the whole experience was bringing them closer together than they had ever been before. At last they had a reason to work and be together and Nellie had never been happier. She could see Jack in his element and understood why his men thought so much of him. He was glad to shake hands as he walked the streets, his larger-than-life confidence blazed out of him like a magnet drawing people nearer, and, combined with his charisma and charm, turned heads and made people believe that here was a politician who cared and who would deliver regardless of the cost.

Two days later Jack was out on the street addressing public meetings around the constituency, up against it, but at his best. Clay Cross was already a strongly established hotbed of socialist fervor, where Conservatives and Unionists and all that they stood for were resented, indeed hated. As the pace increased and polling day (set for 29 October 1923) approached, the words used became more powerful and provocative and Jack's increasing popularity was certainly a worry for the local Labour party. On 24 October, with only five days to go, Jack and Nellie arrived at Langwith for an evening on the hustings in the school hall against the local Labour partisan. As the *Manchester Times* again reported on 25 October, the Liberal candidate had already dropped out of the running, so it was now all about Jack.

Tempers and emotion were running high and it was this sort of atmosphere that Jack enjoyed most, combining the excitement of the challenge and the chase. Working his way around the Shirebrook ward, Jack arrived at Langwith market place around 4 o'clock in the afternoon, where a group of about 100 miners had gathered to hear Jack speak. Flat caps abounded as Nellie and Jack stood on the steps of the library in the evening gloom of a damp October day, flanked by the Labour speaker and Jack's Conservative/Unionist supporters. It had as usual begun to rain and as Nellie began to speak she was heckled from the back of the crowd. 'Why don't you go back to London where you came from!' was heard ringing out across the square, followed by: 'what do you know about life down a pit!' Jack's temper immediately rose in defence of Nellie, as the newspaper recalled, and the colonel shouted in an angry tone, 'If you want to take the rise out of someone take it out of me and not out of my wife!'

Not content with challenging the man in the crowd, Jack then walked down the steps and through the assembled miners (who seemed more than a little taken aback that Jack would not just take the abuse) towards the man he had picked out, who beat a hasty retreat across the square. Jack was clearly in the mood for a fight and the meeting dispersed with Jack evidently angry. The day was not over and there was more to come. After tea with the local Conservative councilor, Jack and Nellie walked through the rain for the 7 o'clock meeting at Upper Langwith School. Arriving just before 7, it was clear that the steam rising from the wet clothes of the 200 or so miners, local shopkeepers and professionals, was mixing with the heat of high expectations. The hall was a-buzz when Jack and Nellie walked in to some applause from the front, and hands in pockets from the back of the room. Whispers had already spread around the town about the previous meeting, and Jack already had something of a legendary reputation about him. Jack, himself, was unfortunately still glowing in the heady mix of emotions that had driven him on in the past to do so many courageous things.

He started the meeting by asking if there were any communists present. Not the most diplomatic start and clearly an attempt to goad anyone of high temper in the room to have a go. There were plenty of takers. 'Yes, we are here!' rang out from the back of the hall, and immediately the tone changed. Jack's supporters jeered, the temperature rose and the atmosphere became tense as Jack took in a deep breath and smiled: 'That's good, you are the men I want to meet.' The Chairman, a Major Lemonby, and his wife stood up and tried unsuccessfully to quieten the hall down as Jack rose to speak. Nellie squeezed his hand for him to calm down. As he started, a shout with a raised fist came straight at him: 'You want chucking out!' and around 100 miners cheered and agreed. Jack, a bit ruffled, stood his ground and according to the newspaper reports, stiffened his back and shouted, "If there is anybody here who can chuck me out, well come and do it!' There was a huge cheer from Jack's supporters and sensing an opening like an old fighter, he managed to get another verbal swipe in and shouted that Ramsey MacDonald (leader of the Labour Party) had been a traitor to the boys at the Front during the war. Not surprisingly, the hall erupted with a mass of shouts and raised fists. Jack stood on the stage and shouted back, 'Yes, yes, a traitor to me and my men!' At this point a man named Watson shouted, 'You're a liar! You're a liar!'

What went through Jack's mind at that moment we can only wonder. Probably a heady mixture of the need to counter-attack, coupled with a desire to defend his honour. Watson cannot have had any idea of the life that Jack had lived up until that moment, but he saw the result of it marching off the stage towards him – and Watson was not a runner either. Jack walked up to him and, looking him in the eye, demanded, 'Take that back!' Watson refused, at which point and without any hesitation Jack punched him hard. The first blow knocked Watson to the side and the second saw him hit the ground hard, at which point the stewards ran up to restrain Jack. What was amazing was that a melee did not follow. In fact, no one ran to Watson's side and Jack's supporters were shocked, as if time had stood still. A few seconds passed and Jack composed himself, saying out loud, 'I am not going to be called a liar by any man. I have fought too long and too hard to be accused of that.' The meeting continued in the quietest calm and the colonel was given a 'splendid hearing' – who was going to shout him down! The next day the *Manchester Times* recorded: 'V.C. Quells Disorder – Interrupter Calls Col. Kelly a Liar – And Pays the Penalty'.

Perhaps the most fascinating result of this extraordinary event is that over the next few days it became clear that a number of men who had served under Jack actually lived in the area. They had mostly been men who had either served in the RIF back from 1915 Gallipoli days, or more recently regulars who had been with Jack in Russia as part of the 2/Hampshires. Interviewed by the newspapers on the character of the colonel, one man said that he felt that the colonel was being shockingly treated in Clay Cross and, 'as ex-servicemen whose interests were ever nearest to his heart, they deplored the unsportsmanlike attitude of many men towards him'. He went on, 'In Russia the men would much rather appear before him than before their company officer, and if his old battalion were in Shirebrook today every man jack of them would be at his side'. He felt Jack had been 'the bravest man in the British army'. A telling and deep insight into the respect held for Jack from the men he so often commanded.

At the end of the day Labour support was too strong for Jack to win this particular battle and he lost the election in Clay Cross – but not before he had taken his vote up from 4,000 to just over 8,000. This was a stirring result, but how much due to his character and performance as opposed to his policies?

Failure, however, left Jack once more subject to his emotions and to his personal battle with peace. A serene existence opened his mind up to the difficulties he had with being at peace with the world. And, of course, now he had the added challenges of missing his daughter and possibly the woman he truly loved and would never meet again. It had been a near-run thing at Clay Cross, but what would happen now with Jack and Nellie?

Chapter 10

The End of His Journey, 1924–31

'I have lived long enough for I die unconquered.'

Epaminondas, who waited until he had heard the Thebans had defeated the Spartans on the battlefield before he ordered a javelin pulled out from his body and died

Whatever Jack decided to do over the ensuing years we can be certain it was not ordinary and he embarked on maintaining a strong public profile with Nellie beside him. For the most part, the two of them made for a sparklingly talented and committed couple. What they lacked on the inside by way of intimacy, they made up for on the outside with compatibility in political action, support for charities and mixing in the social scene around London. There was no way post-war obscurity was going to overwhelm him. Nellie too had blossomed into a confident and outspoken woman, not just in the Primrose League, but in her own right. On 26 September 1924 Nellie is recorded as speaking passionately about Australia and emigration to an audience at Llanishen village hall in Monmouthshire. Jack's name is found in a newspaper article (in the *Yorkshire Evening Post*, 5 February 1925) on local golfing exploits – again, Jack was far from obscure. Apparently, Jack had taken up the game the previous November, from a standing start with the maximum handicap of 30, and by the end of February he was playing off scratch – an almost unheard of feat to accomplish in under four months (especially for someone with so many physical wounds). The article continues:

Scratch in 4 months
Colonel Sherwood-Kelly must have created a world record in rapidity of advancement as a golpher, writes G W Greenwood in The Daily Telegraph. He took up the game only 4 months ago and in 4 months his handicap dropped from the limit to scratch. He joined the Seaford Club and for 4 solid months played 2 rounds each day on 7 days a week with Kneller the professional. During this time Col. Kelly missed only one day – a Sunday. It was golf with a purpose – that of succeeding at all costs in the face of all difficulties.

In peacetime, Jack was now able to show his sporting talents, so much in evidence as a young man back in South Africa. This article perhaps captures the almost myopic resolve of a man determined to win at all costs. His golf prowess is a metaphor for his type of heroism: the calculated, aimed for glory of the victory, no matter what the cost. He also excelled at tennis.

Later in the same year, in April 1925, Jack and Nellie attended sports day at Stowe school in Buckinghamshire, where he was listed as having given a speech and opened the event. Later again on 6 August 1925, Jack and Nellie were present together to open the Royal School for the Deaf (now called the Royal School for Deaf Children) in Margate – indicative of their celebrity status. Two days later, on 8 August 1925, Jack was reported as opening the Margate Fete and then later giving a rousing speech to members of the Royal British Legion in Thanet. The *Thanet Advertiser* stated that after Colonel and Mrs Kelly had made presentations of awards he was asked to speak, and spoke with emotion and thunder about the threats of Bolshevism and the need to maintain the Empire. They were roundly cheered three times by the audience in a standing ovation. Quite a social calendar for them both, showing how they were working together . . . at last.

Nellie too continued to develop her speaking tours and the following year, on 1 June 1926, we find her speaking as a member of the Women's Patriotic League. Perhaps most fascinatingly of all, on 12 June 1926, Nellie was photographed sitting beside the aeroplane of Mary, Lady Heath. Almost a female counterpart to Jack, Sophie Catherine Theresa Mary Pierce-Evans is perhaps a forgotten symbol of the new pioneering woman of the 1920s. Slumbering or maybe simmering before 1914, women such as Lady Heath were unleashed by the Great War and exploded with new confidence into the post-war world. In some respects, Dora was probably someone who wanted a similar life to Lady Heath – independence and freedom from the man's world she had been born into. For Dora it was not to be, but for Lady Heath life was short and a starburst. Born in Knockaderry in County Limerick, she earned a degree in Science at Dublin and had been married and widowed before she was 29. A key founder of the British Women's Amateur Athletic Association in 1922, she was an Olympian as well as a pioneering aviator, earning her commercial licence in 1924. She became the first woman to fly solo from Cape Town to Cairo in around 1927 (carrying only a Bible, shotgun, two tennis racquets – why not? – a fur coat and six dresses). She was one of the best-known women in the world – giving talks on tours across Europe and the USA, where she met the President and Mrs Coolidge. She was reputed to have landed her plane on every flat field in Ireland and for good measure was a dispatch rider on the Western Front. She married three times, set a record of 17,000ft in an open cockpit for a light plane, and reduced to shreds the world record for the women's high jump. To top this all off she was also the first woman to make a parachute jump.

So, in the abovementioned picture we see Nellie, in fur coat and dress, sitting in the middle of a field next to Mary's aeroplane, with the caption: 'At Home with Lady Heath'. We can safely assume that the woman Jack had met in 1914, so quiet and unassuming, had come a long way on her own personal journey. In fact, she may now have even been able to meet Jack on an even keel and gain his admiration. On 11 October 1927, Nellie is recorded as having attended one of Lady Heath's weddings. Mary wore black for her wedding (her favourite colour) and married an iron millionaire from the USA, aged 75 (she was only 30) – so much for social convention for Mary. Like Jack, Mary had little skill or interest in the acquisition of wealth (she died destitute after a fall from a tram aged only 42). Given that there were only twelve guests at this wedding, it is safe to assume that she and Jack had much in common in character, friendship and philosophy on life.

On 31 October 1926, Jack was photographed at Horse Guards Parade in London in full dress uniform, complete with his large medal group and Victoria Cross. On this special day Jack was asked to lay a wreath on behalf of the Ypres League, as part of the then annual commemoration of the sacrifices made at Ypres during the Great War. To be selected for such an honour was particularly special, given the numbers of generals and the like that could have performed this duty, but Jack was heavily involved, as Nellie had been, in the British Red Cross, he British Legion and Talbot House (Toc H). Still gravitating towards the light of fame and respect, Jack was able to maintain an image and station beyond the events of 1919 and his clash with the Establishment.

Clearly, he was not standing still, but still needed something to satisfy his thirst for challenge. Towards the end of 1926 he accepted a job on behalf of Bolivia Concessions Ltd – to build a road across Bolivia. Jack (still resident at the Authors' Club SW1) is listed as leaving Southampton for Buenos Aires and then on to Bolivia on 2 December 1926. We can assume then that the rapprochement with Nellie had lasted through the political attempts at election, but they had simply agreed to be friends and live apart. For the next year or so Jack could be found sweating and driving his men forward to build a road across the jungle and rivers of central Bolivia. He must have nipped back once, though, as the *Cheltenham Chronicle* for 22 October 1927 carries a story about a famous VC in a car smash – indeed it was Jack. Driving a Vauxhall car with a Mrs Riggs of Minchinhampton alongside him, Jack was hit full-on by an oncoming car. There were no charges or indeed injuries, but haring about the roads at high speed was so typical of his ongoing disregard for danger. Sadly, the Bolivia experience was not a happy one, as the company was mismanaged and a court case resulted in 1930 in which Jack was criticized. He was accused of walking out on what he saw as another disorganized mess. His part in all this was successful – not only in building roads and managing men, but in making a name for himself as the VC hero from the

Great War. He contracted malaria and again is on the passenger list arriving at Southampton from Buenos Aires on 6 March 1928.

On the way home, it was clear Jack was very ill and he entered a convalescent home for a while. He was never to be quite the same again, his health beginning to fail after a lifetime of hurt and punishment and his fight against malaria was to be one he was not going to win. How strange that the gas, shells and bullets of world war could not kill him and yet the small bite of the tiniest insect was able to bring him to his knees and ultimately to his death.

Recovering near Bognor Regis, Jack was discovered by Sir Arthur Du Cros, who owned Craigweil House near Bognor. It was here, in 1928, that King George V had been resident whilst recovering from illness. It was also here that Jack found his last employment as agent for the house. Jack was able to live rent-free at Craigweil and found a new role marketing the house to the public. During 1928 and 1929 the much thinner and more worn VC hero could still be found joking and laughing with the 15,000 or so visitors that came through the doors, telling tall tales, always wearing the blue, pinstripe suit, white collars and gleaming shoes. As the months wore on, however, the wounds of past years began to catch up with him.

One of the last references identified with Jack comes with another passenger listing, this time for a cruise aboard *The Duchess of Richmond* to the Isles of the Blest out of Liverpool on 25 January 1930. Again, Jack was listed as living at the Authors' Club, so his time at Craigweil had ended and he was back in London for what was to be the last year of his quite extraordinary life. But it was not over yet. There are references in various narratives on Jack that he went big game hunting towards the end of his life. There is no evidence for this, but the last recorded trip overseas for Jack comes on 14 August 1930. This time (perhaps he had a feeling it was for the last time) he was listed as leaving London for Natal via Suez. Quite an exhausting trip, and given that he travelled first class, most likely funded by Nellie – though he was alone. Still listed as resident at the Authors' Club, Jack possibly went home to say his goodbyes and leave various items with members of the family, such as his sword and medals. One small but maybe noteworthy point is that on every passenger list to date, Jack had described himself as 'Soldier', 'Retired Soldier' or simply 'Colonel'. On this last trip and under 'Profession' he simply wrote 'Nil. Make of this what we will.'

The very last evidence we currently have for recording the events of Jack's life come in two very interesting forms. One is the electoral roll for the Redcliffe Ward in a most fashionable part of London – Chelsea SW10. There, at 28 Harcourt Terrace, is listed John Sherwood Kelly. Clearly well beyond his financial means to rent, this can only have been provided by Nellie to keep him close by, maybe because his health was so obviously failing. The last portrait photograph shows a man whose neck has worn so thin that you could slide your hand into his collar.

So it was that the return from South Africa saw a steady decline in the man. He was 51 and had run his race and not stopped running since he was 12, on that sunny day when he heard the news that his mother had been killed. Jack passed away on 18 August 1931. He had been cared for at a nursing home (which at that time was 31 Queens Gate), opposite Hyde Park, around the corner from the Royal Albert Hall. Again, such an address and such a nursing home could only have been in the gift of Nellie – her love for Jack was simply unsinkable. As Jack faded that summer one wonders if they had time to talk, whether Nellie sat beside his bed and they both looked back on where their lives had entwined and how both had changed. They had moved towards the centre of each other's lives, without being able to live in it. Jack had softened, become more sensitive about his emotions and understood what he had failed to do. Nellie had grown in confidence, had more courage in her beliefs and understood the man she had loved since their first meeting in July 1914. They had fought in war and peace together.

It must have been obvious that Jack was dying as the funeral and all the preparations were in place for the service, which took place only three days later. True to his reputation, the newspapers up and down the country covered the news of his death and funeral, which was held at midday on Friday, 21 August 1931.

> The funeral of Lt. Col. John Sherwood-Kelly VC took place with full military honours at Brookwood Cemetery yesterday. The body was borne to the cemetery on an eighteen pounder gun carriage, manned by men of The Royal Field Artillery. A detachment of Grenadier Guards furnished a guard of honour and the firing party. The banners of the local British Legion were carried in the cortege.
>
> There were no relatives present as they are at present in South Africa. Capt. C. M. Guest represented the High Commissioner for South Africa, Mr Ernest Short and Mr H. M. Walbrook represented The Author's Club and Sir Basil Clarke represented The Authors Lodge.

Short and sweet and to the point. Clarke, his speech writer from 1919, was there. As news of the funeral spread, a whole series of articles were published, not just in Great Britain but also in South Africa, as they caught up with the man that they had written about so often before. Suddenly the power of his reputation came home to those who had taken his actions for granted:

> The death of Lieut. Colonel John Sherwood-Kelly VC in a Kensington nursing home has ended the career of one of the outstanding figures of the war. 'Fearless Kelly' was the nickname he was known by in wartime.
>
> *Daily Express*, 19 August 1931

Lieutenant-Colonel John Sherwood-Kelly VC, CMG, DSO died yesterday in a Kensington Nursing Home at the age of 51. He had been suffering from the after-effects of malaria. Great gallantry made Sherwood-Kelly ('Bomb Kelly' as he was called) a conspicuous figure even among the many whose heroic deeds were an inspiration of the Great War.

The Times, 19 August 1931

Even in Norfolk where Jack had scarcely served (certainly he never fired a shot in anger with the Norfolk's), his death was noted by a large full-page obituary.

VC Hero's Death – War Exploits Recalled
Lt. Col Sherwood-Kelly was awarded the Victoria Cross for conspicuous bravery and fearless leadership in the Great War. He was an acting Colonel of The Norfolk Regiment.

Eastern Daily Press, 19 August 1931

In South Africa, the *Overseas Daily Mail* possibly said it better than anyone else when their headline read:

Lonely Death of War Hero, Lt. Col. Sherwood-Kelly VC – A Lifetime of Fighting.
Lt. Col John Sherwood-Kelly VC, CMG, DSO one of the most gallant soldiers that the Great War produced has died alone and almost friendless in a London nursing home.

Overseas Daily Mail, 22 August 1931

As if to balance things up, a few weeks after the obituaries had been forgotten, a rather fashionable London society magazine, under the heading 'Sporting & Dramatic News' published a short apocryphal story about Jack, sent in by one of their readers:

A story of the late John Sherwood Kelly VC concerns an occasion when he went to a fashionable West End restaurant and ordered a cup of tea. This was brought to him along with a large selection of buns and pastries – as well as a bill for several shillings. The Colonel unhappy with the size of the bill, drank his tea, grimly and reluctantly paid his bill and walked out of the restaurant and into the street holding the entire tray and all the pastries . . .

His grave was not in the centre of Brookwood – far from it. Brookwood is a huge Victorian burial ground with far more unmarked graves than marked, peppered with the tombs and carved angels of the great and the forgotten. But Jack is under a tree, almost on the side of the cemetery, in an unprepossessing plot – until recently with a headstone untouched, except by moss, since 1931. Recently cleaned, it now reads as it should have done all along, with these words underscoring his name: 'One who never turned his back but marched breast forward'. As one walks from the car park over to his resting place, there is a vast, unused, open field with only one or two markers. Amazingly, one such marker is the grave of a soldier of the Hampshire Regiment who served in Russia and died of his wounds in 1921. He was one of the men Jack sacrificed all to protect, and it seems another fitting (amongst many) coincidences of this story. Perhaps Jack's cortège moved unknowingly past this forgotten soldier in this abandoned grave, as his former commanding officer, Lieutenant Colonel Jack Sherwood Kelly VC, DSO, CMG, was wheeled past on his own last parade.

For nearly thirty years Jack's medals were lost, but in 1959 the South African National Museum of Military History wrote to a Mrs I. H. Kelly of Marandellas, Rhodesia (Jack's sister-in-law) transferring £250 to her account for the purchase of Jack's medals for the museum. There was no White Russian Medal (given to all those who fought in Russia in 1918–20, including to Stanley Berrett and all those who admired and followed Jack, but denied to Jack himself) – a typically low and vindictive blow from the Establishment.

And so ended the light of Nellie's life. This once shy and sensitive young man, driven by the lost love of mother and childhood, became a man for all seasons yet a man who could intentionally hazard all that he built. Tall, grand and yet strong and gritty, a combination of fire and water, at one and the same time constructive and yet destructive, able and fulfilled, yet wanting and empty. A man of immense courage, able to give his body over to be bruised and wounded for a just cause, and willing to give it all for just one long shot. A man who typified Kipling's verse and 'filled the unforgiving minute with 60 seconds' worth of distance run'. A man of deep and genuine generosity of spirit and care for others, and yet unable to give of his inner emotions to those who loved him back – a man as predictable as he was contradictory, built of solid rock but with foundations on the sand of his own fears and vulnerability. His life was as full as he could make it, and indeed he lived enough to fill three or four lives over and died as he spent his youth – alone, square-jawed, staring that straight stare that is displayed in all his photographs. He was a man who never blinked first, a man who wanted to balance the books wherever he found them wanting, to the end a man unconquered.

His is the story that keeps on giving. The undertakers engaged to arrange Jack's funeral were Kendall & Sons of 123a Kings Road – again, a very fashionable firm and no doubt funded by Nellie. In their account for £21 0s. 8d. there is a special request to lay the coffin deeper than the usual at 11ft. In addition, the invoice was originally made out for a Mrs Elizabeth M. Coward of Rocke House, Exmouth, but a line was put through her name and it was replaced by Jack's old friend, Frederic H. Hamilton, and his address was listed as Russet House, Tadworth, in Surrey. No sign of Nellie at all.

How Nellie's life unfolded after Jack's death is unknown, but we do know that as late as 1963 she was still alive and writing articles for *Christian Science* magazine under her married name of Nellie Elizabeth Sherwood Kelly – a part of Jack she was not prepared to give up. Angela, we know, went on to have her own life – never knowing who her real father was. We have no notion, either, whether Dora ever told her husband Thomas who Angela's real father was. As one friend of the family put it, 'There were just years of stony silence'.

But Jack still saves the best until last. Throughout the whole rollercoaster ride that is Jack's life, we hold on with fingernails, trying to work out why he behaved in the way he did. We try to assemble a sort of normality that we can only do from our own frame of reference. But Jack's brand of heroism, as we know, bears little resemblance to most, and unless we inhabited the heart and mind of a reckless buccaneer (for in many ways that is what he was) then it is very hard to find points at which we can be secure in fixing a judgement. It is as though he set out to deliberately confuse and evade capture by other people, by friends and certainly by those who loved him and by history itself. Just when you think you begin to understand the man, he lets you into another little secret that throws all your notions up into the air once again. Thus it is, that in the final record available, we have a summary of Jack's last will and testament which says simply: 'Kelly, John Sherwood died 18th August 1931 at 31 Queens Gate Kensington Middlesex. Administration (with Will) London 11th November to Elizabeth Coward widow. Effects £390. 19s. 5d.' Who, we may ask, was Elizabeth Coward?

Notes

Chapter 1

1. *The Standard Encyclopaedia of South Africa*, 12 vols (n.p., 1970), Vol. 8, pp. 632–6. See the *East London Daily Dispatch*, 15 December 1874 and Lloyds Register of Shipping Losses, 1874–5. See also Malcom Turner, *Shipwrecks and Salvage in South Africa 1505 to the Present* (C. Struik, Cape Town, 1988).
2. As recalled by Comander A. J. Bateman, Norfolk, England.
3. 'The Life and People of Lady Frere', an anonymous and undated pamphlet.
4. *Ibid*.
5. The Glen Grey Act was later expanded across much of the Cape region despite huge resistance.
6. 'The Life and People of Lady Frere'.
7. Excerpt from *The Iandra Story – A Romance of Pioneering* (n.p., 1956).
8. *Ibid*.
9. Mary Stawell, *My Recollections* (Richard Clay & Sons, Bungay, 1911).
10. St Andrew's College Cadet Centenary Brochure, 1877–1977.
11. From an article in the *Daily Dispatch* (London SA), 12 May 1989.
12. F. Woods (ed.), *The Original Despatches of Winston S. Churchill, War Correspondent 1877–1900* (Readers Union, n.p., 1975), pp. 19, 30 and 35–7.
13. The *Nongqai*, February, 1918. JSK Archives.
14. For a more detailed survey of the role of Kitchener in the Boer War see George H. Cassar, *Kitchener: Architect of Victory* (HarperCollins, London, 1977).
15. *The Illustrated London News Record of the Transvaal war, 1899–1900*, p. 55.
16. Woods (ed.), *The Original Despatches of Winston S. Churchill*.
17. For a biography of the history of the ILH website article from 'The South African Military History Society', http://rapidttp.com/milhist/lhrcent.html.
18. *The South African Military History Society Journal*, Vol. 10, No. 6. The Diary of 3016 Pte. Horace Bell, 14th Regiment of Hussars. http://www.rapidttp.com/milhist/vol106hb.html.

Chapter 2

1. Jean Coulter, *East London Daily Dispatch*, 12 May 1989.
2. The *Nongqai*, February 1918. JSK Archives.
3. From the personal correspondence of Mr J. Kelly, SA.

4. See www.sahistory.org.za/places/Transkei.
5. From the personal correspondence of Mr J. Kelly, SA.

Chapter 3
1. J. M. Roberts, *Europe 1880–1945* (Longman, London, 1972), p. 143.
2. Richard Shannon, *The Crisis of Imperialism* (Palladin, n.p., 1984), p. 406.
3. From the personal correspondence of Mr J. Kelly in South Africa and also Ian Uys, *For Valour: The History of South Africa's Victoria Cross Heroes* (Johannesburg, Ian Uys, 1973), pp. 261–5.
4. Robert Massie, *Dreadnought* (Jonathan Cape, London, 1991), p. 900.
5. Barbara Tuchman, *August 1914* (Papermac, London, 1987), pp. 96–7.
6. A. J. P. Taylor, *The First World War* (Penguin, London, 1963), p. 35.
7. Robert Rhodes James, *Churchill, A Study in Failure 1900–1939* (Weidenfeld & Nicolson, London, 1970), pp. 62–3.
8. Information on King Edward's Horse is rare although a history was published by Lieutenant Colonel Lionel James (Praed, 1921).
9. I am indebted to the Revd Peter Long of Farnham who kindly researched and provided this information.

Chapter 4
1. See N. Mansfield, 'Volunteers and Recruiting', in Gerald Gliddon (ed.), *Norfolk & Suffolk in the Great War* (Gliddon Books, Guildford, 1988).
2. See P. Bujak, *Attleborough – The Evolution of a Town* (Poppyland Publishing, North Walsham, 1990).
3. Rob Kirk, *The Devils Orchestra – The Story of an Old Contemptible* (n.p., 1997).
4. For more information on the Norfolk Yeomanry see J. Bastin, *The Norfolk Yeomanry in Peace & War 1782–1961* (The Iceni Press, Fakenham, 1986). According to Colonel John Boag OBE, MC, TD DL, the Norfolk Yeomanry kept few documentary records during the Great War. Those that do exist are currently held in the Muckleborough Collection in north Norfolk.
5. An imposing residence in late Victorian style, Margery Hall, near Reigate, is still in existence and divided into flats.
6. The *Cambria Daily Leader*, 12 November 1919.
7. Taylor, *First World War*, pp. 80–1.
8. Noel Annan, *New York Review of Books*, April 1993.
9. A. G. Gardiner, *Pillars of Society* (J. Nisbet, London, 1913), pp. 61–3.
10. Charles F. G. Masterman in Lucy Masterman, *CFG Masterman* (Nicholas & Watson, London, 1939), p. 26.
11. Lloyd George, *War Memoirs*, 6 vols (Nicholson & Watson, London, 1933), Vol. I, p. 395.

12. John Colville, *The Fringes of Power, Downing Street Diaries 1939–1955* (Hodder & Stoughton, London, 1985), p. 125.
13. *Ibid.*, p. 126.
14. W. S. Churchill, *My Early Life* (T. Butterworth, London, 1930).
15. *Regimental History 1/Battalion The Kings Own Scottish Borderers*, September–October 1915, p. 166.
16. *Ibid.*, pp. 166–7.
17. *Ibid.*, p. 167.
18. The Mention in Dispatches was gazetted on 10 April 1916.
19. Major John Gillam, DSO, *Gallipoli Diary* (The Strong Oak Press, Stevenage, 1989), p. 267.
20. Uys, *For Valour* , pp. 261–5.

Chapter 5
1. *East London Daily Despatch*, 22 April 1916.
2. *Ladies Field*, 9 February 1918, p. 369.
3. *Regimental History 1/Battalion The Kings Own Scottish Borderers* (1915), p. 179.
4. G. Gliddon, *When The Barrage Lifts* (Gliddon Books, Norwich, 1987).
5. Captain F. C. Hitchcock, *Stand To – A Diary of the trenches 1915–1918* (Gliddon Books, Norwich, 1988), p. 109.
6. Lyn MacDonald, *The Roses of No Man's Land* (Macmillan, London, 1984), p. 177.
7. *Derbyshire Times*, 3 December 1923.
8. *The Times*, 19 August, 1931.
9. MacDonald, *The Roses of No Man's Land*.

Chapter 6
1. Proceedings of divorce, April 1919.
2. *Ibid.*
3. Private papers of Mrs F. Fouracre.
4. TNA Collections.
5. *The History of The Royal Inniskilling Fusiliers*, pp. 84, 111, 112, 113, 118, 226, 288. From the National Army Museum Nummis Files.
6. Taylor Downing, *Breakdown: The Crisis of Shell Shock on the Somme* (Little Brown, London, 2016).
7. Lieutenant Gerald Herald Hendrick-Aylmer was killed in action on 16 April 1917 aged 19. Only son of Mr Hans Hendrick-Aylmer of Kerdiffstown, County Kildare. He was educated at Billin Grange, Wellington and Sandhurst. Commissioned July 1915, he went to France in July 1916. His name is recorded on Panel 6 of the Arras Memorial in Pas de Calais, France. Also recorded in 'Our Heroe Laochra', South Dublin Libraries.

8. The private letters of Major General C. H. T. Lucas, kindly provided by his family.
9. *Ibid.*
10. *Ibid.*
11. *Ibid.*
12. *Ibid.*
13. Captain D. G. Browne, *The Tank in Action* (Blackwood Press, Edinburgh, 1920).
14. *Regimental Diary 1/Inniskillings*, pp. 84 and 111–13.
15. *London Gazette*, 11 January 1918.
16. TNA.
17. TNA.

Chapter 7
1. Robert Jackson, *At War with the Bolsheviks* (Tom Stacey, London, 1972), pp. 18–21.
2. Basil Liddell Hart, *A History of World War One* (Papermac, London, 1992), p. 180.
3. A. Summers and T. Mangold, *The File on the Tsar* (Jove, London, 1978), p. 244.
4. Lloyd George to Prince Lvov, quoted in K. Rose, *King George V* (Orion, London, 2000), pp. 209–10.
5. Lloyd George, *War Memoirs*, Vol. II, p. 1888.
6. Rose, *King George V*, p. 211.
7. Sun Tzu, *The Art of War*, trans. Thomas Cleary (Shambhala, USA, 2003), p. 59.
8. Michael Sayers and Albert Kahn, *The Great Conspiracy Against Russia* (Boni & Gaer, New York, 1946), p. 3.
9. *Ibid.*, pp. 35–7.
10. M. Kettle, *The Road to Intervention, March – November 1918* (Routledge, London, 1988).
11. Lockhart, British agent, quoted in Jackson, *At War with the Bolsheviks*, pp. 29–30.
12. *Ibid.*, pp. 36–7.
13. G. A. Brinkley, *The Volunteer Army & Allied Intervention in South Russia, 1917–1921* (Notre Dame Press, Indiana, 1966), p. 28.
14. Sayers and Kahn, *The Great Conspiracy*, p. 3.
15. Lloyd George, *War Memoirs*, Vol. II, p. 1891.
16. E. M. Halliday, *The Ignorant Armies* (Weidenfeld & Nicolson, London, 1958), pp. 15–25.

Chapter 8

1. *Regimental Journal of the Hampshire Regiment.*
2. Rose, *King George V.*
3. Rhodes James, *Churchill.*
4. *Daily Express.*
5. TNA.
6. Clifford Kinvig, *Churchill's Crusade: The British Invasion of Russia, 1918–1920* (Continuum, London and New York, 2006).
7. Oscar Wilde, *The Importance of Being Earnest.*
8. Christopher Dobson and John Miller, *The Day We Almost Bombed Moscow* (Hodder & Stoughton London, 1986), p. 177.
9. Quoted in Edmund Ironside, *Archangel 1918–1919* (Constable, London, 1953), p. 117.
10. Major E. M. Allfrey, 'Five Months with 45th Battalion Royal Fusiliers in North Russia', IWM, pp. 1–2; M. Kettle, *Archangel Fiasco* (Taylor & Francis, Oxford, 1992), p. 542.
11. Kettle, *Archangel Fiasco*, p. 145.
12. *Regimental Journal of the Hampshire Regiment.*
13. Imperial War Museum, 74/29/1, Letter of Lieutenant M. S. Moore, 25 June 1919.
14. TNA.
15. *Ibid.*, Kinvig.
16. TNA.
17. With thanks to Mr Richard Berrett for the private recollections of his grandfather, Private Stanley Berrett.

Biographical Chronology

Immediate Family

Father
- John James Kelly born Newbridge, Ireland, 4 June 1850
- Married 30 July 1877 in Queenstown, Cape Colony
- Died 18 August 1926

Mother
- Emily Jane Didcott born Winchester, England, 1 June 1858
- Died 8 August 1892 (The following inscription can be found on a brass plaque in the church of Lady Frere: 'In loving remembrance of Emily Jane Kelly who died at Lady Frere from injuries on 8th August 1892 from the effects of a cart accident. She was a true Christian woman, noble, fond, loving affectionate mother and a staunch friend,' signed Jack)

Offspring
- Emily Nuovo Abele Kelly born Queenstown, Cape Colony, 18 May 1878
- John Sherwood Kelly born Queenstown, Cape Colony, 13 January 1880
- Herbert Henry Kelly (Jack's twin brother) – died 21 July 1893
- Olive Rebecca Kelly born Buffle Doorns, Cape Colony, 10 April 1881
- Edward Charles Kelly born Buffle Doorns, Cape Colony, 28 November 1882
- Percy Dennis Kelly born Lady Frere, Cape Colony, 10 February 1885
- Gertrude Margaret Kelly born Lady Frere, Cape Colony, 5 April 1886 – died 19 October 1935
- Oswald Claude Kelly born Lady Frere, Cape Colony, 5 October 1887
- Clifford Terrance Kelly born Lady Frere, Cape Colony, 26 January 1889
- Ethel Mary Kelly born Lady Frere, Cape Colony, 26 December 1890

Stepmother
- Selena Collins married 11 April 1894
- Died 1944
- Three children:
  - Dorothy Elizabeth Kelly born Lady Frere, 4 April 1895
  - Henry James Kelly born Lady Frere, 29 July 1898
  - Patrick Dermot Kelly born Lady Frere, 6 October 1901

Jack Sherwood Kelly
1880–1913
- 13 January 1880: John Sherwood Kelly born Queenstown, Cape Colony
- 8 August 1892: Mother died in a cart accident
- 21 July 1893: Herbert Henry Kelly (twin brother) died
- 11 April 1894: Father married Selina Collins
- 1894–96: Queenstown Grammar School, Dale College (expelled) and St Andrew's College (expelled)
- 1896: Joined Cape Mounted Police (CMP)
- 1896: Fought in the Matabeleland Rebellion
- 1899: As part of the CMP formed an escort for Sir Alfred Milner on his visit to the Transkei
- Feb 1899: Dismissed from the CMP for insubordination
- July 1899: Joined the Native Department, Cape Colony, after letters from his father pleading for a job for his son
- 1899–1902: Served with the Imperial Light Horse (ILH) and Kitchener's Fighting Scouts in the Boer War – took part in the relief of Mafeking as part of Colonel Plumer's column; operations in Rhodesia, Orange Free State and the Transvaal. Mentioned in Dispatches for bravery numerous times
- 8 January 1901: Commissioned as a 2nd Lieutenant in the ILH
- 5 June 1901: Resigned his commission after an argument with his superior officer
- May 1902: Had been broken to the ranks for insubordination
- Nov 1902–July 1903 – at the age of 22 volunteered for service as a private in the Somaliland campaign in the third expedition against the 'Mad Mullah'
- 1913: Arrives in Belfast to join the Ulster Volunteer Force

1914–15
- 31 August 1914: Enlists in 2/King Edward's Light Horse in London with his brother Edward. Trains and serves with the 12th Service Battalion (he Suffolk & Norfolk Yeomanry) in Suffolk
- 4 November 1914: Appointed to a temporary commission as a lieutenant in the Norfolk Regiment . . .
- . . . Six days later, due to his previous service, appointed major on 10 November 1914
- May 1915: Volunteers for service in Gallipoli. Various mentions as 'Bomb Kelly' during September to December 1915. Assumes command of 1/King's Own Scottish Borderers as acting lieutenant colonel
- 21 August 1915: Severely wounded at Sulva Bay and moved into hospital 22 August–28 October 1916

1916
- January: Part of the Norfolk's withdrawal from Gallipoli
- 2 February: In London and the gazetting of his award of the DSO. Courting Nellie and engaged
- 26 February: Wrote to War Office complaining that he had received no benefit payments for his wounds received in Gallipoli
- 22 April: Married Nellie Elizabeth Crawford Greene at St Peter's Church, Cranley Gardens, London. Nellie resident at 21 Cranley Gardens
- May: Serving in France again with 1/Royal Enniskillen's (Royal Inniskilling Fusiliers?) but severely wounded and saved by Jack Johnson
- May: Evacuated to Rouen and then London by Nellie
- July/August: Recruiting tour to South Africa where the 'old fascinations' returned
- 29 November: Receives his DSO from King George V at Buckingham Palace
- 5 December: Serving as major with the 3rd KOSBs at Duddingston Camp – letter to CO 3rd Bn asking for a transfer to 10th Norfolk's as officers and men of the 1st Bn were also in camp who knew him as CO 1st Bn KOSBs.

1917–18
- 1 January 1917: Awarded the CMG
- 29 March 1917: Takes over command of 1st/Enniskillens (1/Inniskillings?)
- 20 November 1917: Action at Marcoing, Battle of Cambrai, Canal du Nord
- 23 January 1918: Receives his VC from King George V at Buckingham Palace
- March–May 1918: On sick leave as a result of wounds from the Somme and Gallipoli
- May 1918: Second recruiting trip to South Africa. Complaints about Jack's use of bad language at East London
- 6 June 1918: SS *City of Karachi* left Cape Town for England with recruits from South Africa – more problems with discipline and Jack calling them an 'undisciplined rabble'
- 21 June 1918: Court of Inquiry held by Major General Thompson at Military HQ Sierra Leone

1919
- 11 March: War Office minute stating that 'Lieutenant Colonel Kelly is an officer whose tact is not on a par with his gallantry'
- April: Divorce proceedings begin
- April: Volunteered to lead part of the Archangel expedition to North Russia
- 27 May: Landed at Archangel. Parade and Ironside's comments
- 6 June: Arrived Dvina front line with 2nd Hampshire Bn.
- 13 June: Led successful patrol into the interior and personally kills three Bolshevik soldiers

- 17 June: Letter of praise received from General Grogan
- 19/20 June: Aborted attack on Troitskya/death of Captain Gorman. Telephone call from Jack to General Graham: 'feeling shamefully let down'
- 3 July: Brought back up the Dvina using Jack's 'mystery ships'
- 12 July: 2 Companies deployed
- 22 July: Mutiny of Russians and murder of British officers in Dwyers Battalion
- 26 July: Ordered to take over command of the Railway Front and to put down the Russian mutiny
- 26 July: Wrote letter to E. W. Janson, Eaton Square, London on situation and his views, which was opened by the censor. Challenged and serious offence. The same day he writes to Mrs Cameron of Minehead talking about Russia again and sending love to his 'Babe'
- 31 July: Sent his letter to GOC Vologda, reluctant to carry out attack on Red Army Blockhouses
- Wrote to Rawlinson via Ironside (whereas in the past he had run up against authority in the field, he had always came up against junior or middle-ranking officers. This time because of the small size of the expeditionary force it was very fast to be up against very senior officers at General Staff level
- 16 August: Ordered to appear before Rawlinson as Ironside was away
- 18 August: Receives orders that he is to be immediately relieved of his command
- 21 August: Letter from Walshe asking Jack if he wanted his letter to go to Ironside as a private or official letter. Travels home
- August: Reported working for the Southern Railway in Blackfriars against the union strikes in London
- Friday, 5 September: Sent first letter to the *Daily Express*
- Saturday, 6 September: First letter published in the *Daily Express*
- 13 September: Churchill and War Office responds and all newspapers get hold of the story
- 13 September: Second letter published in the Daily *Express* and TUC Congress
- 19 September: Captain Warwick dispatches his letter on Jack to Colonel Thornhill (GSO1) Intelligence
- 22 September: Brigadier General Grogan dispatches his report on Jack to GHQ from his HQ in Archangel – eight points about Jack's 'lack of balance and insubordination'
- 6 October: Jack's third letter to the *Daily Express*
- 28 October: Court martial

1920–31

- 2 February 1920: Staying at the Rubens Hotel SW1. Letter to the War Office claiming expenses for his South African trip in 1918
- 20 November 1922: Article in a newspaper on his being summoned to Windsor Court for non-payment of his gas bill due to his being practically bankrupt
- Start of visits to Nellie's law firm for monthly recovery of shares
- November 1923: Speaking at an election rally at Shirebrook in Derbyshire when Mrs Johnson, mother of Jack, tells him her son was the man that saved his life on the Somme in June 1916/article in the *Daily Mail*, 4 December 1923 about this event
- 6 December 1923: General Election Clay Cross –

Duncan, C. (Labour)	11,939
Sherwood Kelly, Lieutenant Colonel J. (Conservative)	4,881
Thornborough, F. C. (Liberal)	4,488
Majority	7,058
Previous majority	13,306

- 24 October 1924: Thrashes heckler at Langwith in the run-up to the election
- 29 October 1924: General Election Clay Cross –

Duncan, C. (Labour)	14,618
Sherwood Kelly, Lieutenant Colonel J. (Conservative)	8,069
Majority	6,549

- February 1925: Article in a newspaper stating that in four months Jack had reduced his golf handicap from the maximum to scratch!
- 31 October 1926: Lays a wreath as part of the Ypres League at Horse Guards Parade
- 1927: Worked for Bolivia Concessions Ltd. He opened up the country, built roads and railways and established a port 6,000 miles inland. Contracted malaria
- 1929: Worked at Craigwell House near Bognor as the agent of Sir Arthur du Cross, owner of the house, and prepared the house for showing to visitors; 13,000 visited in 3 years looking at rooms used by the king to convalesce
- July 1931: Malaria flares up
- 18 August 1931: Died Kensington Nursing Home aged 51
- 21 August 1931: Buried at Brookwood Cemetery. Full military honours but no family or Nellie present

Index